THE WAY OF PRESENCE

ALSO BY JOSEPH NAFT

Non-Fiction

The Sacred Art of Soul Making

Becoming You

The Radiant Mountain

Fiction

Restoring Our Soul

Agents of Peace

THE WAY OF PRESENCE

Tools and Strategies

JOSEPH NAFT

I.F. Publishing

I.F. PUBLISHING COMPANY
Baltimore, Maryland USA
info@ifpub.com

Copyright © 2017 by Joseph Naft

All rights reserved. No part of this publication may be reproduced, stored in or introduced into a retrieval system, or transmitted in any form, or by any means, electronic, mechanical, photocopying, recording, or otherwise, without the prior written permission of the copyright owner of this book.

ISBN: 978-0-9786109-4-4

Printed in the United States of America on acid-free paper

CONTENTS

PREFACE xiii
1.0 Presence Tools 1
    1.1 Having Feet 3
    1.2 Living Like You Mean It 4
    1.3 Arms and Legs 4
    1.4 Thought Awareness 6
    1.5 Whole-Body Sensing 7
    1.6 An Emotional Life 8
    1.7 Inhabiting Our Body 10
    1.8 Inhabiting Our Mind 11
    1.9 Inhabiting Our Emotions 13
    1.10 Inhabiting Body, Heart, and Mind 14
    1.11 Being Conscious 16
    1.12 Total Presence 17
    1.13 Leaning into Presence 18
2.0 Presence Strategies 20
3.0 Presence Metrics 21
    3.1 Frequency 21
    3.2 Duration 23
    3.3 Intensity 26
    3.4 Breadth 28
    3.5 Depth 29
    3.6 Rating the Day 31
    3.7 Effectiveness 33
4.0 Presence Triggers 35
    4.1 Appointments 35
    4.2 Ad Hoc Goals 37

    4.3 Eating Presence 39
    4.4 The Doorway Exercise 40
    4.5 Walking Presence 42
    4.6 Phone Presence 44
    4.7 Waiting Presence 47
    4.8 Difficulties. .49
    4.9 Money Presence. 51
    4.10 Person Presence 53
    4.11 TV Presence 55
    4.12 Working Presence 58
5.0 Troubles and Purpose 60
6.0 Modes of Presence 62
    6.1 Centered Presence. 64
    6.2 Active Presence 66
    6.3 Sustaining Presence 68
    6.4 Responsive Presence 70
    6.5 Awakened Presence 72
    6.6 Participation Presence. 74
    6.7 Whole Presence 76
    6.8 Creative Presence 78
    6.9 Connected Presence. 80
    6.10 Sacred Presence 82
    6.11 Selfless Presence. 84
    6.12 Multi-World Presence 87
7.0 Basic Inner Work 89
    7.1 Relaxation. .91
    7.2 Inhabiting Our Body 92
    7.3 Inhabiting Our Attention 95

7.4 Inhabiting Our Mind 97
7.5 Living with Heart 100
7.6 Meditation. 102
7.7 Prayer 105
7.8 Inhabiting Energy 108
7.9 Inhabiting Self. 110
8.0 Finding Your Self 112
9.0 The Challenge of Presence 114
   9.1 Hurry and Worry versus Calm Presence . . . 116
   9.2 Presence versus Inertia 118
   9.3 Responsible Presence versus Unreliability . . 120
   9.4 All-In Presence versus Scattered Absence . . 122
   9.5 Engaged Presence versus Indifference 124
   9.6 Grasping versus Just Being 126
   9.7 Task Presence versus Distractions. 128
   9.8 Presence versus Thinking About Presence . . 130
   9.9 Humble Presence versus Self-First 132
10.0 Spirituality at Work 134
   10.1 Presence at Work. 136
   10.2 Excellence 140
   10.3 Ethics. 142
   10.4 Responsibility 144
   10.5 Relationships. 146
   10.6 Communication Presence 148
   10.7 Service 150
11.0 Time and the Timeless 153
   11.1 Linear Time 154
   11.2 Eternal Being. 156

11.3 Eternal Light 158
  11.4 Timeless Patterns. 161
  11.5 Timeless Acts. 163
12.0 Being Yourself 167
  12.1 Being Your Body. 169
  12.2 Being Your Mind. 172
  12.3 Being Your Heart. 174
  12.4 Being Your Personality 177
  12.5 Being Your Relationships 180
  12.6 Being Your Job. 182
  12.7 Being Your Presence 185
  12.8 Being Your I 188
  12.9 Being Your Conscience 190
13.0 Mind and Thought 192
  13.1 Noticing Thoughts as Thoughts 194
  13.2 Who Is Thinking? 197
  13.3 Beyond Thought: The Conscious Mind . . . 200
  13.4 Freeing Our Mind 202
  13.5 Beyond Mind. 205
14.0 The Path of the Path 207
  14.1 Handling Our Peaks 209
  14.2 Profiting From Our Valleys 211
  14.3 Rising Above Our Plateaus 213
15.0 Deepening Our Inner Life 216
  15.1 Silence 218
  15.2 Energy Breathing 221
  15.3 Developing Our Sensation Body. 223
  15.4 The Energy of Higher Emotions 225

 15.5 Fasting and Other Will Tasks 227
 15.6 Cultivating the Heart of Love 230
 15.7 Being Who I Am 232
 15.8 Inner Excellence 235
 15.9 Whole Presence 237
 15.10 Informed Initiative 239
 15.11 The Source of Will is the Source of All. . . 241
 15.12 Persistence: Doing What Matters. 244
16.0 Energy Practice 246
 16.1 Contact with Sensation. 249
 16.2 Breathing Energy 251
 16.3 Inhabiting the Sensitive Energy 253
 16.4 Sensitive Energy in Body, Mind, and Heart . 255
 16.5 Conserving Inner Energy 258
 16.6 Consciousness: The Metacognitive Energy . 262
 16.7 Sacred Light Energy 265
 16.8 Love 267
 16.9 The Transcendent Energy 269
17.0 Transcendence 272
 17.1 Transcending Our Materiality 274
 17.2 Transcending Our Thoughts 277
 17.3 Transcending Our Reactive Emotions . . . 279
 17.4 Transcending Me. 282
 17.5 Transcending Our I. 285
 17.6 Transcending Time. 288
 17.7 Transcending Consciousness. 290
18.0 The Levels of No-Self 292
 18.1 Not Personality. 295

- 18.2 True Self or No-Self? 298
- 18.3 Non-Doing in the Great Self 301
- 19.0 The Way of Wholeness 304
  - 19.1 Fragmentation 304
  - 19.2 The Wish To Be Whole 306
  - 19.3 The Sensitive Energies 308
  - 19.4 Inner Body Wholeness 311
  - 19.5 Body, Mind, and Heart 313
  - 19.6 Conscious Wholeness 316
  - 19.7 I Am Wholeness: Presence Meditation . . . 318
  - 19.8 Living Wholeness 321
  - 19.9 Sacred Wholeness 323
- 20.0 The Way of Integrity 325
  - 20.1 Wobbling on the Way 327
  - 20.2 Lessons of Karma 329
  - 20.3 Respecting Ourselves 331
  - 20.4 Our Word 333
  - 20.5 The Voice of Conscience 336
  - 20.6 Having Principles 338
  - 20.7 Non-Desires 340
  - 20.8 Responsibility 343
  - 20.9 Purity 345
  - 20.10 Unity 347
- 21.0 Living in Flow 351
  - 21.1 Surrender to the Present 353
  - 21.2 Body Flow 356
  - 21.3 Sensory Flow 358
  - 21.4 Fluid Mind 360

21.5 Fluid Heart 363
21.6 Fluid Presence 366

ABOUT THE AUTHOR • 371

PREFACE

In an age and culture focused on status, money, and possessions, anomalies and dilemmas confront us. Once we attain a modest lifestyle, with all the necessities, further personal economic advances do less and less to make us happier, and may even diminish our life satisfaction. At that juncture, how well we live depends much more on our inner state than on our outer circumstances. Foremost among the many determinants of our inner state is whether or not we are actually here, living and participating in our life. Are we letting great chunks of our life pass by on autopilot, or are we present, in the vivid reality of each moment? We all have the same amount of time in each day. The key difference comes in the degree to which we live each of our moments or let them slip away, hardly noticed.

This book primarily addresses the practice of presence: how to be and stay present. How to be here in our life, drinking it all in. How to live more.

The Way of Presence consists of spiritual inner work exercises, each intended for a week-long effort. In this third collection of such exercises, all but a handful are parts of a series, lasting from as few as three to as many as thirteen weeks. Each inner work series offers a context of steps that can lead to greater depth along a particular dimension of the spirit. For a fully robust soul, we need a spirituality that effectively addresses all aspects of our being and gives us the tools, which if applied diligently, will enhance the quality of our inner life. That is what I hope you will find in these pages, a way that enables you to live in presence to live more of your life.

Joseph Naft
August, 2017

THE WAY OF PRESENCE

1.0 Presence Tools
(Introduction)

To actually change our level of being, two possibilities present themselves. We can leave it to the normal course of our life. Every life has its share of triumph and failure, love and defeat, health and sickness, gain and loss, pain and pleasure. Through all of that, we inevitably grow into some measure of wisdom, life wisdom, and along with it some transformation of our being. It is a slow process.

There are ways to intentionally accelerate our transformation. Principal among these are the various spiritual traditions and paths. What makes the difference between the journey in life and the journey in life on a path is the application, personally, directly and repeatedly, of spiritual practices. This requires effort, within our mind, heart, and body, and is thus often referred to as inner work.

One important subset of inner work practices deals with presence, becoming more present, more often and for longer periods, more broadly, more deeply, and more intensely. There are many, many practices that can and do prove effective. Some work for certain people, and some suit others. One person typically needs more than one practice to develop various aspects of presence and to ensure the practice does not become stale or perfunctory. We ourselves must be directly, viscerally engaged for the practice to be beneficial or effective. So we try various practices and go deeply into one that fits us. And then while keeping up our work with that practice, we also learn and work with another. Gradually we master several practices, at least to the level of being able to enter them at will and in almost any circumstance. Eventually we establish a whole toolkit of practices familiar to us and at our ready disposal. Of course, we use common sense and refrain from inner work in life critical or dangerous situations, such as driving or chopping vegetables, that require our full attention.

Continuing our inner efforts, coupled with our own creative and persistent application, the practices reveal their deeper levels to us, while our being grows and deepens. In contrast to this high goal, some of the practices will seem like trivial tricks or gimmicks. Yet in those cases, it is their very simplicity and concreteness that enables us to respond directly and quickly to the inner impulse of awakening that reminds us to practice presence. That impulse vanishes rapidly, so we need to be ready for it by having one of presence tools in our pocket, as it were, and immediately engaging with it. We refrain from wasting energy on upbraiding ourselves for having forgotten to be present and instead, as soon as the impulse of awakening arises, we respond by picking up our practice yet again.

This series of Presence Tools will offer short descriptions of various presence practices, with a brief rationale for each. The rationale matters, because our way is one of understanding, born of experience. It is necessary to know, in theory, what the practice is and why we engage in it. More than that cannot be written. So for our understanding, and being, to grow, the theory needs to be coupled with the actual, sustained, and repeated experience of the practice. Because it is impossible to reduce an inner experience and all its nuances to words, the tool descriptions will of necessity be incomplete and have holes. Through creativity, intuition, trial and error, we fill in those holes and fill out our understanding and our being.

1.1 Having Feet
(Presence Tool 1)

Our body is our primary connection to the present moment. Through staying in contact with our body, we stay in contact with the present. Though we aim toward contact with our entire body, it is easier to begin with a part. And because we can bring more intense awareness to a part than when we spread our awareness throughout our whole body, we often return to focusing on a part, even after long experience with this type of inner work.

Our feet offer a useful target for awareness. They have many nerve endings and are thus quite sensitive and a ready source of sensory feedback. We begin by simply putting our attention in both of our feet and holding it there. We might practice this for some minutes during a sitting meditation at the beginning of each day, just to get the feel of sensing our feet, and to prepare a foundation for practicing awareness of our feet during the day.

Holding our attention in our feet awakens and draws the sensitive energy into them. This energy makes our feet vivid and alive, almost as if we had an inner foot in addition to our physical foot. When we walk on feet full of sensation, we walk on a fire that lights, vibrates, and warms without burning. When we walk on feet full of sensation, we actually have feet.

We can practice having feet at any time, sitting, standing, or walking. When we remember to do this, we just immediately bring attention to our feet, or expand our attention to include our feet. And we try to sustain that.

For this week, please practice having feet.

1.2 Living Like You Mean It

(Presence Tool 2)

Living in presence means living like you mean it. It means having your intention in whatever you do. It means having yourself in whatever you do. It means doing whatever you do.

In presence, we do not passively let life happen to us, or let the now slip unnoticed into the past, lost forever. We jump in with both feet. We are here. We are attention and intention, alive in this moment. We live our life, rather than letting life live us.

The difference may seem subtle at first. But with practice it comes clear. The ancient spiritual question "Who am I" is subtle. But the related question "Am I here?" is easier to get hold of. Though awareness matters, this is not essentially a matter of awareness. It is a matter of who is aware or whether anyone is aware. Is there just an awareness with no one watching, no one home? Is the watcher so diffusely spread into the awareness that effectively no one is watching? Or "Am I here?" Am I seeing what I'm seeing? Am I doing what I am doing?

Or is my life happening without my participation? And when I am not here, participating in my life, am I truly living? To live a full life, means first to be here, living our life, to be our attention and intention, in every moment.

Am I here? For this week, please live like you mean it.

1.3 Arms and Legs

(Presence Tool 3)

Presence Tool 1 addressed the importance of being in

contact with our body to anchor our presence in the now. We began with Having Feet. The broader that body contact is, the more effective it can be. So we now move into practicing contact with our arms and legs.

We start with our right arm, from shoulder to fingertips. By bringing our attention into our right arm and holding it there, we become aware of the arm from inside it. We come into organic, visceral, direct contact with the life in our arm. As the contact deepens, the arm comes alive in our perception, growing vivid, filled with a vibrating energy that we call sensation. We say we are sensing our right arm.

Next we leave the right arm and focus on our right leg, from hip to toes. We sense our entire right leg for a time. Then we move to our left leg, then our left arm. Next we sense both arms at the same time. Then both legs. Then all four.

The foregoing can be profitably practiced in sitting meditation, to get a strong taste of it. We can also practice sensing our arms and legs as we go about our day, whenever we have some spare attention. Say we start with our right arm. Inevitably our attention will lapse and move to something else. The next time we remember this Presence Tool, we sense our right leg. The time after that, our left leg. And next, our left arm and so on. If we forget which limb we are on. We choose one at random and start from there.

Sensing anchors us in the here and now, and tunes us into life. It is a simple but remarkably powerful approach to presence. For this week, please practice sensing your limbs.

1.4 Thought Awareness

(Presence Tool 4)

While body awareness is an essential anchor, full presence requires more than that. For many of us, our experience of life is dominated by our thoughts. Yet we are so identified with our thoughts, that we regard our thoughts as who we are, or as the most direct expression of our real self. For example, when the thought "I" comes, we believe it is us or at least expresses us. All of that is an illusion that keeps us locked in a small world. A major step toward true inner freedom comes with the piercing of the illusion of thoughts as self.

Toward that freedom, we practice being aware of our thoughts, as thoughts. Ordinarily we drift along with our thoughts, sometimes aware of their meaning, but rarely aware that any particular thought is just a thought, just a mental word sound or a mental image. We do not usually see thoughts for what they are, namely just thoughts, because we conflate them with our self.

The practice of thought awareness is best begun in sitting meditation. We first establish our presence in our body, through relaxation and sensing. After becoming settled in our body, rather than lost in thoughts, we maintain a background contact with body sensation, while putting our foreground attention into our mind to notice our thoughts. We see each thought arise, occur, and pass away, often quickly prompting the next thought to arise, occur, and pass away. We may notice that the thoughts have meaning, but for the purposes of this practice, we do not engage with that meaning. We keep attention to the bare fact of a thought arising, occurring, and passing away. It is like watching a text stream scrolling through our mind. Rather than being concerned with reading and evaluating the text, we just see the ongoing, endless stream itself. If we find ourselves being carried off in that thought stream, we reestablish contact with our body and then return to the practice of thought awareness.

Once we acquire the taste of seeing our thoughts as just thoughts, we can extend this practice into our day beyond the sitting meditation. When we notice that we are engrossed in a stream of thought, we rouse ourselves to see that the thoughts are just thoughts and nothing more. In particular we see that our thoughts are not who we are, though they implicitly claim to be. Simultaneously sensing part of our body, like an arm or a leg, while watching our thoughts, helps us stay grounded in the present moment, rather than being carried away in the thought stream.

For this week, please practice seeing your thoughts as thoughts.

1.5 Whole-Body Sensing

(Presence Tool 5)

Having practiced sensing parts of our body, we now turn to extending our sensation into our whole body. This is one of the major and most effective tools in the practice of presence. The quality of wholeness occupies a special place in the spiritual path. The practice of whole-body awareness, whole-body sensing, ushers us into a wholeness that encompasses much more in breadth and depth than our body.

One way into this wholeness is to build it up. Again, starting this in sitting meditation allows us to focus exclusively on this effort and establish a strong taste of it. We sense each of our limbs, then all four limbs. Then we add the sensation of our torso, though we do not try to sense individual organs, so as not to interfere with their instinctive functioning. Finally we add the sensation of our neck and head. At this point, we have a complete sensation of our entire body. We maintain that and sit in the fullness of our whole body.

With practice, we become able to go directly into whole-body sensing, without building it up piecemeal. Though when we do that, we still have the challenge of strengthening the sensation throughout our body and of maintaining our contact with all that sensation. We spread our attention through our whole body and keep it there, even as we go about our day.

This offers us a broad and effective foundation for presence. Plus, it just feels right. It feels as if we have finally come home into our body, as if sensing our whole body is the way we are meant to live. It feels like a state that we want to have as our new normal.

For this week, please practice whole-body sensing.

1.6 An Emotional Life

(Presence Tool 6)

Feeling our way through life, our emotions guide us. We feel the poles of approach and avoidance, pleasant and unpleasant, desire and repulsion, curiosity and boredom, happiness and sadness, confidence and fear. Our emotional heart acts as an intuitive sensor perceiving and responding to whatever comes along. We do not need to think about whether to like something or not. We just like it, don't like, or don't care. The immediacy of our emotions gives them great power. We inherently trust our heart to point the way.

This all sounds fine. So what is the role of spiritual inner work with regard to our emotions? Where does presence come into our emotional life?

We tend to collapse into any emotion that reaches a certain threshold of intensity. We get lost in it. We disappear. The emotion takes us over. Yes, we have an internal monitor performing functions like stopping any violent impulses that arise in conjunction with the emotion of anger, for example. But here we are not concerned primarily with such extreme cases. Rather, we look to the everyday experience of feeling and being lost in that feeling.

In some cases, that might be a good thing, like becoming totally absorbed in a moment of playing a musical instrument or in participating in a sport. Those are cases of heightened awareness. But the usual thing is that when we lose ourselves to an emotion, our life is narrowed thereby, our field of view diminishes, our presence weakens.

We seek to feel what we feel, so that we are here, feeling it, we are here, in the feeling. We do not seek separation, our mind on one side and our heart on another. That destroys the spontaneity of life. We seek conscious participation. Rather than disappearing, we are here in our heart, in our life. We feel our emotions as emotions. We do not wall off the unpleasant, unwanted emotions. We feel whatever we are feeling. We open our arms wide and embrace our life, our heart in all its manifestations. And in that way, we reintegrate our disparate emotional parts, the disowned pieces of our self. And by integrating our emotions, we heal and become whole. And in becoming whole, we become our self, here in presence, here as presence.

In the heart of presence, love comes, because nothing blocks it. Joy comes. Awe and wonder come as our eyes are made new.

We usually regard awareness and consciousness to be associated with our mind, our head brain mind, the one that thinks. This practice, however, is not concerned with thinking about our feelings. It concerns awareness, which goes well beyond our thinking mind. By allowing ourselves to feel what we feel, we bring a direct, emotional awareness to our feelings. We reclaim what we have cast aside. We become more unified, while broadening our contact with life.

For this week, please feel what you feel.

1.7 Inhabiting Our Body

(Presence Tool 7)

In Presence Tool 2, *Living Like You Mean It*, we addressed the question of "Am I here?" Now we put a specific target for that question, making it more practical and concrete: "Am I here in my body?" We work to be here in our body, to be the one sensing our body, to inhabit our body. We have practiced sensing our whole body. In doing so, we may be more or less present, in our body.

Now we turn to making it more. We feel that "I" am here in my body, that "I" am sensing my body, not just that there is this body or that there is sensation in this body. I occupy my body, continually. I stake my claim to the whole of my body, moment to moment. Doing this, I realize that I am the one experiencing being in my body, I am the experiencer.

If I do that for one moment and then abscond in the next, falling absent from my body, I am lost again. There may be experience, but no one is here to receive that experience, to engage with it. Experience is empty without an experiencer.

Inhabiting our body does not require tension. It just requires presence: my presence in my sensation, in my body.

The result is truly a wonder. Suddenly life grows vivid. We have a strong impression of our body and of being here in this place, in this moment, in this body. What my body does, I am doing. Or rather, my body does what I do. Or better yet, there is no separation between me and my body. I am fully in my body. More particularly, I am fully in the sensation of my body, in the sensitive energy filling my body. I and my body are unified in full awareness.

In this way, my body serves as the platform for my presence. I can be here, because my body is here. The stronger my contact with my body, the stronger my presence. If my sensation is weak or partial, I can nevertheless inhabit what there is, and by doing so, the sensation strengthens and spreads. Then I can say to myself "I am here in my body."

For this week, please practice inhabiting your body.

1.8 Inhabiting Our Mind

(Presence Tool 8)

We tend to believe that our mind is defined by our thoughts, that our mind is our thoughts. In those fleeting moments when there are no thoughts, it seems as if we have no mind. But we also, and more accurately, consider a moment of no thoughts as indicative of an empty mind, which implies that our mind is more than our thoughts. We rightly say that thoughts run through our mind.

Generally we are not present in our mind. The thoughts usually run on their own, thinking themselves in an automated, reactive, self-generating, and haphazard way. Except when we intentionally focus our thoughts on some problem or issue, we are at best spectators, passively aware that thoughts are running on, and we not fully present in our mind.

When we work to be present in our mind, to inhabit our mind, several different modes are possible, with varying results to match. The most obvious is when we actively impose ourselves on our mind. Consider the mind to be like an ocean, whose surface waves are the thoughts. Active presence quiets the surface from above. It is as if we sit on the surface of our mind and pacify it by force of will. This can work for a brief time, but then our energy wanes, our intention wavers, and suddenly we vanish again.

Passive presence takes a different approach, entering the ocean of mind from below. We relax into our mind, without an active agenda. We let the thoughts run on as they will, while we slip between, behind and under them into the peaceful, deep waters. This can be wonderful, giving us a glimpse of freedom. But the very passivity of this state leaves us vulnerable to getting attracted by and taken into the surface waves of thoughts. One moment we are relaxed and at ease, and the next we are drifting away on the current of thoughts.

A middle way opens to a substantive and more sustainable presence. We enter our mind in a relaxed way from below, while remaining vigilant to be in this moment in our mind rather than carried off with thoughts. This fusing of active vigilance with passive relaxation, gives a distinct third approach. We are here, in the whole of our mind, surface and depths. We are relaxed enough not to burn through our energy reserve too quickly, and even to allow more energy to well up from the depths. At the same time, we are vigilant, present. We do not need to suppress the thoughts that do arise. Instead we see them as just the surface phenomena that they are, while we inhabit both surface and depths.

Practicing this is easier at first in seated meditation. Begin by using some technique to focus your attention and allow the rush of thoughts to subside. Then bring the passive relaxation and active vigilance. Later, you may find yourself able to access this state as you go about your day. The question is: do you own your mind? Or is it owned by every passing thought?

For this week, please practice inhabiting your mind.

1.9 Inhabiting Our Emotions
(Presence Tool 9)

Just as there exists an ocean of peace beneath our thoughts, that same ocean lies beneath our usual emotions. By our presence, we can connect our everyday heart with that sacred heart of the world, because presence spans all the levels, from above the surface to the spiritual depths. In that way, we discover the source of equanimity, joy, awe, compassion, love, and our kindred connection with others. In the heart of presence, we create an opening for those non-self-centered emotions to enter our experience.

The hallmark of inhabiting our emotions is equanimity: we are fully here and at peace with ourselves and our world. And that equanimity allows the other deep emotions to flow through as appropriate and necessary to our immediate situation. Within the heart of peace, joy, love, and compassion find room to arise. Not all the deep emotions are pleasant, but they are all uplifting, connecting us with the sacred. Grief is one example of such an emotion.

Another quality shared by all the deep emotions is that they are not about us, personally. They are not centered on us.

They are not self-referential. Rather, the deep emotions come through us, from beyond us. To the extent that we are open to and welcoming of these sacred emotions, they inhabit us. It is right to say, that we, as our higher self, our real I, inhabit our emotions as the deep emotions.

Equanimity has a special place in this rainbow of emotion, because it paves the way for the rest. Our self-centeredness has no claim on or place in equanimity. When we are here, inhabiting our emotional heart, we connect with the ocean of peace that manifests to us as equanimity. We see and accept things as they are, without falling into indifference or passivity. We act, with vigor, to change things as necessary. Yet we do so from equanimity and conscience, not from a need to score ego points or to be in control.

Ego is like a mirrored surface on the ocean of feeling. From above, we only see ourselves and our emotions are centered on ourselves. From below, the deep emotions are reflected back down and cannot make it to the surface of everyday life. Presence breaks through this mirrored surface, dissolving it. We inhabit our emotional life. We do not recoil from it, nor do we center it solely on our personal desires and antipathies.

For this week, please inhabit your emotions. Be here, in your emotional heart. This means more than awareness of our emotions. It means occupying our emotions, being in them. And as the surface emotions subside, we are left in peace. And in peace, the other sacred emotions come up from their hidden source.

1.10 Inhabiting Body, Heart, and Mind

(Presence Tool 10)

True presence embraces wholeness, transcending all forms of partial presence. Neither inhabiting our body, nor inhabiting our heart, nor inhabiting our mind reaches wholeness. We need all three simultaneously. We can approach this effectively from below, from part to whole. We can practice inhabiting our body, our entire body, establishing our presence here. Then we can add a second part, inhabiting our body, plus our mind or heart, depending on our disposition at that moment. After establishing presence in two parts, we add the third, so that we practice inhabiting body, mind, and heart all together. Once we have experience and a clear taste of what it is like to inhabit body, heart, and mind, we have the option of diving into it directly, entering all three at once, rather than building up piecemeal.

Perhaps surprisingly, this three-fold configuration proves more stable than engaging any one of the three alone. With our mind, we can easily be carried off by thoughts. But if we are also anchored in our body and heart, we can more readily maintain moment-to-moment presence in the face of our thought stream, with all its scenarios and stories. Similarly, our emotions seduce us with their immediacy, urgency, and valence. Again, though, body and mind presence help us stay centered in front of any emotions that arise.

To be clear, when we speak of inhabiting body, heart, and mind, we do not only mean awareness of body, heart, and mind. Inhabiting means that we are here in our body, heart, and mind, as the one who is aware, the one who acts, the one who participates, the one who is. We have a visceral sense of agency, of immediacy and ownership, here in our body, our heart, and our mind.

For this week, please practice being here in all your parts.

1.11 Being Conscious

(Presence Tool 11)

After we sit in meditation for a while, our thoughts and sensory perceptions slow down, our body settles into sitting without moving and without the urge to fidget, our emotions quiet down. We seem enter a zone characterized by a lack of action and perception, as if we were asleep. Yet we are not asleep. We are wide awake in this stillness, this quietness, this peace. Very gradually, we come to realize that there is more here than a mere absence of what we are accustomed to see, think, and feel, more here than just the absence of tensions and stress. We begin to suspect that the stillness and our awareness of it are aspects of something, not just nothing.

But this something is very different. It is not a thought, but more like the capacity to perceive thoughts. It is not an emotion, but more like the capacity to have emotions. It is not a bodily or other sensory perception, but more like the capacity to perceive our senses. It is the blank screen on which our life unfolds, the blank screen that comes alive in displaying all the contents, all the details and events of our life. Under all our perceptions, there is this blank screen.

We give this cognitive stillness the name of consciousness. It is a form of inner energy without boundaries. It has the qualities of stillness, peace, and equanimity in our body, mind, and heart. But its preeminent quality is cognition, the general capacity to perceive. By turning our consciousness back on itself, we can perceive it. To do that, we simply relax back into this inner stillness and rest there, fully alert to this unfamiliar space.

In this vast, inner spaciousness, we have room to spread out. Without boundaries, we have nothing to shape or defend. Fully cognizant in this inner, pre-sensory space, we just are.

With practice, we can learn to be in that consciousness, to be in that inwardly free space, even while we also perceive our ordinary senses and act in the midst of life. Consciousness is always here in us, if we can but remain open to it. We can live our life fully, while residing in consciousness. Again and again we lose contact with that cognizant stillness, that pre-sensory spaciousness. Again and again we re-enter it.

For this week, please be conscious, be in the cognitive substrate behind all experience.

1.12 Total Presence

(Presence Tool 12)

Combining our prior efforts on inhabiting body, heart, and mind, with that of being conscious, enables us to begin our work on total or complete presence, which encompasses three levels, three worlds. The first is at the level of time, the world of our senses, our body, our emotions, and our thoughts. The second is at the level of eternity, the timelessness of just being, of pure awareness, of consciousness, wherein nothing is happening, where we just are. The third is the world of will, our source, the source of our I, of who we are.

Total presence unites all three levels in us; it brings the timeless into time. Bridging that gap is who we are, what we are built for. Our will, our I, originates in the spiritual realm of pure action, decision, and choice, well beyond ordinary time. Through the medium of consciousness, which is timeless in an eternal, is-ness sort of way, our will crosses from pure action into time. We cross into inhabiting our life, participating as the one who is aware, the one who chooses, the one who acts in time. Thus our will, our I forms the central pole, bridging and uniting the three levels in us.

What does this mean in practical, experiential terms? Starting from below, we begin by opening our awareness to embrace our entire body. Then we also include our mind and heart. Taking a step up, we relax into the cognizant stillness of consciousness, the pure awareness surrounding and permeating us, beneath our perceptions of body, heart, and mind. At the same time, we maintain awareness of our body, heart, and mind. It is as if we find ourselves in a spacious cognizance that includes all of our parts.

Then comes the crucial, stabilizing step of bringing our self, our I, our will, our attention into contact, passing through the cognizant stillness and into our body, heart, and mind. To some degree, this has already happened in the earlier steps. But now we make it explicit to ourselves that "I" am here in this. We make it, we make our self, robust. We stand here in ourselves, in our body, heart, and mind, in our consciousness, as our self, as our I, as our attention.

For this week, please practice total presence.

1.13 Leaning into Presence

(Presence Tool 13)

The defining human quality is our power to choose. And one of the defining measures of our life is the degree to which we choose to live it. So often we are indifferent to particular moments, like the simple routines of our life. Or if not indifferent, we might rather not be experiencing this moment, we might rather have it end soon so we can move on to the next situation, the next moment. Behind our indifference, dislike, and rejection, we hide our inner face from too much of our life. And that is our opportunity, our opening to live more fully.

We can choose this moment, this precious, singular, once-in-a-lifetime moment, as it is, warts and all, pleasant or unpleasant, routine or unusual. We can choose to live this moment. We can choose to be here, to participate in this moment, to experience this moment. Even if we do not like it, or do not care, we can still make this moment the time of our life, which it certainly is.

This is not to say that we should not work to improve ourselves and our circumstances. But we would be well served by not allowing our dissatisfaction to keep us from living the life we have.

Our entire life is a finite series of moments. Each one matters, because it happens only once. Each one that we do not experience, or only half-experience, effectively shortens our life, because that moment is lost to us forever. Each one that we do experience enriches us, regardless of its particular content or circumstance, because we make it ours. This is my time. This is my life, all of it.

To be clear: we know that our senses continue to function, more or less, in every waking moment. The question is whether and to what extent we ourselves are in touch, in contact with what our senses are bringing us. If we ourselves are in contact, we call that being present or having presence. So to be in contact, we choose our life as it is right now, we turn our inward face, our attention, our self, fully toward this moment. We arrive here with both feet. We lean into presence. Whether or not we like where we are, who we are with, what we are doing, or how we are feeling, we have this power to choose to live it fully, to be here in it, to participate in it, to make it ours.

By choosing this moment, we transcend the fog of indifference or rejection that all too often enshrouds us. Leaning into this moment penetrates that fog and reclaims that bit of life for us. We inwardly step forward into now and ride that crest of the endless wave of time.

We lean into our body. We lean into our mind. We lean into our heart. We lean into our senses and our experience.

For this week, please practice leaning into presence and thereby lean into your life.

2.0 Presence Strategies
(Introduction)

The previous inner work series, Presence Tools, offered a graduated and comprehensive set of methods for the practice of presence. Presence does take practice. We may have a strong intention to practice presence, but life gets in the way, we get distracted, we forget and lose contact with that intention. We need meta-methods, or strategies, to support our inner work, our use of the Presence Tools, to close the intention-action gap. These Presence Strategies are not the work of presence itself, but rather enable that work actually to take place.

Presence strategies come in many forms, but can be broadly classified into two types: metrics and triggers. Presence Metrics provide us with ways to measure our efforts of presence, at least in an approximate, subjective manner. These metrics give us specific feedback on how well we are doing with regard to presence. Because presence takes place in our inner world, it is easy to fool ourselves about the degree of our presence. For example, we may think that we are present all the time. But when we start to look at our situation more carefully, we see that we are not present all the time. Presence metrics help us gauge where we are and thereby help us see where we want to go.

Presence Triggers remind us to practice presence. We set our intention to practice presence in specific situations. When those situations arise, they may trigger our work of presence. Presence triggers come in many forms, limited only by our creativity in generating new ones that are particularly applicable to our own lifestyle, that will actually remind us to practice within our daily life. Presence triggers give us a way to form useful habits, habits of coming into presence in specific situations. Depending on our particular nature, some of the triggers will grow into positive, long-term habits, if we make the necessary effort. Other triggers may be useful for a limited time only, and then grow stale. The metrics can help us determine which triggers work for us.

So this inner work series on Presence Strategies will be divided into two series: Presence Metrics and Presence Triggers. We begin with the Metrics.

3.0 Presence Metrics

3.1 Frequency

(Presence Metric 1)

Frequency of presence connotes how often we return to ourselves, how often we remember to be within ourselves and make the effort to be present. We aim to decrease the lapsed time between falling out of presence and coming back to it. Every activity in life transforms into an opportunity for practice. Former sources of frustration, such as waiting in line, become openings into which we pour our spiritual effort. Whenever we notice that we have fallen out of presence, out of consciousness, we immediately rouse ourselves back into the moment.

To gain some clarity on the actual frequency of our inner work efforts, we can simply count them. One approach to training in presence involves setting a daily goal of a certain number of instances of presence and then counting how many times we come to presence that day. This can be partly observational: incrementing the count whenever we notice that we have somehow, without premeditation, risen to presence. The other part is intentional: whenever we remember our task of presence and our goal, we immediately take that opportunity to return to presence and then increment the count.

The count itself, though, is just a measure, important for the goal-oriented specificity and commitment it enables, but not as important as the act of coming to presence which it records. We begin modestly, setting as our goal an easily achievable number of times in the day that we will be present. Gradually, over a period of weeks or months, we increase the daily number and fill our waking hours with more instances of presence. The counting gives us a way to quantify our inner work, engage our will in fulfilling our daily goal, and make our spiritual path a little more concrete.

As an example, take the exercise of sensing each of our four limbs in turn: cycling through the right arm, right leg, left leg, and left arm. We set ourselves to repeat this exercise a particular number of times during the day – say five or ten. Whenever we remember the exercise, we turn to it, increment our count, file the count in our memory, and then leave it until the next time we awaken to the exercise. Instead of sensing we could work on general presence, a heartfelt prayer, or some other practice. To simplify, we choose one practice to count for the day and we set the daily number each morning.

If it should happen that we reach the end of the day without having made our frequency goal, we carry through on our commitment by not going to sleep until we finish. This might, for example, require a period of focused inner work where we allow ourselves one count per minute. Sticking to our commitment for the day keeps the whole process alive. Otherwise the practice of counting our inner work quickly loses its potency.

Such definite repetition of any spiritual exercise works to gradually stretch our attention, open our perceptions, collect our energies, strengthen our will, and dispose us toward the path. Starting anew at a count of zero each morning enlivens our practice by permitting us a fresh start every day, while keeping us humble by the mere fact of beginning again. The counting itself ties together our day of inner work, making the separate repetitions into a single act of will. Most importantly, counting concretizes our efforts, moving our inner work from the potential to the actual.

For this week, please use counting to measure and enhance your work of presence.

3.2 Duration

(Presence Metric 2)

Now we turn to the question of the stability of our presence: how long does any given episode of presence last?

In actual practice, we find that presence is short-lived — very short. We may momentarily surface into the vivid life of presence, only to have some thought, from the endless stream passing through our mind, come along and grab us, so that we lose ourselves on a mental tangent, our presence dissolved. Or something we see or hear takes us. The variety of ways we lose presence knows no bounds.

The first step toward extending the duration of any given episode of presence is to notice how long our presence does last. However, this is not as relatively simple as counting the frequency of presence. The obvious way to measure the duration of anything is to time it. Look at the seconds tick by on our watch and see how long we are there. Unfortunately, that simply will not work for several reasons.

First, trying to time our presence with a watch is too awkward and disruptive of the flow of our life. Our work of presence needs to fit into our life. The work of presence is inner work and can run in parallel with whatever we are doing outwardly, except for the usual caveat that when engaging in life-critical tasks, like driving, we keep our entire focus on the external task. Stopping to gaze at our watch whenever we come back to presence would disrupt the flow of life, and quickly become a burden.

Secondly, it is doubtful that we could actually time our presence even if we wanted to. The problem comes at the end. When we lose presence, we do not notice the loss. Indeed non-noticing is non-presence. We simply are no longer here, no one at home to notice that we are not present. When we do wake up and notice that we were not present for a time, that waking up is the start of a new episode of presence. We were not there to note the end of the last episode of presence, so we could not time it.

The solution to the riddle of becoming aware of the duration of presence is two-fold. First, we do not seek an objective, clock-measure of presence: we only look to having a subjective measure. How long does it seem to us? In particular, we do not need to think of it in terms of how many seconds, or if we are very steady, minutes. We look at relative duration of presence. Was it longer or shorter than prior episodes of presence? If we can gain a sense of that, it gives us a direction for our inner work, the direction of maintaining our presence for a little longer than before.

The second part of working with duration is try to increase it. When we awaken to a moment of presence, we aim to extend it to the next moment and the moment after that. We aim to stay here, in our body, as ourselves. We can work at that directly, simply by maintaining our intention to be present on a moment-to-moment basis. We can practice this intention to stay present in sitting and then also in daily life. The moment-to-moment factor is crucial. We seek to not allow gaps. It is not easy and we can only work on that briefly. But by doing so, our ability to stay present grows.

A less direct and more artificial but still effective approach is to count breaths. We practice awareness of our breathing, particularly the sensations of our breath at the tip of our nose and upper lip. We count each exhalation if we are in contact with it. The counting, though, is secondary to the awareness of each breath. We count up to ten and then begin again at one. If we lose the count or lose our awareness of the breath, we begin again at one. This practice, normally done at the beginning of a sitting meditation, quickly brings us into a relatively stable presence. After we are able to stay with the breath without losing the awareness and the count for several cycles of ten, we can drop it and proceed with the rest of our meditation practice. At that point we might want to combine the work of broadening our presence to include our whole body, mind, and heart, while keeping the unbroken, whole-body, breath awareness as an indicator of continuity of presence.

We can also try this breath counting as a way to temporarily increase the duration of our presence during our day, when we do not have other strong demands on our attention.

The result of practicing moment-to-moment presence is a much stronger and more continuous presence, a presence that is not as easily disrupted by passing thoughts or other events, a presence that can engage in activity and sustain itself, a presence whereby we can be fully here, living and experiencing our life vividly.

For this week, notice the duration of your presence and work to increase it, to make your presence more continuous.

3.3 Intensity

(Presence Metric 3)

If we look at different instances of presence, different moments when we are here, we notice they are not all inwardly the same. One way that moments of presence differ is in terms of intensity. I may be alert, but just how alert am I? I may be present, but just how present am I? How vibrant and vivid is my awareness in this moment? To what degree am I in contact with what my awareness brings to me? To what degree am I here? To what degree am I, right now?

The practical question regarding intensity of presence is how to increase it. One approach consists of increasing our inner energy. Many kinds of spiritual practices help with that, including, for example, doing a morning and/or evening meditation, participating in a worship community, an inner work group or a spiritual retreat, and breathing energy. Not wasting our energy, in tensions or harmful stress, in physical over-indulgences, or in destructive emotional storms, helps conserve the energy we have. The quality and quantity of our inner energy certainly impacts our ability to be present.

But the true key to intensity of presence is the in-the-moment will-to-be, the will to be more present right now. Can I be present now? Can I be more present right now? And yet again even more present? If we actually try this and practice it, through trial and error we begin to get a taste of the nature of the effort required to intensify our presence.

One false avenue toward more intense presence is that of increasing tension, inner or outer. Tension has no place in presence and should not be confused with intensity. Tension merely wastes our energy, thereby diminishing our ability to be present. We cannot intensify our presence by making ourselves tense within.

We can find a hint of how to be more present by its similarity to the effort of extending the duration of a given episode of presence. Both engage the same will, our will to be present. The difference is in the will to stay present versus the will to be more present. The two are complementary, supporting each other, similar yet distinct.

Another clue to the nature of the effort to be more present emerges from the effort to sense more strongly. This is more readily accessible. If we bring our attention to our right arm and hold it there, the sensitive energy accumulates in the arm, making it more vivid. Simply by staying with our attention in the arm, the sensing continues to grow stronger. But it can also grow stronger by our intention that it do so, by putting ourselves more into the arm. This reflects the fundamental effort required to be more intensely present, which is not only about drawing in more energy, but more so about strengthening our will-to-be right now, in this moment.

Efforts to intensify our presence attune us to the various degrees of presence. This teaches us to measure our presence by its intensity. For this week, in any given moment of presence, be even more present.

3.4 Breadth

(Presence Metric 4)

Sometimes we need to focus and we do so intentionally. In certain meditation methods we practice just that: focusing our attention, that most useful of our inner tools. In presence, however, we can both focus on whatever we need to focus on and simultaneously spread wide the umbrella of our presence. In presence, focus brings its object into the foreground, while allowing everything else to stay in awareness, albeit in the not-so-far-back background.

So in a moment of presence, we can ask ourselves how inclusive our presence is. Does my presence embrace everything in this moment, inwardly and outwardly? We can look at that first in terms of our body. Does my awareness extend to the whole of my body? Am I in contact with the sensitive energy throughout my body?

How about emotions? Does my presence include my emotional state, be it peace and equanimity, love, indifference, anger, lust, or greed? Whatever the particular emotion is, am I in contact with my emotional nature as it is right now, with how it feels to feel my feelings? Or am I pushing my emotions away, rejecting what I do not want to feel, not admitting to myself how I feel?

How about my mind? Am I aware of whatever thoughts may be running through or reacting to what I see or hear? Am I aware of my thoughts as just thoughts? Or are they happening disguised as what I take to be my own ongoing commentary and narration of my life? Am I aware of the attitude underlying my current state? Are these current thoughts intentional or automatic?

Am I in contact with all my senses? Am I seeing what I'm seeing, hearing what I'm hearing? Am I in touch with my immediate situation? Am I responding as necessary?

Am I here with the whole of myself?

So we can measure our presence from the viewpoint of its breadth. How wide is the embrace of my presence in this moment? Repeatedly noting the breadth of our presence attunes us this aspect of it. And the very practice of looking at our presence in terms of its breadth changes it. If we look for a broad tent of presence, we find our presence expanding its reach.

For this week, notice the breadth of your presence. Widen your presence to embrace the whole of yourself and your surroundings. Set the walls and barriers aside. Open your inner arms of presence and be whole.

3.5 Depth

(Presence Metric 5)

Do I have a center right now? Who or what occupies my center? Is it the mostly random stream of automatic, self-generating thoughts that sound like me? Is it I, am I here in my center? Is it something beyond I? Am I open to, and in the presence of, my sacred source?

One way to gauge our presence concerns how deep it is, how deep we are. The telling question is: who is present? Who is seeing what my eyes see? Who is hearing what my ears hear? If the answer is no one, just our thoughts or emotions, then this is not presence. This is our will fragmented to such an extent that every passing thought or emotion successfully claims to be me, to be who I am. This fragmented state is the zero line of our scale of depth.

The next clear mark up the scale occurs when we experience ourselves as being in our center, as being the one who sees what we see, who hears what we hear, who does what we do, who thinks what we think when we think intentionally. If we are here, at home in ourselves, in our body, mind, and heart, in our sensation and consciousness, then we have a center and we are present in it. In that condition we are unified as our I. We actually live our life, rather than our life living us.

Between the zero line of fragmented non-presence and this I-centered presence, there are various intermediate, partially unified states. We enter those when we make efforts to be in contact with our body, or our mind, when we make efforts to be wholly present, but are not quite there. In these intermediate states we still wobble and are not settled in presence, not even temporarily. These states also occur fleetingly when we are surprised or shocked by some unexpected event. We are bumped up, into presence. But, if we do not know the taste of presence and the methods for intentionally coming into or maintaining it, we fall apart quickly, back to the zero level, to non-presence.

There also exists a higher kind of presence, beyond our I. For that we need to let go and abandon ourselves. We drop our I into the depths beyond it. We open ourselves toward the direction of inwardness, beyond thought, emotion, and sensation, even beyond the stillness of consciousness. We reach deep within and ask that the door be opened to us. And we allow the higher, the sacred, to flow into us, as us. Our center expands to be everywhere and nowhere.

This is the direction of our work in depth. At first, when you drop everything, what is left is you, your I. To go further, we need to drop even this I, this wonder that is us.

The depth metric is a measure of what world you are in, of the state of your will: fragmented, partially unified, unified I, or the Sacred Self. For this week, please measure the depth of your own presence.

3.6 Rating the Day

(Presence Metric 6)

Time is precious. How we live today creates our future. Do we spend our time profitably in developing our soul? To answer this, we could use a daily measure, based on our presence metrics.

Taking stock of our inner work helps bring clarity to the apparent fuzziness of the spiritual path. Because the path only partly belongs to our ordinary world in space and time, we do not readily see its contours. By regularly assessing our practice, we can see our true situation more clearly.

Here is one approach to this. At the end of each day, at bedtime, look back to see the extent to which inner work, spiritual practice penetrated your life during that day. How often were you present, for how long, how deeply, how broadly, how intensely?

You need not make this a highly detailed review. Simply note your overall impression of the quality of your inner life during the foregoing day. To make it more concrete and to obtain a measure for day-to-day comparisons and goals, rate the day on a 0 to 10 scale, with 0 standing for no presence at all, and 10 representing your ideal of presence practice. The one absolutely necessary ingredient in this review and rating process is complete honesty with yourself, the willingness to see your life as it actually is.

This important and effective practice can be found in a number of wisdom traditions. It dates back at least five hundred years, for example to the time of the Khwajagan, the masters of wisdom of Central Asia, among whom were the founders of some of today's Sufi orders. This daily evaluation helps us identify our obstacles to and opportunities for inner work. It helps us realize our true position on the spiritual path, thus encouraging us to redouble our efforts to practice more, to practice wisely, to practice with heart.

So at the end of your day, take a look back to see how you were inwardly. One clue can be found in how you are at that moment, as you retire from the day. The day is over and with it the time for active efforts. So here you are. In this effortless state, to what degree are you present? To what degree is your body alive with sensation? To what degree are you aware of your thoughts and emotions, of the stillness and equanimity beneath them? To what degree are you here? The quality of our presence at the end of the day is a strong indicator of how well we have worked that day.

Some of us start our day with a meditation period, which may result in a state of centered presence we can carry into the day. If we work at presence during the day, it builds up even stronger, so that by the end of the day, we are effortlessly here in body, heart, and mind. If on the other hand, in terms of inner work, we just coast through the day, making no intentional efforts of presence, then whatever presence we gained in our morning sitting will dissipate long before we go to bed. How we are at any moment is partially a function of our prior efforts, our prior practice.

For this week, at the end of each day, please rate the quality and quantity of your work of presence during that day.

3.7 Effectiveness
(Presence Metric 7)

We have looked at six ways to measure our inner work of presence, six different views. One of the primary reasons for gauging our presence in these ways is to see what works. We have available from various spiritual traditions an abundance of proven techniques for bringing ourselves into and maintaining a state of presence. Yet what works well for you, may not work for me. What works for you today, may not work for you tomorrow or next year. What works in one situation, may not work in another. To assess all that, we now look to combine our various metrics into one overriding meta-metric: effectiveness. Using this effectiveness measure enables us to experiment with the methods in our toolbox of presence and see which work best for us. The practice of presence is an art, but gauging the effectiveness of our approach puts that art on a sound foundation.

Sometimes habit and momentum cause us to carry on using a presence technique long after it has stopped being effective or optimal for us. In other cases, we find ever-growing depth and value in a particular technique as we continue to engage in it over months or years. Checking on ourselves, in terms of the frequency, duration, intensity, breadth, and depth of our presence and how it varies day-to-day, shows us how effective our practice is. Then we can try changing our practice and seeing how effective that change proves to be. We bring our full intelligence to bear on our inner work. We sort out what feels good, comfortable, or familiar from what actually makes a difference in our ability to be present.

No one, no spiritual teacher and no book, can tell us what practice is best for us. They might show us practices and advise us, but only we ourselves can judge what fits and what works for us. Though we seek out and profit from spiritual companionship and communal practice, self-reliance remains an essential element of our way. To rely on ourselves means that we understand that no one can do our inner work for us. It also means assessing our inner work as best we can. Ultimately, self-reliance develops our contact with our own I, the core of true presence.

In our path toward presence, we do not seek escape into eternal bliss. In seeking a better life, we do not give ourselves entirely over to the material world of time. Presence puts us right at the interface between the eternal and the temporal, honoring both and giving each its due. We bring the depth of our spirit to our actions in time. We are here. Yet we do not know this place very well, this shoreline of the sacred. But now we have a sense of how to measure our presence and thereby pierce the fog that envelops our perceptions. When we can see and know our own presence, then we can find ways to enhance it.

For this week, please notice the effectiveness of the various ways you work to be present.

4.0 Presence Triggers

4.1 Appointments

(Presence Trigger 1)

We have studied and practiced methods and tools for establishing presence. And we have looked at various metrics to assess the quality and quantity of our presence. This still leaves us with the crucial problem of remembering to initiate our work of presence. Do we go about our day without practicing presence, even though we know how to do so and how to assess our efforts?

What we need are triggers that will remind us in the midst of our busy or not so busy lives, remind us to practice presence now. Rather than waiting for spontaneous moments of awakening into presence, which only come haphazardly, we develop intentional triggers that will awaken us. So now we begin to study and practice a series of such triggers. In doing so, as we learn the possibilities, we also become able to devise our own presence triggers, suited to our capabilities and circumstances. All the presence triggers depend on our taking the time to create a clear intention to awaken to presence whenever that trigger occurs.

We start with a simple, though not necessarily easy, way to trigger presence. We set up, in advance, appointments for ourselves, times during our day at which we intend to practice presence. We do this in the morning, at the start of our day, perhaps at the end of our sitting when we have heightened clarity of intention.

There are at least two approaches to using appointment triggers for presence. The first is the straightforward one of making an appointment with ourselves for definite times of the day. For example, we could say that we will practice presence at 10:00 AM, 3:00 PM, and 8:00 PM, or other times that fit our life. Then when those times arrive, we engage in one of the presence practices from our inner work toolkit. If we miss the exact time, but remember about it later, then we just practice presence at that moment of remembering.

We may be tempted to set a reminder alarm on our phone or watch. This might work, but it has two problems. First, such external reminders tend to become ineffective after a while, as we just start ignoring them. Second, we want to build an inner force of presence, an inner source of remembering to practice, not have to rely on artificial means. The growth of that inner source itself becomes a central aspect of our spiritual work.

The second type of presence appointment is situational. We choose an event or circumstance we will very likely be in sometime during the day, perhaps more than once. And we set ourselves, in advance, to practice presence when that circumstance arises. Perhaps we know that we will go to a particular place today or that we will do a particular thing. We set our intention to practice presence at that moment, when it comes. This approach leaves the field wide open for us to experiment with various appointments for presence.

The important thing, anytime we do remember to work on presence, is to actually do it, to come back to ourselves, to come back to being here. When we remember, be it by appointment or otherwise, we immediately engage in one of the presence tools and we work to sustain and deepen our presence. If we remember and yet dismiss that remembering or let it slide, then the moments of remembering will come less often and soon enough we will altogether stop remembering to practice presence. We need to honor that moment of re-awakening to the possibility of presence, every time.

Setting appointments to meet ourselves in presence can be powerful and effective. It can happen that we suddenly come to, right at the time or situation that we set hours earlier. It is a gift we give our future selves.

For this week, please practice setting and keeping appointments to practice presence.

4.2 Ad Hoc Goals
(Presence Trigger 2)

Short-term presence goals can help. Say you are out for a walk or a jog or a bike ride and you decide to be and stay present. You might choose a landmark that you will soon pass, like a tree or a pole, an intersection or a building. And then you work to maintain your presence until you reach that landmark. Once you reach it, you immediately select the next suitable landmark and stay present until you get there. This type of practice has the great advantage of being concrete and immediate. The circumscribed nature of the effort enables us to bring more intensity and more continuity of presence, at least for that brief time.

The endless other examples of short-term goals of presence include: until the next commercial break in the TV show, until you reach the front of the line you are waiting in, until you finish brushing your teeth, until you finish doing the dishes or just this dish, until the end of the conversation or the meeting or just this sentence you are speaking or reading. We use our creativity and intelligence to find such ever-present opportunities and adapt them to support our inner work.

We can transform our ordinary activities into occasions for inner work by choosing to practice in particular situations and events as we enter them. For example, I am about to go into the grocery and suddenly remember that this offers me a chance to work. So I decide, on the spur of the moment, just before entering the store, that I will attempt to practice full awareness of my body through sensation during the entire period I am in the grocery. Then as I shop, I keep returning to my intention to practice and keep strengthening my contact with the sensitive energy in my body.

Similar possibilities abound in which we can choose discrete events, on an ad hoc, opportunistic, non-premeditated basis, to be venues for inner work: going to a party, a concert, a commute, a walk, a meeting, a meal, doing a household project, pumping gas, taking a shower, performing minor tasks like taking out the garbage or combing our hair, and so on. The power of this method lies in the fact that the inner task is limited to one time interval, which becomes a field for our will, for our intention. Because we can envision the entire event ahead of time and because it has a clearly defined duration, we can fill the event with our intention to practice and thereby bring stronger, more frequent effort to bear on our inner work than might otherwise be possible.

For this week, be prepared to respond to the unexpected impulse to pursue your inner work during a situation or event you are about to begin or already in. When you recognize the opportunity, let this recognition be a presence trigger for you to set yourself to practice presence during the event. As you go through it, stay in touch with your intention and actually practice for the duration of the event. If you lose your intention, then, as soon as you remember, return to working to be and stay present.

4.3 Eating Presence

(Presence Trigger 3)

Eating with presence means in part to actually taste our food as we eat it, to be aware of its aroma and texture, aware of chewing and swallowing, aware of bringing the food from plate to mouth. Too often we are not in contact with our food as we eat. Intentionally tasting our food helps us to appreciate and enjoy it.

However, eating with presence means more than just tasting our food: it means to be fully present while eating. In presence we are in contact with our entire body, at home in it. We are aware of the thoughts and emotions running through us. We are aware of our reactions to the food, our desires. And most importantly, we are in ongoing contact with our self; we are here, the one who is eating. We become the intention to nourish our body through eating.

The delight that food naturally and rightly gives can easily lead us to fall into identification with eating. Sometimes the desire for food overpowers us into anticipating the next bite rather than focusing on the one we are currently chewing, ironically decreasing the taste experience and satisfaction that we derive from eating. In that situation our food eats us; we are just passive beneath the desire.

Saying a blessing prior to eating can remind us to eat with presence. It puts us in touch with our dependence on and indebtedness for our food. It reinforces our connection with the Earth and with the society that brings us more than we ourselves grow. Ultimately we may eat with respect and even reverence.

So if you are so inclined, say a blessing before your meal, and use that moment to come into presence and heartfelt gratitude, to prepare yourself for the sacred and enjoyable act of eating. A brief blessing, whether done inwardly for ourselves, or outwardly with our tablemates, can create the tone of presence for the meal. Even without a blessing, it helps if we set our intention to eat with presence at the beginning of the meal. We eat with respect for our food, as our essential lifeline.

During the meal we stay aware of the visceral, bodily act of eating, of bringing the food to our mouth, of its aroma, of biting into it, of chewing, of its taste and texture, and of swallowing. We stay aware of our inner reactions to the food, the liking or the disliking, the wanting, the craving for the next bite, perhaps even the gratitude. We stay aware of our whole body and ourselves, of I am eating.

Something unexpected may begin to open when we eat with full presence. Besides the well-known nutritional components of our food, there are spiritual energies within the food we eat. By eating with presence, we gradually come to be aware that presence unlocks those energies from the food and enables us to absorb them as food for our soul. When we eat inattentively, we miss this important opportunity.

How we eat is an indicator of the state of our soul. We work to develop mealtime as a trigger for presence. We let each meal remind us to enter the occasion with presence, to be the one who is eating. For this week, please practice eating presence.

4.4 The Doorway Exercise

(Presence Trigger 4)

To remind us to reawaken into presence, we can work to form certain simple, positive habits. One such is to come into presence every time we walk through a doorway. It sounds and is simple. But it requires a sustained effort of active and self-cognizant intention to get to the point where doorways do remind us to be present.

The exercise is this: as we walk through a doorway, we bring our attention into being in our body and into being here as our self. We let the doorway remove the fog of half-awareness and random thoughts that usually surrounds us. As we walk through the doorway, it is as if we were walking through a curtain of energy that shimmers right through us and reinvigorates our contact with our body.

The difficulty is that doorways come upon us unannounced and that we pass through them rather quickly. So we might remember about the doorway exercise only after passing through. This is unlike, for example, eating presence, wherein we might remember to be present at any time during the extended period of the meal and then be able to work on presence for some of the remainder of the mealtime.

Doorways are too quick for that. We need to be alert and aware of the doorway as a trigger for presence before we reach it. Nevertheless, if we remember about the exercise after passing through a doorway, we can just turn to presence right then. The important thing is to be present and to work on being present more. Doorways can help us with that.

The doorway exercise can teach us valuable lessons. For example, we can be in a room, knowing that soon we will walk out the door and intending to be present when we do so. Then by the time we actually move toward and into the doorway, we have lost contact with that intention to be present and forgotten the exercise. This shows our distractibility. It shows how easily our intentions evaporate. It shows that to make an intention effective, we need to get fully behind it. So we try again and maybe the next time we do remember to be present at the door. And this shows the value of persevering.

Each morning, we set our intention to work on this doorway exercise that day. Even if we remember it very few times, or even just once, it will be of value. If we persevere, doorways can become a frequent trigger for us to be present.

For this week, please practice being present whenever you pass through a doorway. Be in your body as the one who is walking through that doorway.

4.5 Walking Presence

(Presence Trigger 5)

That majority of us fortunate enough to be able to walk can make double use of walking by practicing presence as we walk. If we pursue this powerful practice often enough and persistently enough, the act of walking itself gradually becomes a trigger reminding us to be present, here and now.

In walking presence we are not just going somewhere, we are also already here, in mid-stride. Walking presence begins in our body, with direct awareness of our feet and legs as they move, of the muscles in our legs as they flex and release, of the changing form of our feet as they adapt to each portion of our step and to the contours beneath them, of our arms swinging in coordination with our legs, of the rhythms of our steps, of the effort of going uphill and the relative ease of going down, of the quality of our breathing as it responds to our pace.

All these aspects of body awareness in walking can be

enhanced and interwoven by the practice of sensing while we walk. Sensing is body awareness plus. What we add is contact with the sensitive energy in our body. We can best become familiar with sensing in quiet sitting meditation by putting our attention into a hand or foot, an arm or a leg, and holding our attention there. Gradually that part of our body grows more alive and vibrant and we become aware of the energy within it. Through persistent practice we become able to sense our entire body and not just while sitting quietly but also in movement, for example in walking. So as we walk we practice, as continuously as possible, being aware of our body and of the sensitive energy within it. Though this is the essential foundation and in itself can change our state dramatically, there is yet more to walking presence.

    We do not walk with blinders on; we need situational awareness, even in the ordinary manner of walking. But with walking presence, we take in the whole scene around us, whatever or whoever is there. Persisting, this leads to a global awareness, an entry into the field of consciousness. Consciousness has no boundaries and through it we open to wholeness, both the whole of ourselves and the whole situation surrounding us. We open to the wonder of being alive, to the beauty of this world, to the freshness of this ever-changing moment, to our mind and our body. Everything, inner and outer, is embedded in this one broad field of consciousness, this holistic continuum underlying all our partial perceptions of this and that. In walking presence, we are alert and alive. And again there is yet more.

    We usually treat the event of walking like taking a taxi. We tell the driver — in this case the automatic part of our mind and body — our destination and then we sit back to go along for the ride, daydreaming all the while. Rather than be a heedless passenger when we walk, presence brings us fully into the action, as the one who is walking, as the walker. Presence means doing what we are doing. We see what we see. We hear what we hear. We feel what we feel. And when we walk, we walk. We have the sense that "I am walking, I am taking this step." We become ourselves, walking.

All this may sound complicated, but it is not. The practice of walking presence does build up, layer by layer: from body awareness, to sensing, to consciousness, to I am. In the end, though, it is simple and natural and a joy: just fully here, walking.

Sometimes we walk only a few steps and at other times much further. To be present in walking only a few steps, we need to prepare, to enter presence before we even start. For longer walks, we can use the walk itself to generate and deepen presence as we go. Either way, short or long, we walk so often that walking offers an important opportunity to insert more presence into our day. And the more we practice walking presence, the more the act of walking itself reminds us to be present: we start walking and we spontaneously remember "here I am, walking."

For this week, walk in presence, let the act of walking remind you to be present.

4.6 Phone Presence
(Presence Trigger 6)

One advantage of having phone calls trigger presence is that incoming calls happen randomly. So if we can train ourselves to respond with presence whenever the phone rings, we can then bring presence into moments that might otherwise lack it entirely. The incoming call side of the practice is this. Whenever we hear our phone ring, or feel it vibrate to announce a call, we immediately become aware of our body and of ourselves as being here and now. Then we maintain presence until the end of the call. As we reach for the phone, we stay present, in our body, as our self. As we speak and listen, we stay present, in our body, in our heart, in our mind, as our self. And we keep that up until the call ends.

The call triggers us into presence. If we forget to rise into presence when the phone first rings, then perhaps we remember at some point during the call. And we work at presence from that point on. If we lose our presence and then notice that during the call, we just immediately come back into presence.

One kind of question that arises here is whether it is possible to work at presence during a conversation without feeling somehow at least partially removed from the conversation, as if our work of presence itself were creating a barrier between us and the other person, or distracting us from the conversation. The answer is that presence brings us more into the conversation, more into contact with the person we are speaking and listening to.

In presence, we are not so distracted by our thoughts reacting to what we are hearing or planning what to say next. We are just listening, taking it all in, fully focused on the conversation. In presence, when we speak, we not only hear ourselves talking, we are also in what we say. We mean what we say and what we do not mean, we do not say. In presence we embrace both viewpoints: our own and that of the other person. We see the whole situation more clearly and respond more appropriately than when we are just reacting from a narrow part of ourselves.

The practice for placing a call is similar. When we notice our intention to make a phone call, we immediately become aware of our body and of ourselves as being here and now, and we set our intention to maintain presence throughout the call. As we start the call, we are there, in contact with the act. As the other person answers we are there, in contact with our body, our mind, our heart, our self, and hearing what they say. And so it continues until we end the call.

This is not an easy practice for two reasons. First is the challenge of remembering to practice phone presence. If we persist with the intention to have the phone awaken us into presence and carry through on that whenever we remember it, then gradually we accustom ourselves to having phone calls trigger presence.

The second challenge is becoming able to be present while in a conversation, though it is somewhat easier while listening than while speaking. In listening presence our mind quiets down and we just listen carefully. The difficulty there is the reaction we have to other person and to what is being said. We have thoughts and emotions kicking off in response. While they are speaking, we are planning what to say next. All that takes us out of listening presence, distracting us into what is happening inside us rather than what we are hearing.

In speaking we tend to get lost in what we are saying. It seems to us that we do not have enough attention to both be present and to speak. The difficulty here is our belief that we need to split our attention between speaking and presence. We can resolve this by just bringing one unified attention, one unified will into the act of speaking. We speak from the whole of ourselves. We are the one who is speaking. There is no duality of speaking and presence. There is just one: speaking presence. There is not intention and attention, there is just one will. Our unified will entrains our entire awareness, body, heart, and mind, into one wholeness: speaking presence. And with practice we extend listening presence and speaking presence beyond phone calls, into conversation presence in any situation.

For this week, please practice phone presence. Let the act of receiving or placing a phone call remind you to be present during that call.

4.7 Waiting Presence

(Presence Trigger 7)

Waiting used to be a problem. Standing in line at the store, we would fight off the boredom by scanning the tabloids or other products waiting there with us or we would ruminate on our bad luck of getting in the wrong line, coming to the store at the wrong time, or the injustice and inefficiency of it all. But now waiting is an opportunity. We just grab our smartphone and have an array of things to do while we wait our turn. Another option, though, is to have the situation remind us to focus on presence while we wait. The waiting itself can trigger us to remember ourselves and be present.

Looking more carefully at these interludes, these gaps in time that we call waiting, we see this as the low-hanging fruit of off-the-cushion inner work. The feeling of incipient boredom can be a potent reminder that we have both the time and the inner resources available to focus on presence, at least at that moment. Waiting can remind us to be here while we wait. That work of presence while waiting, removes the feeling that waiting is wasted time and fills the period with meaning, with vivid life, with something productive and nourishing for our soul.

Sometimes we wait inwardly, even while fully occupied outwardly. This can happen when our outer activity does not require our full attention. Take the example of exercising. Maybe during a particular exercise session we are looking forward to it being over, waiting for it to end. This type of inner waiting is also a good opportunity for presence, because it signals that we have inner resources, attention and cognizant energy, to spare. We can turn that to constructive use by practicing waiting presence right then.

We wait: in line, for our ride, for the bus, the train or the airplane, in the waiting room. We wait for the waiter. We wait for the class to start or the commute to be over, for the work day or week to end. We wait for a break, for our ship to come in, for the computer to boot up. So much opportunity. So much time ready to be put to constructive use.

We tend to equate waiting with impatience and boredom, twin emotions of rejection, rejecting our life as it is in this moment, and most tellingly, rejecting just being. We want to do something or be entertained, somehow to fill our time, to fill the silence or to rush on to the next thing. We rightly abhor wasting our time. But busyness alone does not help; it just masks the more fundamental problem: that we live without presence, that we live without being here to experience our life in the full richness of each moment.

When we wait, we not only have time, ordinary outer time, to kill as it were; we also and more importantly have inner time. Just as outer time is the framework of action in the physical world, inner time is the framework of action in our inner world. The inner action we seek in this particular mode of spiritual practice is to become and stay present while we wait. Waiting provides the opportunity for that inner action.

When we notice that we are waiting for something,

then instead of sinking into boredom or resentment, instead of breaking out the smartphone, instead of scanning the tabloids, we can move into presence, as completely as possible. With practice we become able to enter full presence all at once. Until then, we take a stepwise approach and build up our presence.

We start with our body, with awareness of our body, sensing parts and, if we can, the whole of our body. We take time to strengthen that direct, visceral contact with our body, to raise that sensitive energy. To this we add awareness of our emotional state, of what's happening in our chest and solar plexus. To that we add awareness of our thoughts as they come and go. Then we enter the cognizant stillness behind our thoughts, our open, spacious consciousness, whereupon we see that we are not our thoughts or our emotions. To all of that we add ourselves: we enter the moment as I. I am here, now. I am the one who sees what I see and hears what I hear. And then we maintain this fullness of presence, as we continue to wait. This is waiting presence.

For this week, don't just wait, be there.

4.8 Difficulties

(Presence Trigger 8)

Life brings us joy and also, inevitably, brings us troubles. Our problems come in all shades and sizes. At one end of the spectrum are the minor annoyances, like misplacing our keys, catching mild a cold, or getting stuck in traffic. At the other end are the major ones, like losing our job, having a serious illness, getting divorced, or seeing a family member dying. The more peace we have inwardly, the less we are touched by annoyances; we just sail right through. But as the severity increases, we all have a limit where the difficulty does disturb or even shake us.

That disturbance may be brief, as with the more minor problems. Or it may be protracted in the face of a major problem. Without waiting for a deathbed conversion, we can work to have our unexpected and unwanted difficulties deepen our inner life. When we are in dire straits, we may naturally turn toward the Divine. We may ask for help from that Constant, Loving Friend. And those situations may jar us into a stronger, more lasting presence. Conversely, the depth and strength of our presence determines how we respond to difficulties, what we can bear.

We might ask whether a particular serious problem was *meant* for us. If we approach our difficulties with openness, we may be able to extract meaning from them and in that sense make them *meant* for us. We can extract meaning from difficulties on several levels. On the basic level of life skills, we ask what caused this difficulty and what we can learn from it, how it can inform our future actions. On the psychological level, we notice our tendency to ruminate over the situation and to whine, complain, blame, and terribilize. We see how our rejection of pain, how our attachment and clinging cause so much of our suffering. Perhaps we see a way to accept and move forward. On the spiritual level, our own suffering can give us compassion for the suffering of others. It can awaken us to reassess our life, to see what really matters to us. It can remind us to be present, to be here in ourselves, for ourselves, and as ourselves, in both suffering and joy. Both by necessity and opportunity, a time of troubles can be a time of renewal and rededication to our spiritual inner work.

In presence we can find refuge from our difficulties. When a disturbing problem comes up, we can train ourselves to meet it with presence. If we stay on our surface, in our perseverating thoughts and reactive emotions, we are easily battered by the vicissitudes of life. If we go into our depth, we have a chance to maintain, to stay ourselves. The only caveat here is that we should not abuse our inner work, our presence, by using it as an escape from facing and responding to our difficulties. Presence can and rightly does help us escape from clinging and identification. And presence enables us to be here to meet the challenges that confront us.

Our work for this week is to make our difficulties into triggers for presence. Whenever we have a problematic situation arise, be it minor, moderate, or severe, we turn to presence.

4.9 Money Presence

(Presence Trigger 9)

Regardless of how much we make or have of it, and regardless of whether we need or want more of it, money plays a key role in our life. In its multiplicity of forms, we often deal with money. We tend to have inner and outer conflicts and tensions on issues around money. We tend to be attached to and identified with money. We tend to allow the amount of money we earn or have to define us, whether overtly and consciously or in subtle and unrecognized ways. All these factors make our money dealings a ripe target for presence.

The basic practice of money presence is to be present whenever we deal with money in any of its forms. When we make a purchase at a store, we come into body awareness, sensing our body as we dig into our wallet or purse, count out cash and hand it to the cashier, or pull out and swipe a card or put it into the reader, or tap our phone to complete the transaction. We are there, in our body, in that action, not just in our mind thinking about it. When we buy something online, we sense our body as we key in our credit card information and click the buy button. When we pay a bill, we sense our body as we write the check or click on a website to pay it. On pay day at work, when we review our direct deposit pay stub or receive and cash our check, we sense our body as we do so. Any time we pay or receive payment, we let that act trigger us into presence, an organic, in-that-moment presence.

Of course, true presence is much more than body awareness. But sensing our body is the foundation of presence and is concrete enough for us to know with relative clarity whether or not we are actually doing that bit of inner work. So we start with sensing as we deal with money and then add awareness of our thoughts and emotions in those moments, the tensions in our body, and then we add a sense of wholeness, a sense that I am here doing whatever it is I am doing with money. We are present.

We can also notice when we are just thinking or even obsessing about money and let that noticing trigger us to be present at such moments. We see our thoughts and we are in our thinking mind. We see our emotions and we are in our feeling mind. We are here, thinking and feeling about money.

To be clear, our intention and the purpose of money presence is to be present. This is not a magical way to create abundance. As our self-awareness around money grows, money presence may or may not heal our relationship with money. It may or may not help us find a way through our money problems. But whether or not we have issues with money, this practice can help us to be present in more situations than might otherwise be the case.

For this week, please practice money presence.

4.10 Person Presence

(Presence Trigger 10)

Very few live as hermits; the rest of us are social beings. We need each other in so many ways and we discover ourselves in relating to others. The natural and true way to relate to another person is to be present with him or her. We touched on aspects of this in an earlier installment of this series on presence triggers: Phone Presence. There we practiced speaking and listening presence. Now we seek to take a step beyond that to actually being with the other person: here I am and there you are and we are here together.

This is different from just listening to the words that come from a person's mouth. It is entering the space that embraces us both. You say what you say. I think and feel what I think and feel. Then I say what I say. But all of that happens in this one space that we share, within this one awareness that we share. We begin to experience that your awareness and my awareness are not separate, that one field of consciousness enfolds us both.

This both requires and enables us to be at ease with the other person. To the extent I am concerned with the impression I am making, with what you think of me, and to the extent I am concerned with what I think and feel about you, and to the extent I am enmeshed in some presumed hierarchy in which we occupy different rungs, then I remain locked in myself and cannot simply be here with you. But if I see that you are a person in the very same way that I am a person, neither better nor worse, neither higher nor lower, but one and the same, then I can be with you. I am myself. You are yourself. Both unique, but both the same in that one life flows through us, one consciousness embraces us.

This is the inner relationship between us all. It holds true regardless of whether we are lovers, family, friends, colleagues, acquaintances, total strangers, or even enemies. In this inner relationship, there are no strangers, there are no enemies, there are only persons, whose essential, spiritual, core personhood has the same roots as our own.

The practice of sensing brings us into contact with this moment, so that we can occupy the same time and space as the other person. However, to be in the field of consciousness that embraces both of us, requires more than sensing alone. It requires contact with the silence in our center, with the stillness beneath our thoughts, emotions, and physical sensations.

Essentially, this is a stillness of our will, an inner stance of receptivity and openness, a willingness to just be here. Consciousness itself is open, having no boundaries. So whenever we adopt an inner attitude of openness, we thereby align ourselves with consciousness. And if we can see that inner spaciousness as more than just an absence of thoughts and noise and events, then we can enter the vast, cognizant stillness of consciousness.

The cognizant stillness at the base of my mind, my being, is the same cognizant stillness at the base of your being. That is the field we are in. And by the act of just being, of just being present with another person, we enter that shared field.

This works best when we have time. But it can also come in snippets, in the fleeting hello, in the brief interaction, in the quick exchange of pleasantries. If we are ready, if we are in contact with the stillness, then when another person comes into our space, we are there to share our inner space with them, no matter how briefly.

Each person is unique and even awe-inspiring, as the bearer of a piece of the Divine. So whenever we are with anyone, by their mere proximity to us they can awaken us to the wonder of humanity and bring us up into presence. Seeing another person, we rise out of our inner monologue into the presence of the hidden sacred within them. And by our sameness, it reminds us of the hidden sacred within us.

For this week, please practice person presence: be fully there whenever you are with another person. Let the fact that the other person is there trigger you to practice presence.

4.11 TV Presence

(Presence Trigger 11)

We spend much of our precious time being entertained: by TV, movies and video, music and concerts, sports, novels, and so on. We consume all these with little thought to the effects on our life and particularly our inner life. Can we bring more value to our time as a spectator?

A primary way we measure the quality of any entertainment is the degree to which it engages us, mentally and emotionally. If it's good, it invites us to surrender to it for the duration. And if it's good, we accept. That is the bargain. We give our mind and heart to the show, the movie, concert, game, or novel and let it play us. For that period we live as that event. Its images form themselves in our minds. Its emotions form themselves in our hearts. The show moves us; it lives us. We allow ourselves to be passive receivers, passive participants. Our life for that time is the show.

This we usually consider good entertainment. The

drama, the thrill, the suspense, the horror, the righteousness, the anxiety and fear, the romance and humor, the beauty, the reversals, and the breakthroughs: entertainment stimulates us with a wide repertoire of emotion and spectacle. No wonder it can be so addicting. We experience it all in ourselves as our own. Indeed it is our own experience, for those moments. We surrender, putting ourselves into abeyance, and let the show take us, letting it drive our perceptions, feelings, thoughts, and mental images. The entertainment industry has gotten very good at this, keeps getting better, and will continue to become more effective, more immersive, as new techniques and technologies come into use.

So where does this leave us, if we aspire to a spiritual inner life? One answer, that doesn't offer much help, is that there are the rare few works of entertainment, certain great music, a few movies, and others that rather than take us out of ourselves, actually serve to bring us to ourselves, calling us to presence. But those are rare. The great bulk of entertainment takes us away and scripts our time and experience for us.

Another answer is the monkish one of eliminating our TV watching, our movie going, our music listening. Rather than make our life dull, that would enrich it; the ordinary would become more vivid. But the fact is that most of us, including those who yearn for a spiritual inner life, do not aspire to become monks, nuns, or hermits. We seek a path into the spirit, while living an ordinary life in our times. And the ordinary life of these times in the developed world certainly includes consuming entertainment, or rather being intermittently consumed by entertainment.

So the question becomes: can we bring inner work into our periods of entertainment without diminishing our enjoyment of the show? Can we, for example, give our mind and heart over to the show, while keeping some presence in our body? A partial presence to be sure, but presence nevertheless. Instead of living completely vicariously in the show, instead of the show totally living us, we also live a parallel time, a real time, in the present, in our body. We let our mind be shaped by the images of the show and our heart informed by the emotional tenor of the show, while our body we keep as our own.

Of course, this is much easier said than done. It takes a clear and decisive intention, formed prior to the show and sustained during it. Without that, we very likely will disappear within the first minute and only reemerge sometime after the show ends, with a vague, uneasy feeling that we have somehow lost our time.

It's been a long day. We're tired and just want to zone out in front of the TV. Is there any chance of presence? Well, yes: we can relax into our body and set a simple intention to stay in contact with our body. Presence does not need tension and can even be effortless. But it does need the will to be. Presence may arise accidentally, unbidden, but quickly evaporates without our intention to be here. So in front of the TV, we can relax into a larger awareness that includes both the show and our body. Almost inevitably we soon forget our body and get lost in the show. Our inner work then is to return again and again to that body contact, whenever we notice we have lost it. And at the commercial breaks or at changes of scene or when we turn the page in our novel, we can take the opportunity to reaffirm, to renew our body presence and carry that into the next segment.

While we base our entertainment presence in body sensation, the core of presence as always, is the ongoing experience of "I am here," the direct perception that I am here, watching this show, in touch with my body. The body contact ensures this presence has some reality to it and does not just evaporate nor descend into a fantasy, a pseudo-presence, where we accept a pretense, an assumption of presence, even when there is none. "I am here, in contact with my body and watching the show."

Entertainment is not inherently destructive to our inner life. But there is an opportunity cost to those hours a day we spend in front of the TV or otherwise being entertained, unless we use that very same time to build our soul, through presence. We may even find that the more present we are, the more we enjoy the show. So when we do relax into some entertainment, we can also practice relaxing into our body, into ourselves, into our I.

For this week, please be there to enjoy the show. Let entertainment trigger you into presence.

4.12 Working Presence

(Presence Trigger 12)

Most of us work, whether at a job or in our home, whether paid or not. For our present purposes, we consider work to include both our jobs and recurring chores, from simple personal hygiene to cooking, cleaning and maintaining our home and possessions, caring for our family, planning our budget, paying our bills, shopping, and all the rest. So much of our life requires us to be actively engaged, managing and shaping our immediate surroundings to meet our needs and desires. We shall refer to all of that by the name of outer work, or just work, in contrast to inner work. And our inner work aim will be to be present while we work, to have our work remind us to be present.

Some types of work, say for example the work of a surgeon, a nurse, or a teacher, already require presence, require us to be there and fully engaged, a natural presence. We leave those types of work as they are, without trying to add any other form of presence to them. But many kinds of work leave us with spare attention that we can turn toward presence. And every type of work has some down time, interludes during which we can relax into presence. In these cases, we can utilize our Presence Tools to practice while we work.

Inner work and outer work go hand in hand. To a large extent, our jobs define us. They give us a way to be productive, to serve society and ourselves. There is a great dignity and fulfillment in work, regardless of the particular type we do. That is one of the fundamental lessons of the Bhagavad Gita. Bringing presence into our work, engages us more fully in what we do. And by being more fully engaged, we naturally bring more quality, a sense of excellence to what we do. At the same time, the more engaged we are, the more satisfaction we derive from our work. External quality in our actions, enhances our inner quality of experience, and vice versa. And though our jobs may define us, only in presence do we truly become ourselves.

Our inner work of presence needs to be concrete and specific. If we say to ourselves that today I will be present as I go about my job, we may have great difficulty realizing that aim. It is too diffuse, too general, too encompassing to be feasible. We will have a much better chance of bringing presence into our job, our outer work, if we choose specific routines or duties during which we will practice presence. Once we establish some regularity of presence in those duties, they can serve as a foothold for presence at work. Then we can add other aspects of our work into which we bring presence.

In time, as we repeatedly touch the timeless stillness

of being present, the moments coalesce. One vastness underpins our work day. We move and act in that vastness. We pay attention and seek to be effective in our duties, all in the inner freedom of presence.

This inner work series on Presence Triggers certainly does not exhaust the innumerable possibilities for imbuing the situations of our life with the power to awaken us, to remind us to be. Each of us can invent and develop presence triggers that suit us, that work in the particulars of our own life and with the characteristics of our own temperament.

For this week, please work on developing specific domains of Working Presence as presence triggers. Beyond this week, please establish presence triggers in your life, either from this series or of your own creation, or both. Use these wake up calls to come back into presence, to come back to being yourself.

5.0 Troubles and Purpose

When faced with serious troubles, what do we do, how do we respond? The most natural response may be to withdraw into ourselves, to lick our wounds as it were. This may or may not be an effective coping mechanism. Perhaps we need to reach out to others, friends or professionals. Perhaps we need to take an active role in resolving or mitigating the troubles assailing us. But a great deal remains out of our control and despite our best efforts we may be left with pain or loss. Do we just give in, wallow in it, and perhaps descend into depression?

There is a big difference between giving in and accepting. In giving in, we passively lose ourselves to the troubles, falling underneath them. Acceptance, by contrast, has an affirmative aspect, where we acknowledge that this trouble is part of how our life is right now, but not the whole of it. If it is a serious trouble, it may seem to be all-encompassing. Still, one way to keep moving, alongside and despite the trouble, is to live with purpose.

One level of purpose is personal. It is right to seek a personally satisfying life, to do what we enjoy, to fulfill our dreams and develop our potentialities, to engage with friends, family, and colleagues, to take care of our body and satisfy it within the boundaries of non-harming, to work and produce to support ourselves. So in the face of troubles, we may be able to reach for solace in pursuing our personal purposes.

A second level of purpose is serving other people. Within the real limitations that might be thrust on us by our troubles, we can still embrace the purpose of serving and caring for others, even if only by a smile. We do what we can for our family, friends, and our society. This matters because it raises us out of the self-involvement that becomes particularly insistent in times of trouble. Service connects us more deeply with the world beyond our body, mind, and ego. Service makes us useful. In the same vein, we take care, to the extent we can, not to impose our own suffering on others, nor to infect them with it. However, when truly necessary, we gratefully allow others to serve us, providing them the opportunity to be of service.

A third level of purpose is serving the sacred. We do that by our inner work, be it of kindness, presence, prayer, or simply letting go of our suffering. All inner work serves the sacred by purifying will and transforming energies. The question for us is whether we allow our troubles to displace and block our inner work. Inner work in the face of trouble has even more value, because it requires greater motivation, greater intention.

Suffering is our normal reaction to pain. Though it does not diminish the pain, inner work requires us to sacrifice our suffering. If we dwell on our suffering and self-pity, we lose the little energy and will left to us by our troubles, and have nothing with which to be kind or present. Nevertheless, even with that nothing, we can still pray, if only to ask for help. This is the positive side of trouble, that it can purify us, stripping away the baggage of self-centeredness and egoism. Rising from the ashes with a cleansed heart, we approach the sacred through kindness, presence, and prayer.

When times of trouble come to you, as they to do to us all, please see if you can carry yourself through by engaging with purpose.

6.0 Modes of Presence
(Introduction)

What is presence and how do we come into it? At its fundamental core, presence is a conscious relationship with the world. That relationship can take many different forms. To help us see and understand the forms of presence, we begin with an intermediate but useful abstraction: we explore the underlying dimensions of presence.

First, we note the six general classes of action that underpin how we relate to our world.[1] There is a class of *Expansive* action that leads with active will working on a medium to achieve a result. *Unifying* action begins with a need or opportunity that draws action to achieve harmony. *Freedom* begins

---

1   See the presentation of the six triads in J.G. Bennett's Dramatic Universe, Volume 2.

in a release of constraints to allow latitude in action. *Order* begins with the license to construct a pattern of action or existence. *Identity* begins with an inchoate potential released and shaped into a unique wholeness. And finally, there is the class of *Interaction*, an active impulse allowed contact with a field or medium for its action.

As we said, these classes of action are rather general, and so give us little specific guidance on their own. Toward that, we add the dimension of higher and lower, the more sacred and the more material, the refined and the dense. In particular, we look at *Essential* action and *Personal* action. By Essential, we refer to the higher or Sacred in its action on us. And by Personal, we refer to our own action within the domain we can influence.

Putting all that together, we have six classes of action, each with Essential and Personal modes, to give twelve types in all. And we apply these twelve types to the field of presence, to reveal twelve modes of presence. This is where all that abstraction starts to have a direct impact on how we understand our experience and conduct our inner work. The following table shows the modes of presence:

Action Class	Modes of Presence	
	Essential	**Personal**
Expansive	Creative	Active
Unifying	Sacred	Responsive
Freedom	Spontaneous	Awakened
Order	Multi-World	Sustaining
Identity	Whole	Centered
Interacting	Connected	Participating

In the coming weeks, we will experiment with each of these twelve modes of presence. For this week, please look at your own work of presence and its various flavors and aspects. How do you come into presence? Does it descend on you unbidden? Do you rise into presence? Do you choose to be present? Do you choose to stay present? Who is the you that is present?

6.1 Centered Presence

(Modes of Presence 1)

Centered presence occurs when out of the chaos, we emerge. Inwardly, we live in a realm of chaos and noise. Our mind operates that way. Random thoughts bounce off each other, endlessly. Things we just happen to hear or see generate more thoughts, again in a never-ending chain. Some events, inner or outer, trigger our emotions, which then drive our thoughts. Where are *we* in all this?

Prior to presence, we are not in any of this. We are nowhere to be found. In effect, we do not exist. And then something unseen takes place. The spirit of our inner work enables us to assert ourselves, to be ourselves, to rise out of the chaos of our mind, to be at the center of it all, to be the center. Then here I am, centered and present. All the goings-on are still going on, but now we are here, as the center. Before, there was no center. Now there is.

How can this become our inner work of centered presence? First, our chaotic mind needs to include some willingness and intention to be present, as well some understanding of what it means to be present. Even when that intention and understanding are not activated, not front and center, their potential nevertheless sets the stage, raising the possibility. Then a moment brings an enabling trigger that reminds us of presence, showing us that we could be present right now. This allows our intention to transition from being dormant in the background into actually being present.

The simplest mode of presence is to be the center of oneself. We feel alive, no longer submerged in and at the mercy of the stream of perceptions. We emerge from that stream to stand in it. We are here, the seer of what we see, the hearer of what we hear, the doer of what we do. And that makes the whole stream of perceptions much more vivid, simply because now there is someone here to receive it all. Life no longer just happens, passing on its own. Now we are here living it.

In centered presence, we feel our own identity. We become ourselves, not in some abstract, long-term way, but right now, in this moment, here I am, in the midst of my life, as the center of my experience. We are conscious of being ourselves, but not in a reflexive, self-contemplating, looking-into-the-mirror-of-our-mind kind of way, not saying "Oh yeah, that's me alright." We are not centered on ourselves in a self-centered or narcissistic manner. It's not about me, it's about I. We face forward, as we ourselves live our life in this moment. We are the one who is responsible. We are the one who is there for the people in our life. We are the one who chooses our choices, who decides our decisions, and who directs our attention. This is a very different life than our life on autopilot, without us as our center.

Yet sometimes we are here, and sometimes we are not. Our inner work is to be here, to be our center, more and more. We make our intention, our aim: to be centered. Then whenever an opening into now comes, we are ready to emerge as ourselves, as our center. We are ready to experience our life, to live our life.

For this week, please practice centered presence.

6.2 Active Presence

(Modes of Presence 2)

Inner work requires initiative. Active presence begins with our choice to be present. "Now is my time to be here." When we choose to be present, however, we are immediately confronted with the issue of how. Where do we stand in the field of this moment, in the stream of time and perception? If we do not know where to stand inwardly in order to be present, if we do not choose where to stand, if we do not know how to stand in presence, then our choice to be present is barren. It is at this point that methods and training come into play and prove their value.

To begin, we stand in our body, in direct, visceral contact with our body. We sense our body. Sensing means paying attention to our body, to the point of having an immediate, organic, sensory contact with our body. We can start with focusing on a hand or a foot and over time progress to sensing our entire body. What matters in this for active presence is that our body is a place to stand. More specifically, we stand in the sensation of our body, in the sensitive energy that mediates our direct experience of our body. Our body sensation is always in the present moment. So standing in body sensation leads naturally into presence, because it puts us here and now.

But we do not lose ourselves in sensing. We know that we are here in this body, in this sensitive energy. We know in ourselves "I am sensing." In this way, sensing becomes a platform for presence, a place to stand. We are more than sensation. We can have contact with higher energies as well.

Indeed, the very energy that enables us to choose to be present, to initiate presence, to pay attention to our body, to be in this moment, is the conscious energy. This is the cognizant stillness underlying all perception and thought. It is our fundamental awareness, on which all our sensory experience plays out. When we feel that we are, when we feel the simple and direct experience of just being, we are more or less in the conscious energy.

Sensing our body puts our sensitive energy in its proper place. Our thoughts can also be made of sensitive energy. However, thoughts ordinarily mix with and mask our more fundamental cognition. Sensing our body helps stratify our energies, so that we can stand in sensation while being in consciousness.

At the core of active presence, the axis on which presence revolves, is the one who is present, the one who is actively choosing to be present, namely our "I." We feel and experience that I am here. Our intention to be present, and the associated attention, are our will, our I. Our I ranges through our entire presence, through our consciousness, our sensation, and our body, mind, and heart. I actively decide to be present and the power behind that choice organizes, stratifies, entrains and relates all my parts, the whole field of experience, into this one presence, into being able to say in truth "I am here."

For this week, please choose to be present, please practice active presence.

6.3 Sustaining Presence
(Modes of Presence 3)

The duration of an episode of presence matters. Can we extend our presence by even ten seconds before we melt back into the stream of perception, thought, and emotion? Active presence, where we strengthen our intention, standing behind and as our effort to be present, standing in full will-to-be, though powerful, is difficult to sustain. The energy runs down, we get distracted, and we're gone. Nevertheless, active presence is important and has its place in balanced inner work.

But there is another way. If we want to be present, not just momentarily, but to stay present a little longer, the key is to relax into being here. We relax our body, sense it, and relax into the sensation. We notice our thoughts and relax into the cognizant space behind them. We relax into the equanimity behind our more superficial and fleeting emotions.

This approach to presence engages a different side of our will, namely understanding and insight. We can allow ourselves to live in our fundamentally open and free awareness only to the extent we understand it through seeing and experiencing it. Our practices of meditation and active presence build that seeing, that understanding and insight. And then we know in our core what consciousness is. We know in our core what happens when we passively follow wherever our thoughts and emotions lead us. We know in our core that our sensation body is always now and is our proper home. These are the elements of understanding how to live in presence.

That understanding enables us to relax into presence, relax into being here, into being ourselves. If we allow our presence to spread wide, to embrace our whole body, our mind, and our heart, that broad extent gives us a little more stability. So when some hot item reaches out to us from the stream of perception and thought, we can stay in presence, instead of being swept away and submerged in that stream.

Being present is certainly a fundamental aspect of a life well-lived. This moment, each moment, only happens once. It comes and goes. Are we experiencing it fully? Asking ourselves that question helps motivate and remind us, for this moment. But what about the next? Motivation is an expression of our will, and as such it is the core of presence. If the strength of any other concern overshadows our motivation to be present, we will not sustain our presence. Understanding enters to show us that we can care about both, that being present does not preclude or interfere with other life concerns, and that those other concerns need not displace our wish to be present. We can live in presence and live a full life. Indeed, the more we live in presence, the richer our life becomes. This moment, every moment, is part of our life. Are we experiencing it fully?

Our understanding combines with that motivation, bringing us to this moment of relaxing into presence. And here we are! All good and sacred qualities, begin and take root in presence. Though presence puts us in touch with the timeless, the depth of that contact depends in large part on time, on how long we stay present. So we relax into, and live in, the here and now.

With practice we can learn to sustain ourselves, to face our life, to be. For this week, please practice sustaining presence.

6.4 Responsive Presence
(Modes of Presence 4)

When we see how often we are lost in the stream of thoughts, lacking presence, inattentive, half-aware, it moves us, kindling our need to live more completely, more vividly. We could try seeking new experiences whose very newness awakens us. Certainly, there is no harm in going after new experiences. But there is a more effective approach to the fundamental problem of half-awareness: upon noticing our own absence, we actively respond by choosing presence, choosing to be in this moment fully. In this sense, we do not need to seek new experiences, because in presence each moment is made new.

It may be the thousandth time we are washing the same dish, but instead of being inattentive, bored, daydreaming, or wanting to be finished, we live it. In presence we are in contact with our all our senses. We hear the splash and feel the warmth of the water, the hardness and weight of the dish. We notice its fragility. We feel our hands in action. We notice the colors and shapes of the dish, the sink, the water, and we feel that we ourselves are there, washing this dish. This is a moment made vivid, as each moment can be, if we live it in presence. Knowing this is possible, the contrast with a moment of half-awareness makes us wish for more. And we act on that wish by moving into presence.

When someone we care about is in difficulty, we respond. Sometimes this calls for action on our part. But often it simply calls us to be there for that person. We see the need. We may not possess the requisite expertise or ability to alleviate the difficulty. We can, though, offer ourselves, as a kind and supportive presence. We can just be there. Our own inner stillness and attentiveness have a subtle but important impact.

When we ourselves are in some difficulty or confronted by a significant challenge, we may need to respond with action. Our tendency may be to panic or react. But action backed by presence is more complete. When we are there, doing what we are doing, being the one who is doing it, the quality of what we do trends upward. The difficulty elicits this positive and appropriate response from us, rooted in presence. Here I am, doing what I need to do.

The entire field of experience spreads before us in every moment of our life. We are surrounded by and embedded in our experience, just as we are surrounded by and embedded in our immediate space. Can we enter the field of experience with presence? That field is a vast, endless opportunity for presence. It cries out for us to make something of it. Only if we are there, does experience matter. Otherwise, it may be wasted; our time and our life pass us by.

The upshot is that if we enter our experience with presence, the result is a meaningful moment. And meaningful moments make for a meaningful life. Whenever we wonder about the meaning of life, about the meaning of our own life, we can look to presence as a way toward answers. Certainly, what we do matters. But how we do what we do, in particular the degree to which we are present, underpins all meaning. Meaning flows from responding with presence to the possibilities, situations and moments of our life.

For this week, please practice responsive presence.

6.5 Awakened Presence

(Modes of Presence 5)

There is a simple version of awakening, one comes to us more often than we might think. One moment we are lost in thoughts or a TV show or whatever, and the next moment here we are, as ourselves, in ourselves, aware of body, mind, heart, and surroundings. This is not our grand image of Awakening, seeing the angels in heaven. Rather it is an almost ordinary experience of suddenly, inexplicably, without any intention or action on our part, coming back to ourselves, to being ourselves. The sense that this is almost ordinary lulls us into discounting the significance of such moments, with the result that too often we let these awakenings pass, while we quickly fall back into half-awareness.

Awakened Presence may be triggered by some random impression from our surroundings, or by some not so random impression, such as viewing a great work of art, hearing music that reaches into us, seeing a beautiful scene in nature, coming into contact with an inspiring person or someone we love. There are also the presence triggers that we intentionally develop. And sometimes there may not be any apparent trigger: out of the blue we just come back into ourselves.

In any case, here we are, more awake than we were just a moment ago. We can, and usually do, just enjoy it, relishing the luster it reveals in our life. Then we coast on that enjoyment, but not without a consequence: we let this sudden presence dissipate and dissolve.

That happens because we may not recognize the moment of presence for what it is and do not realize that we could intentionally strengthen and sustain it. Or we do recognize the moment for what it is, and fail to make something of it. If we do recognize the awakening when it comes and if we do so choose, we can step into this unintentional, momentary awakening, and transform it into intentionally active or sustaining presence, thereby stretching the duration of our presence. The awakening comes as a gift and an opportunity. Our inner work is to put it to good use by extending and deepening our awakened presence.

For that, we use the methods of presence, such as sensing our body, feeling our emotional state, being cognizant of our mind and other perceptions, not-identifying with any of that, and being ourselves, the one who is here seeing what we see and doing what we do.

This unbidden, random awakening raises us temporarily out of our state of half-awareness, and suddenly here we are. Being here again is not ordinary, but does seem normal. It is normal, or should be normal, because that state of full awareness and being the one who is aware is the fully human state. It also seems normal because it is timeless. So that when we are relatively present, it seems like we have always been this way. And when we are our in ordinary state of non-presence, we do not notice how we are. This leads to the illusion that we are always present. If only.

Our work for this week then, is to notice when we do awaken, to realize that moment of awakening for the gift and opportunity that it is, to realize that it is not our ordinary state, and to value it accordingly. Instead of being half-alive, we are fully alive, at least for that moment. And then once we have noticed and valued our moment of presence, we make something of it, not let it, not let ourselves, slip away so easily. We work to stay present, to extend and deepen our presence. We rise into life and we stay alive. Inevitably, we do slip back. But just as inevitably, another opportunity will arise.

6.6 Participation Presence
(Modes of Presence 6)

Have you ever tried to be present while you do something, for example while you speak? Whenever we do anything, there are at least two ways it can go in terms of presence. The most typical way is that we get lost in what we are doing. This does not mean lost in the transcendent sense of becoming one with the action, but rather lost in the sense of absence of intention, half-awareness, and autopilot functioning. An alternative is to stay present while we do what we are doing, being the one who is doing it, participating in it.

Two factors determine which of these ways any particular action will go. The first is our will: whether or not we are making a conscious and intentional choice to do what we are doing and whether we continue making the ongoing choice to stay in it while we do it. The second factor is the freedom and inner peace to carry that out.

In participation presence we are engaged but not lost in the action and we are present but not aloof. We are right here in the midst of our life. Being present means being here now, not somewhere else in our thoughts or mental images, not riding away on an emotion divorced from what is in front of us. Participating means our presence is in the action, not the artificial presence of an observer, surveying the scene as if from a distance, from a perch above it. We do not need to maintain distance to be present, we can be in the thick of things, in our body, in our immediate surroundings, with whomever is with us, all as it is in this moment. We jump in with both feet and live our moment.

And although we are engaged, we carry within us the equanimity and peace that enable us to stay ourselves, stay aware, neither shrinking from nor disappearing into what we do and see. We do not try to use presence to escape our troubles. When difficulties come at us, we are right there. We let them flow through us, without hooking us, while we do what we need to do. When the beauty of life unfolds before us, we are here to receive it and let it flow in joy, appreciation, and love.

To have that enabling equanimity and peace within us requires inner work. The most effective for this is a daily period of silent meditation. That gradually trains us to be at peace within our inner chaos. In meditation, no matter what is arising in our thoughts and emotions, we stay with the practice, for example watching our breath or sensing our body. We let the thoughts and emotions come and go as they will, while we stay present to the practice. We slowly descend beneath our inner chaos into the layer of peace and equanimity that surrounds us. We learn to come back to that peace even when not sitting in meditation. The more we soak in that unshackled peace, the more our being expands to incorporate it into our daily life.

So when we choose to be present and to stay present as we participate in our life, the peace that envelops us keeps us from being knocked aside or distracted away from our intention to be here as we involve ourselves with each moment of living.

In the example of speaking, if we try to be present as an observer of ourselves, we find it interferes with the act of speaking, making us awkward, stilted, and self-conscious. But if we enter the speaking, if we are present as the one who is speaking, it feels natural and complete; it gives a wholeness to the act of speaking, a wholeness that is not there without our participation presence. We speak from and with the whole of ourselves.

For this week, please choose to participate consciously in your life. Please practice participation presence.

6.7 Whole Presence
(Modes of Presence 7)

Having worked with the six Personal modes of presence, we now come to the six Essential modes. The personal modes concerned our own action within the domain we can influence, whereas in the essential modes the higher or Sacred acts on us. Our work is to prepare ourselves for this higher action on us, open ourselves to that, recognize it when it comes, and transition to a personal mode of presence as the higher one fades.

We begin with Whole Presence. As the name implies, this gives us a sense of wholeness, not just wholeness of body, which itself is a wonder, but a greater wholeness that incorporates our body, mind and heart, our senses, our will, and consciousness itself. And because consciousness is all-pervasive, this greater wholeness includes all that is within our immediate environment and perception, the world around us at this moment.

This is a wholeness that we enter or that comes over us. We are not able to manufacture it, but we can open to it. How? We start by opening all our perceptions to let everything in, through a broad and choiceless awareness that includes ourselves and all our immediate surroundings.

There is a close affinity between consciousness and space. All that we see and hear is in space and in consciousness. Space is the framework, the field of our experience. Everything occupies space. All events happen in space. Although physics teaches that space is malleable, we experience it as all-pervasive, timeless, and constant. In this direct and all-inclusive way, space gives the unity of wholeness to our experience. By opening to space we open to consciousness, and vice versa.

This notion is not meant to be taken in a theoretical way. It is not meant for thinking about. It is meant for direct perception, for practice. By opening our mind and senses to the field of space around us, within, beneath, and behind everything, we open to the unity and wholeness of all we experience in this moment. We are wrapped in the free embrace of space. Space is in us and in everything we see. And behind everything we see, there is more space. That perception is key, because it shows us directly that space envelops everything and connects everything in its vast and immediate wholeness. As we open our perception to space, as if we were opening our inner arms wide, we open ourselves to the great unity of all.

But there is even more to this. Consciousness occupies that same boundless field. And being in that, we find our heart touched by the Great Heart of the World, in an upwelling of love from our very roots. We feel embraced by the Sacred, in Whom we live and move and have our being.[2] Again, we do not need to try to manufacture this feeling. It comes naturally when we open to the vast and spacious freedom that surrounds us.

This boundless presence is our presence. But at the

2   Acts 17:28

same time, it is greater than us. We extend to the limits of the whole because the wholeness is indivisible. We are also just a particle embedded within that Greatness, but a particle with the special qualities of consciousness, intelligence, heart, and uniqueness.

For this week, please practice opening to this essential Whole Presence.

6.8 Creative Presence

(Modes of Presence 8)

There are many modes of creativity in life, from solving minor everyday problems to making works of art, music, and literature, to invention and scientific discovery. The preliminaries to creative endeavor include gathering the expertise, skills, knowledge, and materials necessary to carry out the creative act. That may take many years of study and practice. One approach to putting those hard-earned prerequisites to use is through creative presence.

Armed with the prerequisites, we turn our attention to the problem, challenge, or field in which we are choosing to work. We give the issue the appropriate amount of consideration and thought. Sometimes that is enough. But if not, we can move into the practice of creative presence, the essence of which is holding our attention in front of the challenge or opportunity. We stay there, letting the various ideas and associations percolate through our mind. We connect with the stillness under all that. And we wait in that gap before acting. We wait in presence, creative presence. We do not wait passively; we wait with our attention loosely and silently directed toward the question or challenge. This gives form to the chaos of our mind and, like a magnet, creative presence draws the new insight. We stay with the challenge in an active way, until a moment of inner letting go comes, providing an opening through which the creative force can enter and show us how to deal with the challenge.

The prerequisites and all our experience provide the raw materials. The stillness provides an arena in which the smallest elements of those raw materials can recombine in a multitude of expressions, one of which may rise to the top as the creative diamond in the rough. When we notice and recognize its potential, we can then test, cut, and polish that diamond to yield the beautiful and/or useful.

If we just keep on thinking and ruminating in our ordinary way about the question or challenge, we are less likely to come to the truly creative insight, because ordinary thinking uses expressions that are too long and too fixed to yield the truly new. The creative process, by working at a more elemental level, allows for many new combinations to form in the depths of our mind and heart, and bubble up into awareness.

As stated earlier, creative presence is one approach to creativity, and certainly not the only one. Ordinary thinking about the challenge can pave the way for new insights. Such thinking is typically part of the preparation for creative acts. Furthermore, creative insights can occur in any context, from crises to dreams to wild passions. Nevertheless, the creative presence approach blends with and extends our spiritual practice. From deep inner work, the resulting quiet, clear mind and peaceful heart offer excellent conditions for the creative impulse to enter us and be recognized.

Some creative endeavors, such as art and music, may incorporate an element of expert improvisation in the medium. Creative presence can play a role even in these cases, because improvisation is built on full engagement in the creative act, improvising from a quiet mind and a focused being.

For this week, whether confronting a minor problem or engaging in a playful or serious creative endeavor, please practice being there intentionally in creative presence.

6.9 Connected Presence
(Modes of Presence 9)

There are several levels of being connected with others. At one level, we feel that we ourselves are connected with the other person, I connect with you. I am here and you are there and we relate to each other as people, equally people, separate but connected, boundaries intact.

At the deepest level of connection, there is unity of will. This occurs, for example, in a true and totally committed marriage. We also find it in the relationship between a loving parent and their child, where the parent's wish, commitment, and actions invariably serve the welfare of the child, even at the expense of the parent's own welfare. There are cases of such unity of will among soldiers in battle, within a high-functioning team, and in some instances of communal worship.

Connect Presence resides at an in-between but still profound level of connection: you and I merge into the one consciousness, the one space, the one reality that embraces us both. In this case it no longer seems as if there is a locus of being, namely me, connected with another locus of being, namely you. Instead we are both part of the one being.

At this level we do not need to assert our separateness, our individuality, our uniqueness because we are both part of the Great Unique. We relax into just being and our ego is no longer an issue. In such moments, we do not need to define ourselves, to tout our experiences and abilities. We do not need to impress others or ourselves with how special we are. We just are. And if I am, then you are also. So we are both just being, taking part in a very deep form of connection.

One surprising thing about this connectedness of being: it is not as rare for us as we might imagine. We have moments where the conversation stops and our mind quiets down, we relax and we just are, with others, who occupy the same plenum of consciousness, spaciousness.

For that moment we are not driven by our ego, whose main function is to maintain our separateness. Ego works effectively through our thoughts, convincing us for example that we are our name. But when our thoughts grow quiet for a moment, we temporarily cease believing that we are anything, and we can just be. We do not need to convince ourselves that we exist, that we are something. We can just be. And if I am, then you are also; not as someone separate from me, someone with a different name. No, we are two people beyond name, beyond words or symbols, two people embraced by the one life that flows though all.

How to come toward this connected presence? The key is to be in the stillness when we are with others. The stillness does not demand that we define ourselves or limit who we are. Typically, this can only occur during lulls in the conversation, because speaking and listening usually bring us to the surface of our being, lost in what we are saying or hearing, lost in opinions and attitudes, lost in our self-image, ego, and name. Moments of silence let all that subside. Or, if our presence is strong, we may be able to be in the stillness behind the words even while in conversation. Few of us become monks and take a vow of silence. So unless we make a particular effort, we only come toward connected presence occasionally: the rest of the time connecting in the usual ways, for example by conversation.

When we are in the inner stillness, our inner world expands into the outer world. Our boundaries dissolve and we are connected with all that is around us: people, trees, and everything. We occupy one reality, the spacious consciousness that pervades it all. No need to reach out; we just relax into that. With our personal walls in abeyance, we enter the whole scene. And although there are many other vivid elements of the scene, including other people, the distinctions are overshadowed by the fact that we are here together.

For this week, please practice Connected Presence.

6.10 Sacred Presence

(Modes of Presence 10)

Sacred Presence means worship on the go. The essence of prayer is receptivity, surrender and openness to the Sacred. In the context of presence during our normal activity, receptivity means actively directing our inner opening, our deepest desire, toward the Divine. This type of surrender is not passivity; it is not giving ourselves over to indolence. Nor does it mean an empty repetition of a phrase, mantra or sacred name. Rather, in sacred presence, we walk through life in touch with the sweetness of the Sacred, as if a secret back door to our heart were open from within to allow the higher to warm and nourish our soul.

We practice first in the contemplative stillness of sitting. Here the repetition of a phrase, mantra, sacred name or prayerful melody can help move us toward the essence of worship, toward opening our heart to the Sacred. This can take years of devoted practice and can be made part of our regular meditation.

Perhaps toward the end of each sitting we set aside a period for worship, for delving into the recesses of our being to open our heart, to let go of who we think we are, to let go having anything, of being anything. We point ourselves, our entire inner world toward the Sacred. We point ourselves ever deeper into the core of our being, into who we are, into the source of our attention, our will. This requires a subtle blend of actively directing ourselves deeper and receptively opening to what we may find there. Beyond words and images, we let ourselves be drawn beyond ourselves, into the unknown in our depths. And there, the loving heart of the world awaits us.

As we continue with this, day after day, year after year, the hard kernel of our ego, of our separateness begins to melt. Its absence creates a wordless gap in our center, through which we can welcome the Sacred. At this point we are moving beyond the props of words, mental images, prayers, or repetitions, to the essential act of opening and surrender, of giving ourselves over. Then the Sacred is present in us, through us, as us.

After we become able to connect in that way, we can carry that ability, that desire into our life. Even in the middle of doing something outwardly, we can open our heart to the Sacred and let the Sacred be present in us. This is palpable. It is not just an idea. We feel it, vividly. It warms and energizes us, as if we were tapping into the great reservoir of the spirit. We feel cleansed. We know the rightness of this state and wish to make it our station, readily available in our new-normal mode of living.

Toward that, we practice this opening to the Sacred,

as stated earlier, in the context of presence beyond the sitting cushion. That means full body awareness: being in our body. It means awareness of our mind, being in the cognizant stillness behind our thoughts. To this presence in body and mind, we add the turn toward the Sacred through opening our heart. Body and mind give us a place to stand and to be the one who is standing. Opening our heart makes it worthwhile, gives us the reason to be, to be present. The strength and purity of such a welcome moment gives the Sacred a place to stand, a place to be present, in us, as us.

For this week, please practice Sacred Presence.

6.11 Selfless Presence

(Modes of Presence 11)

The self that we are without in Selfless Presence is our small self, our self-referential, self-serving, self-centered ego. In its place we enter the great Self. Like the awakening of Awakened Presence, Selfless Presence can occur spontaneously, without our recognizing the reality of it. But Selfless Presence goes beyond Awakened Presence: in the latter we are ourselves, in the former we transcend ourselves. There is no inner voice, no attitude attributing all to us, measuring all by us, referring all to us. We may start a creative action, practice it, nurture it, but the point comes when we allow the action to continue on its own, without our interference, with our intentionally directing it. Rather than us doing what we are doing, the action is being done through us. Our role is to initiate and get out of the way, get out of our own way.

The questions for us are how to come to selfless presence, how to go beyond our ordinary sense of self, and why.

First, why. There are levels of good reasons for working toward selflessness. The most basic is that so much of our inwardly negative and destructive thoughts and emotions, as well as our outwardly negative and destructive actions are driven by a mistaken view of who we are, by a futile attempt to build, feed, criticize or defend our illusory self. Even a slight amount of seeing through that self, though perhaps a painful shock to our world view, yields enormous benefits in terms of reduced stress, increased happiness, and improved relationships.

Another reason is that by living from our ego, we are living a lie. Our ego is an illusion. Thus, it can never be truly satisfied, fulfilled, or at peace. Ego is built on wanting, on desiring, and on the pretense that this self-centered attitude is who we are. Paradoxically, we can never be fully ourselves as long as we are driven by ego, identify with ego. Ego is a mask that hides us from ourselves and from others. When we get beneath ego, we can just be, without all the posturing, pretense, and demands.

The deepest reason is that ego is an aberration of the spirit, taking what is most precious in us and misusing, stealing, and wasting it, in service to a superficial separateness. Our innermost Self, our I, our will, is an emanation of the truly sacred Will of the World, the Divine source, the mountain of Purpose from which we all spring. Ego blocks, twists, and pollutes that channel. It is not just an embarrassment to and diversion from true humanity; it is a sacrilege.

So what can we do about it? How can we work toward relief from our ego? The prime way is to see through the illusion repeatedly, until we know in our heart of hearts that our ego does not have any real existence. When we look to see who we are, we find nothing. This is not because we do not know how to look or where to look. This is not because our perceptions are clouded. It is because when we look to see ourselves, there is nothing to see, nothing to find.

Take the example of our thoughts. We think I. I will do this. I hate that. I want this. If we look to find ourselves in that I, we find only a thought, a thought that we can be aware of. So there is something deeper than that or any other thought. Yet all day long, thoughts spin this web of who I believe I am.

But quiet meditation shows us that thoughts are just thoughts. We first learn that we do not need to act on them or believe them. Then we learn that they usually generate themselves, automatically, without our thinking them or directing them. Seeing thoughts as just thoughts, as just mental chatter, starts to liberate us from egoism, because patterns of thought are the body of our ego. They tell us the stories that define us, or rather that we believe define us. They express the attitudes and world views that define us, or rather that we believe define us. But all these attitudes, world views, stories, beliefs, and other thoughts are just thoughts. When we can step back, allow them to flow through our mind without falling for them, we see that we are not our thoughts and, indeed, not our ego.

Our thought patterns are so familiar they sound like us. They are so intimate, that secret voice in our head, that they seem to be us. But they are not us. Meditation helps us see. And that seeing sets us free, at first intermittently, until one day we see the illusion so deeply that we cannot forget. The thoughts may continue, but they no longer convince us that they are us. Going further with meditation and presence, we live more and more in the cognizant stillness beneath all thought.

There are many other ways to transcend ourselves, among which are service, prayer, and creative endeavors. All the ways are enhanced and made more effective by the effort to live in presence, in contact with our body, mind, heart, and Self. We learn to shift our identity from that small voice in our head, to the great world we live in, to being a particle of the Sacred. In selflessness, we still take good care of our body, our family, our society, our job, but without all the angst. And in doing so, we reconnect with and serve the Sacred.

For this week, please practice toward Selfless Presence.

6.12 Multi-World Presence
(Modes of Presence 12)

The notion of worlds as distinct modes of living and experiencing deepens our understanding of ourselves and our life, while offering us direction to guide our inner work. Consider four states. In one state we are stressed out, either by worrying about some unwanted, impending event or by not wanting to be in the situation we are currently in. In another state, though perhaps dealing with the same external situation, we are inwardly at peace, naturally joyful, fully aware, and aware of our self, aware that we ourselves are here. In between these two, a third possible state finds us in contact with our senses, our body, our thoughts, and our situation, not overcome by worry, but not at peace either. And below that one, we have the state where we operate on autopilot, enthralled by the self-generating, ceaseless commentary in our head and living by habit.

Ordinarily we think of these states as belonging to the same realm. One day I feel very much alive. Another day I'm alive, fully aware, and at peace. On a third day I'm feeling lost and on a fourth I'm neither here nor there, just in a habitual limbo. We assume these vastly different states are part of the same level of living, since all four are still me. Certainly we prefer not to feel stressed and worried, but we do not consider that state to be part of a fundamentally different realm than being at peace.

Nevertheless, we can learn a great deal from starting to see these states as belonging to altogether different worlds. Naming them helps. The world in which we are worried, stressed out, or otherwise lost to ourselves we call the World of Delusion. The world of ruminating, associative thought, automatic emotional reactions, and habitual actions we call the Autopilot World. The world in which we feel alive and in contact with our body, mind, heart, and senses, we call the World of Sensory Contact. The world in which we are inwardly at peace, naturally joyful, fully aware, and being our self, our I, we call the World of Consciousness. And there are also the higher spiritual worlds that we may come toward by opening our heart and will to the Sacred. Life in each of the worlds has a very different tone and character.

One way to characterize the spiritual path, the way of inner development, is as climbing the ladder of the worlds. The more together, open, and pure we become, the deeper the worlds that open to us. This does not mean that we leave a lower world behind to live solely in the next higher world. Rather, we discover the ability to move between the worlds, to live in more than one world. After all, we cannot abandon taking care of our body, the development of our conscience stops us from abandoning our duties and obligations in any realm, nor do we abandon those we love. We do, though, leave behind our identifications and attachments as we climb.

So our ongoing inner work of meditation, presence, prayer and the rest develops our ability to live in more than one world. But what does that mean? What if you could bring to any situation the inner state most appropriate to that situation? Much of our day might be spent in the World of Sensory Contact, experiencing our life and doing what we need to do. Some of our time we might let ourselves relax into autopilot daydreaming. As for the World of Delusion, we might set it aside altogether, after seeing how wasteful time in that world is, how it drains our energy, damages our relationships, and muddies our view of the past, present, and future. When we need to be fully there, we become conscious, perhaps in communicating with another person, undertaking a difficult or creative task, or making an important decision. For those inclined to prayer, the higher sacred worlds beckon us beyond ourselves, toward the Sacred Light and the underlying Unity of all.

We move among the worlds as appropriate to fulfill our inner and outer life. This multi-world presence transforms this life. We know the meaning of inner freedom and become able to be as we need to be, without attachment to any of it.

For this week, please explore Multi-World Presence.

7.0 Basic Inner Work
(Introduction)

Our goal may be to develop the exemplary human qualities of love, compassion, integrity, kindness, wisdom, patience, and joy. But those qualities cannot be grafted onto us from the outside, cannot be built on just any foundation. So they are inherently difficult to acquire directly. Instead, we seek to raise our level of being and purify our will through practical methods of inner work. By doing so, we enter the way of transformation, a way that leads us to the transparency of spirit and openness to the sacred that allows those higher qualities to shine through us, illuminating and warming our life and all we touch.

Regardless of how much or how little experience we have with inner work and spiritual practices, it remains necessary to keep the basics in sight and to return to them frequently. The building blocks of our inner work create the foundation for our inner life and spirituality. Without a strong foundation, all the rest crumbles. We cannot build that inner foundation and then forget about it. It is like eating: it makes everything else possible and we need to keep at it for the rest of our life. We continually need to reinvigorate our basic inner work and stay with it, for it feeds our inner body. Without that nourishment our inner life withers. Our hope for a vibrant and fulfilling inner life depends on a strong foundation.

In the coming weeks, we will explore some of the basic types of inner work. Just as our physical body will not stay healthy if we give it only one type of food, our inner body needs a variety of inner work to develop its various capabilities into a balanced, harmonious, and stable whole. Nevertheless, each type of inner work is a piece of the spiritual hologram, containing aspects of all the other types. So each type is important on its own and as a preparation for the others.

The diversity of inner work also helps us through the dry spells. When we lose the ability or interest to engage in one type, or it grows stale, we may find that we can pursue another type. This keeps things fresh and moving, as the various kinds of inner work support each other in the overarching journey of developing our soul.

Another reason to keep after the basic forms of inner work is that they evolve as we do. The more we work with each type of practice, the stronger and deeper we are able to go with it, often in unexpected and surprising ways. This proves invaluable in the continuing renewal of our drive to practice.

Engaging with the basics promotes humility. We do not consider ourselves to be experts in the moment-to-moment work of the spirit. Rather, we are all beginners, starting again in each moment, looking to see what is there, what is new, how we can improve. No matter how much experience we have, we stand as a novice before the great mystery of the spirit.

7.1 Relaxation
(Basic Inner Work 1)

We begin our exploration of basic inner work with the practice of relaxation. The first level of relaxation involves relaxing our body. While we all do that when we go to sleep at night, the practice of relaxation trains us to relax consciously and to live in a relaxed body. One advantage is that when we relax we do not waste our physical and inner energies on tensions. That releases those energies for more productive uses, like nourishing our inner life.

With that we can already see that our physical tensions often are manifestations of emotional or psychological tensions. When we are worried, angry, afraid, harried, frustrated, or otherwise in a knot, it shows up in our body, most often in our face, or shoulders, or abdomen. Relaxing our body thus engages the interplay between our physical tensions and our emotions. If we can relax our body, then our emotions tend to relax. If we can relax our emotions, then our body tends to relax.

We can work at this during a sitting meditation. We sit

upright and comfortably, in a posture that will not put us to sleep, a posture that we can maintain for the duration and that will help us stay alert. We direct our attention to our face. We notice the tensions there and let them go. We do not rush this; we relax into relaxing. And we continue this process throughout our body, from the top down. We put our attention on each part, notice the tensions there, and let them go. We relax our scalp and neck, our shoulders, arms, and hands, one part at a time. We relax our chest, back, and abdomen. We let the tensions drain out of us. We relax our legs, upper legs, lower legs, and feet, one part a time. Then we go through the entire body one more time to relax further.

We practice this regularly, daily at the beginning of our morning meditation. It is an excellent prelude to other meditation practices. It helps bring us inner and outer calm, from which our spiritual work can proceed.

Later, we notice opportunities for moments of this relaxation practice during our day. While tensions can be useful or even necessary in preparing us for action, they usually just waste our precious energy. We may find chronic tensions in various parts of our body and learn to let them go. Likewise, when we notice any unnecessary tension, chronic or episodic, we practice letting it go. We feel a little less subject to the exigencies of life, a little less at the mercy of every passing situation. We discover that we can at least have some impact on our formerly unconscious responses.

For this week, please practice relaxation.

7.2 Inhabiting Our Body

(Basic Inner Work 2)

One great advantage of utilizing our body as the arena for our inner work is that it is always here and now. Unlike our thoughts and emotions, our body never strays from this moment. All of its sensations and attractions arise here in this moment. And our inner work, our spiritual work needs to be based in this moment. So the question becomes how to base *ourselves* in our body. For that, various effective techniques have been devised and refined by generations of people engaged in spiritual practice. It is only when we begin work with such methods that we see the extent to which we are not based in our body. For the most part we are in some thought or emotion, or perhaps outside of ourselves altogether, in something we see or hear or think about. Coming home into our body enables all our inner work.

A second great advantage of our body as a focus for basic inner work is its organic, visceral, physical nature, which makes our body easier to stay in contact with than our thoughts, emotions, or other capacities. Because of this, contact with our body gives us a viable and potentially stable foundation in the present moment. Again, though, the question is how.

Sitting quietly, slowly and systematically relax your entire body, checking and relaxing each part. After you have relaxed your body, begin the following exercise.

Place and hold your attention in your right hand. When you notice that your attention has wandered, simply bring it back to the hand. Have a direct perception of the hand, from inside it. Thinking about the hand or visualizing it does not help with sensing; it moves us into our mind at the very moment we are aiming to be in our body. Just keep your attention in your right hand. After a few minutes of this, notice the difference between your immediate perception of your right hand

and your left hand. The right hand may be more alive, more vibrant. In contrast, the left hand seems relatively empty.

This difference is due to the presence of the sensitive energy in your right hand. The act of holding your attention in the hand has drawn that energy into it. We say that you are *sensing* your right hand and that it is full of the sensitive energy.

Now move your attention into your right foot and hold it there for a few minutes. Gradually the sensitive energy will begin to collect in your right foot. You will be sensing your right foot. Next sense your left foot and then your left hand.

In time, you will acquire the taste of sensing, so that you can easily recognize its presence or lack thereof. Then you can begin sensing entire limbs. Putting your attention in your right arm and holding your attention there in the whole of your right arm, the sensitive energy will spread throughout the arm. Next, sense your right leg, then your left leg, and then your left arm.

If you persist with the practice of sensing, your perception of and facility with it will grow. Then you can shift into sensing both arms or both legs, or all four at once. And then practice sensing your whole body, all four limbs, as well as your torso and head. In sensing your torso, however, keep to a general overall sensation of it, rather than trying to sense particular inner organs, so as not to interfere with their automatic functioning.

When you become able to sense your whole body, a qualitative shift occurs. You can then inwardly take possession of your body, be in your body, inhabit your body, in a new and powerful way. We sense our whole body and we inhabit it; we are here in our body, in the whole of it, and we work to stay in it.

Importantly, this practice fits well with our life beyond the meditation cushion. Except for life-critical activities that demand the whole of our attention, like driving, we can sense and inhabit our body as we go about our day. This brings a new and vivid richness to our life.

For this week, please practice inhabiting your body.

7.3 Inhabiting Our Attention

(Basic Inner Work 3)

The exercise of inhabiting our attention is a truly remarkable one, for it very directly enables us to become ourselves. First though, comes the more straightforward exercise of attention itself, in particular actively directed attention, as opposed to the passive type that is drawn from us by external events, such as watching TV or other entertainment. We may pay attention to a TV or a video on some screen, but generally we are simply acquiescing to that, not actively making any effort beyond putting ourselves in front of it. The creators of TV and other video entertainments are masters at grabbing and holding our attention.

Video games, on the contrary, despite their dubious and often violent content, do require active attention, an intentional and ongoing engagement. But they also have an element of drawing your attention to their action, as do some other, similar situations, such as listening to a lecture or a speech.

One way to come toward a pure exercise of attention is through various meditation practices. A prime style for this, taught in Buddhist circles, is following your breath. Among the breath-following meditations, the one that focuses on the nostrils and upper lip is perhaps the most effective for training and stabilizing our attention.

Sit quietly and comfortably relaxed, though upright. Put your attention on the sensations your breath makes on your nostrils and upper lip. Count the exhalations 1 to 10 and then begin again at 1. Continue the counting the breaths in that way. Keep the counting in the background, while the foreground of your attention stays in contact with the sensations of the breath at the nostrils and upper lip. Keep your attention focused to just that area, as the breath passes back and forth.

The associated counting helps ensure that you remain focused. On the first breath, count 1 gently in your mind, when you exhale. On the second breath, count 2. And so on to 10. Then start again at 1. Each breath is natural, unforced. Let your breath set its own pace and length. Do not drive the breath with your counting. Let the breath drive the counting. When you lose the count, simply and immediately upon noticing that loss return to the breath and the count beginning at 1. In a given meditation session, once you reach the state of having been with the breath for an unbroken 5 or 6 cycles of 10 breaths, you can drop the counting and just stay with the breath sensations or move on to the next part of your meditation practice.

As an intermediate step toward inhabiting your attention, you can at this point work to keep your attention steady and stable, unwavering moment-to-moment. Remain relaxed while doing this. Hold your attention there on your breath.

Now, go all in with your attention. In fact, become your attention, be your attention. You may discover that this comes naturally, because you are your attention. You are not your thoughts, not your emotions, not your body, and not your awareness. You are your attention.

The practice of inhabiting your attention is to be there

in it, to ride it, to be it, to stay with it. Wherever you look, there you are. Whatever you listen to, there you are. Whatever you do with intention and attention, there you are. You no longer need to look for yourself, because you are the one who is looking, you are the looking.

For this week, please practice inhabiting your attention.

7.4 Inhabiting Our Mind

(Basic Inner Work 4)

Inner work regarding our mind begins with thought awareness, in particular, awareness of thoughts as thoughts. That is different than simple awareness that there are thoughts running through our head. We often know that we are thinking. The issue is that we believe that we are generating our thoughts intentionally, all our thoughts. And with that belief comes the assumption that our thoughts speak for us, speak our mind, even that we are our thoughts. In short, we identify with our thoughts. This running commentary on our life is ours. We believe that we are the commentator embodied in our thoughts.

The difficulty is that sometimes this is almost true, but most of the time it is not. Most of the time, our thoughts generate themselves. They associate somewhat randomly, bouncing off each other, our sensory impressions of the moment, and our memories. Our thoughts run automatically in long-established patterns. No one is thinking those thoughts; they think themselves. They run all our experience through their filter, coloring and creating our view of life and the world, coloring and creating what we take to be our very self. The great majority of the time, our mind is idling, turning over with automatic, associative thoughts that speak only for themselves, not for us.

However, there are times when we do think our thoughts. The distinguishing factor is intentionality. Are we intentionally considering some topic, weighing the pros and cons of some situation or decision, pondering a problem, or planning what we will do or say? In such cases, we are thinking our thoughts; they do come from us. Yet even then we are deceived: we mistake the thoughts for the thinker. We identify with and believe we are our thoughts.

Our identification with our thoughts is deeply ingrained. Thought patterns are the patterns of our personality. Automatic thought reactions seem to our reactions. Yes, our thoughts also drive our feelings and our feelings drive our thoughts. But it is our thoughts that interpret how we feel and set our course of action.

This remarkable, multi-purpose, powerful tool that is our thinking mind is perhaps our most important capability for dealing with the world around us. It sets us apart from other animals and has enabled us humans to dominate all life on the Earth and adapt our environment to suit our needs and desires. No wonder we identify with it.

Nevertheless, it is a lie, a false, though fundamental, assumption. We are not our thoughts.

The way to begin to realize this and, more importantly, to learn to be independent of and unconstrained by our thoughts, is through quiet meditation. Without the practice of meditation, we might never understand the possibility of living beyond thought, we might never see ourselves as the thinker who thinks our thoughts when they are intentional and not automatic.

We sit quietly, relaxing our whole body, and then sensing our whole body. Established in this bodily anchor in the present moment, we can practice noticing our thoughts as they come and go, without going with them, without thinking them or pushing them away. We just let our thinking mind relax, let it slip into idleness and seemingly random thoughts. Gradually as we watch our thoughts come and go, come and go, we start to notice gaps between them.

Who am I when there is a gap in my thoughts? I see the gap, so I am not my thoughts. I can be in that gap, in that stillness between and behind the thoughts. Even when there are thoughts, rest in that stillness. The one who is resting in that stillness, the one who is seeing the thoughts and the gaps between them is me, my I. This is the same one who thinks my thoughts when I intentionally think them; the same one who sees what I see and does what I do. Stepping behind and out of our thoughts frees us from the enslaving illusion that we are our thoughts. We drop the heavy and consuming burden of believing we are our thoughts and instead come into our Self.

This meditation needs a good deal of practice. We need to marinate in that inner stillness until our identity shifts from our thoughts to our I, to the one who can use our mind to think. In the process, we learn to inhabit our mind, to inhabit the cognitive stillness that is our mind prior to thought. Our thoughts may run through our mind, but they need not disturb the cognitive stillness that sees them. We have dropped a part of our false identity and gained an important measure of inner freedom. In meditation, this comes intermittently and temporarily, until the day when we see through our thoughts so clearly that we no longer identify with them, whether on the cushion or off in our life. We do not need our thoughts to be ourselves.

For this week, please practice inhabiting your mind. Practice coming into the inner stillness, resting in that inner stillness, while letting the endless stream of thoughts pass by. They are, after all, just thoughts. Their only power over us is the power we give them.

7.5 Living with Heart
(Basic Inner Work 5)

Just as there is a range of value of our thoughts, from passing, automatic ones, to our deepest, intentional contemplation to unexpected creative vision, there is also a range of value in our emotions. Our emotions define what matters to us. Some indicate long-term, recurring themes showing what is truly important to us. Others are fleeting, indicative only of a passing concern or interest.

Inner work on emotions has two levels. One is dealing with all that can go wrong with our emotions. The other concerns refining our emotions as a path into the Sacred. We all know various ways our emotions can cause us problems. One such class is where a particular emotional state overwhelms us, especially in a protracted or recurring manner. For example, a legitimate concern can become an ongoing anxiety that colors our whole psyche. Or a passing unhappiness or ennui becomes a persistent depression. Or a minor insult elicits a festering anger or a debilitating self-doubt. And so on with self-pity, greed, jealousy, envy and the rest. Looking at such problematic emotions from the perspective of our spiritual path, we see that they can drain the inner energy we need to practice presence, they come from and strengthen our self-centeredness, and they can subvert our intention to engage with the methods of the path. But those methods themselves can be our salvation.

Big-mind meditation helps us learn to accept all that

arises in us, without feeding the problematic emotions. The same is true for the practice of contact with body sensation. We just let the emotions come, be there, and go as they will, while we sit and see. We do not run from these emotions, nor allow ourselves to be run by them. We let them be. We let ourselves be. We honor our emotions as part of us. We own our emotions. This accepting, loving attitude toward ourselves helps heal us. The months and years of spiritual practice lead us toward inner peace, a vast peace that undergirds every moment.

In some cases, however, problematic emotions persist strongly enough and long enough to block our inner work and require us to engage professional help in the form of psychotherapy or prescription drug therapy. Note that we do not recommend marijuana for those pursuing a spiritual path, because of its long-term draining effect on inner energies.

The healing of our emotional nature is a process, which in a spiritual context is sometimes called purification. Self-acceptance, as noted above, is part of that. Another is letting go. For example, we see anger coming up in us as a reaction to something or someone. Having seen that movie before, we know it generally leads nowhere constructive. Can we let it go before it snowballs in strength? Can we see it and move our attention and interest to some constructive response or to just ignoring whatever is eliciting our anger? Can we recognize that the anger is not who we are? Can we step aside and not allow the anger to define us? If we can let go of the anger, we make room in our heart for the positive, we learn and earn a heart of peace. A similar approach can also help with all the other destructive emotions.

However, a heart of peace does not mean coldness and indifference. If anything, we care even more. But now our emotional response to the world is based in peace.

As our emotional heart heals and our prayer and meditation deepen, higher emotions come to us more frequently: love, joy, equanimity, compassion, kindness, awe, humility, and more. Such emotions come from and connect us with the spiritual underpinnings of the world. Notice that these higher emotions are not self-referential, self-centered, or ego-driven. The deeper we go, the more our heart fills with these jewels of the spirit.

We can cultivate the higher emotions, which come to each of us, at least in small doses. When we notice an impulse of compassion arising in us, we can welcome it, make room for it, let it pervade our heart and whole being. The same holds for love, joy, kindness, and the rest. Too often, when we note one of these higher emotions, instead of welcoming it, we squash it because it does not fit with our usual world view and personality pattern.

Owning our emotions enables us to inhabit our heart. To be here fully means to also be in our emotional heart. This can be the heart of peace, a stance of readiness for whatever life brings, a stance of openness, embracing, and connectedness. When we enter presence, we enter with our whole being, including our heart. We live with heart.

For this week, please practice purification and living with heart.

7.6 Meditation

(Basic Inner Work 6)

A cornucopia of styles and forms of meditation fill the spiritual marketplace. Why should we meditate and how shall we choose among all that is available? Millions of people meditate, so we can safely assume there must be some value in it. Indeed, the value has been studied scientifically to show health benefits, stress reduction, and positive changes in the brains of meditators. However, some researchers into the science of meditation freely admit that science cannot gauge the spiritual effects of meditation, which have been taught for millennia and only become evident in a person's direct, inner experience.

Somewhat surprisingly, the choice of which style or form of meditation to engage in is not as important as whether one actually does meditate and the time devoted to it. The time factor can be broken into duration, frequency, and longevity.

By duration, we mean how long any particular meditation session lasts. The effects increase exponentially with the duration. We might say, for example, that 60 minutes of uninterrupted meditation is worth more than four 20-minute sessions. Or that a 90-minute meditation is worth more than four 30-minute sessions or two 60-minute sessions. Or that after a two-hour sitting, you feel like you have just returned from a 10-day retreat.

The longer one sits, the deeper one tends to go. What happens in the later minutes of a 60-minute sitting generally, but not always, far surpasses what happens in a 30-minute sitting. Each moment of a given session builds on the previous moments. So the lesson here is to gradually build up the time devoted to our morning sitting, as long as we can make it fit within the duties, demands, and loves of our life. If during an extended meditation session, our body grows too uncomfortable from sitting in the same position, we can slowly, and while maintaining the continuity of our meditation, stand up and continue meditating in a standing position. Perhaps, after a while, we sit back down, slowly and while maintaining our state.

A good duration to aim for is one hour, when you can make the time for it. Longer is even better, but shorter is also good and definitely worth doing. An hour can be a workable compromise between our need to develop our spiritual nature and our need to live an active, productive life. For some, though, an hour may not be feasible. For example, parents of young children may find it challenging to set aside any regular time for meditation. But the selfless duties of parenthood accrue their own spiritual merit, as do many other kinds of duties, particularly those whose benefits go beyond ourselves. Nevertheless, if we can find time to meditate, it can help us perform our duties well.

Frequency refers to how often we meditate. First and foremost is to establish a daily practice, in which we have a substantial period of sitting meditation every day. Preferably we do this early in our day, so as to establish an inner tone for the rest of the day. Frequency, though, also has its own inherent value independent of duration. So if we can stop to meditate a number of times a day, even for just a few moments each time, this has a profound effect. Each time reestablishes our connection with the inner peace of our morning sitting, our connection with a deeper world, and helps us carry that into our life.

Longevity, in this context, is how many years we have been practicing meditation. Our spiritual work is for a lifetime. We do not reach a point where we can say our spiritual work is complete, for two reasons. One is that our personal transformation has no upper limit. The second is that every bit of meditation produces spiritual energies and acts that feed not only ourselves, but also the great spirit of the world. That need and opportunity never ceases. Meditation works on us slowly but inevitably. It builds and builds. It changes our brain and transforms our being and our life. The more years and decades we practice meditation, the more profound the effects, both for ourselves and in the quality of what we produce for the spirit.

Meditation has been shown to change our brain structure and function. Yet we should not consider that to be the limit of meditation's effects. Our normal nervous system gives us various powers of perception, including seeing, hearing, touching, smelling, tasting, and awareness of thoughts. The physical transformation of our brain through meditation opens new powers of perception, the perception of realms of the spirit.

The substantial, frequent, enduring practice of meditation transforms our life. Some of the effects have been shown to appear in as little as two weeks, while others build up over decades. Our morning sitting enables us to start our day centered, present, and free.

For this week, please reinvigorate your meditation practice.

7.7 Prayer

(Basic Inner Work 7)

"You shall love the LORD your God with all your heart and with all your soul and with all your might." Deuteronomy 6:5

All and any prayer connects us with the Sacred. That is the basic intention behind every prayer, regardless of the type, be it asking for something, praising or thanking God, or contemplating or opening to the Divine. Prayer has an immediate and direct effect on the person who is praying. The mere fact of recognizing a higher power diminishes our egoism and leads us toward true humility. Thus prayer helps purify us, while purity of heart, in turn, enables us to pray more deeply.

The most common type of prayer is petitionary, wherein we ask for something. We might also praise or thank God in the type known as worship. These kinds of prayer usually involve words, whether spoken or chanted aloud, or just rendered as thoughts in our mind.

How can we deepen our prayer? Consider first how much of you is engaged in the prayer. Is it only in your thoughts or on your lips? If you are saying a prayer, are you simultaneously thinking about something else? Is your heart in it? Can you bring your heart into it? So that while you say or think your prayer, you also feel it. Can you bring your body into it? So that while you feel your prayer, and say or think it, you also are fully in contact with your body and including your body in the process of praying. Your thoughts, your emotions, and your body are all praying together, as one.

A further question comes: am I praying or is this prayer happening in me but without me? Am I fully engaged in the prayer? Am I behind it? Am I the one who is praying? Am I here, using all my capacities of body, heart, and mind to pray? Is the prayer fresh in this moment? Or is it just going by habit on its own?

Besides being fully and wholly engaged in the act of praying, we try other types beyond petition and worship. For this, place and direction are key. There are many sacred places conducive to prayer, from certain places in nature, often designated as such by native peoples, to the many houses of worship that we have built. The primary function of all these sacred places is to move us into that most sacred space of all: the temple of inner stillness within each of us. That vast temple is always there and always available, though usually hidden behind our endless thoughts and reactions and sensory impressions. Meditation also helps us find that sacred space. Going into that stillness, we pass through some of the veils separating us from the Sacred.

Yet to cross the next gap, we must go beyond the stillness itself. We work toward opening a direct connection between ourselves and the Sacred. Opening to the Sacred is an act of prayer. This does require full engagement, but does not necessarily require words. Here we immediately confront the issue of where to look, of what direction to open to. Some use one of God's many names as a means of orienting themselves toward the Sacred, an approach that certainly can help. Truly, though, the direction is a mystery. One way to look is into and through our spiritual heart, which encompasses our entire being and opens into the Sacred.

We also look into and through our own most inward core, our I, back behind the one who sees what we see, who does what we do, back behind the one who chooses what we choose, back behind the one who directs and focuses our attention. The reason is that our very own will is a ray of the Divine Will. That connection may be overlooked or ignored or even twisted, but can never be broken. If we delve deeply into ourselves, into our own root, we delve toward the Sacred. In this place and in that direction, our prayer is the act of exploring with heart.

Afterward, we sit quietly for a time, letting our being digest the results.

For this week, please renew your own practice of prayer.

7.8 Inhabiting Energy
(Basic Inner Work 8)

Spiritual energies pervade our inner world. The quality, quantity, and degree of organization or disorganization of these energies determine the quality of our life, both inner and outer. Much of our inner work concerns developing our ability to perceive energies and the right use, accumulation, digestion, and organization of energies.

One rudimentary and indirect way to perceive our energy level is to judge how alert, awake, and present we are. Energies largely determine all that. Through this metric of how alert and awake we are on a given day, we can begin to see that how we live affects our energy level. This may be obvious in the ordinary way, but to help ourselves along the spiritual path we need to pay even more attention to it. This is managing our life to manage our energies.

Clear examples include the energy effects of how well and how much we eat, sleep, and exercise. The use of tobacco, drugs, or excessive alcohol reduce our energy level. Part of our spiritual path is to conduct these aspects of our life like an experiment, with the aim of maximizing the quality and quantity of our inner energy. Many people try to do that to some extent. But we want to see into the subtleties of how various bodily actions affect our ability to be present, to meditate, to maintain ourselves in the face of adversity. We notice how emotional storms affect our energies and that drives our effort toward equanimity. This is all uniquely individual and changes day to day and year to year. The point is to have our body produce inner energies and not waste them.

When we fill our body with the sensitive energy and inhabit it, we form what is, momentarily at least, like a second or inner body made of that energy. By inhabiting our body, we are actually inhabiting that energy, which mediates and enables our direct, visceral contact with our body. It is akin to wearing clothes: we create this inner clothing that will carry us into the spirit, like in the parable of the wedding banquet.

We learn to focus our attention on the air we breathe and extract the energy within it. We send that into our body to help build our reservoir of sensitive energy, to provide the material for our inner body. And as we do that, we maintain our presence in our inner body, we inhabit our energy body, so as to be there to receive the additional energy we breathe.

We learn that the inner stillness is not an absence of sound, thought, and movement. Rather it the very substance of our consciousness, the conscious energy. We lean back into that cognizant stillness. We open into its vast space without boundaries. In that space, we marinate in peace and equanimity. We let our spirit, our soul, our self spread wide, with no holding on. This welcoming ocean of peace abides within us.

In the deeper realms of prayer, we open our spiritual heart. As we address our yearning toward the Sacred, a sparkling energy of light and love flows into us from behind. It warms our heart and fills our being, transforming us in the process.

In the deepest reach of all, we share our very identity, our self, with the Sacred One. And in those moments, though the energies cascade down into us, we realize that our identity with the Sacred matters even more.

While all this inner work with energies seems personal, it is much more than personal. It affects the world around us, in positive ways. Indeed, all true inner work is an act of service, service to the Sacred and service to our society. How that works is for each of us to see and discover.

For this week, please delve more into your own inner work with energies.

7.9 Inhabiting Self

(Basic Inner Work 9)

Certain fundamental questions never seem to go entirely away. Who am I? Am I here? What is the purpose of life, particularly my life? Does it even have a purpose? We cannot find the answers to such questions in something we read or hear. Even if what we read or heard were the true answer to one of the questions, delivered by a reliable source, it would still not really satisfy us, because of our lingering doubt. Those foundational questions are so basic that we can only answer them for ourselves, in ourselves, by living the answer, by being the answer. And even then, our answer evolves over time, as we do.

Am I here? Instead of just us asking ourselves that question, we could turn it around and practice being here to the point where we can say, in full-throated truth, I am here. Then not only do we know we are here, but we also know who we are, experientially. Some may think this too hard. Others may think it very easy. The reality lies in between. The hard part is to see through what we are not, yet believe ourselves to be.

For example, we are not our body. We can be aware of our body, which shows the distinction between our body and the I that is aware of it. We can direct our body; again we note the distinction between our body and the one who directs it. What we see in the mirror is our body, not our self.

We are not our mind or emotions, our thoughts or daydreams, our tendencies, our likes or dislikes, our knowledge, skills, memories or personality. We are not our opinions or beliefs. We are not our world view. We can be aware of our mind and emotions and the rest, which shows the distinction between them and the I that is aware of them. We can direct our thoughts and, to an extent, direct our emotions; again we note the distinction between mind/heart and the one who can direct them.

But our body, mind, and heart make a compelling case that they are who and what we are. After all, our mind thinks I. So isn't our mind who we are? Not so. The thought of I is not I, is not our will, is not the one who sees what we see, thinks what we think, and feels what we feel. The thought I is just a thought. Yes, it points toward who we are, but is no more who we are than is a finger the moon it points toward. A similar situation exists with our body, on which our very life depends, and with our emotions, which sometimes show us what we care about. We may drive our thoughts. We may have our body speak or act for us. We may have our emotions embody our concerns. But even though the actor may enter the action, they are not the same.

Contrary to how it may seem, we are not always here and we are not always ourselves. Those illusions come from the fact that whenever we notice ourselves or our surroundings, we are here. But we are not always noticing. We spend far too much of our life in a fog of automatically flowing, associative thoughts and daydreams, or ruminating on some outrage or lost in some entertainment.

The good news is that we can actually practice being here and being ourselves, even in the midst of thoughts and entertainment. We can practice presence. We begin with staying in contact with our body as the foundation for presence. We pay attention to notice any thoughts and emotions. And we come fully into ourselves as the one who is paying attention, the one who is in contact with our body, the one who is noticing our thoughts and emotions. That one is who you are. We practice being that one. We practice inhabiting our self.

Whatever we do, we practice being the one who is doing it. We do not let our actions just happen by habit or reaction. We practice being the actor. Whatever we see, we practice being the one who is seeing it. We do not let our seeing, our experience, just evaporate with no one at home to receive it, to experience it. In these ways, we actually live. We do not lose our time. Life does not pass us by. We inhabit our life. We inhabit our self. This is presence. This is I am.

This practice takes intention and effort. It takes experimentation and exploration to understand it. But it changes our life at a fundamental level, even if just for a moment. For this week, please try inhabiting your own self.

8.0 Finding Your Self

We may spend many years looking for ourselves, trying to discover who we are. To want to find ourselves seems natural, wholesome. But our inability to do so, to be certain about who we are, seems perplexing, even paralyzing. Are we so hidden that we cannot see who we are? Or perhaps, as the Buddhists say, we do not even exist, we have no self. Or are we here, but unrecognized? This fundamental conundrum can cause a great deal of grief, especially if we substitute some unconstructive pose for who we really are.

In trying to know ourselves, it is difficult to know where

to start, where to look, because so much stands in the way. We have an ever-growing heap of memories, but they are not us. We can know our endless stream of thoughts, but they are not us. We can know our body, with all of its actions and sensations. It is our life, but it is not us. We can know our emotions, but they are not us. We can know the many desires whispering and tugging at us, but they are not us. We can even see and direct our awareness itself, but we are not our awareness. It is not possible to know our self in the same way we know anything else. We cannot know ourselves that way for a simple reason: we are the one who knows. We cannot see ourselves, because we are the one who sees.

We can, however, be ourselves. We are our will. The most direct way into being our self, our will, is to be our attention. That is something we can experiment with. For example, we can hold our attention steady on an object, a thought, or a part of our body. Then as we do so, we get behind and into our attention itself. We become our attention. We become the one directing and focusing our awareness. The stronger our attention is, the stronger we are.

We work to discover, in our own direct experience, what it actually means to be our attention. And then we practice that. And we can practice being the one who sees what we see, the one who does what we do, the one who thinks when we intentionally think and the one who feels what we feel. In short, we are the one who is present when we are present, the one who experiences what we experience.

We may spend years trying to discover our true calling, what we are meant to do. Yet our first calling is to become ourselves, to be ourselves. Everything else flows from that. How can we know what to do, if we do not know who we are? We begin to see what we are not, but had believed ourselves to be. We see that we are not our thoughts, desires, or personality patterns, and we see, with the Buddhists, that all of that is not our self. And we practice being our self, our will, our attention, our I. We practice presence, and being the one who is present. Life flows. We practice love, and being the one who allows love to flow through us.

For this week, be your self.

9.0 The Challenge of Presence
(Introduction)

Those who have attempted to be present or to be mindful as much as possible during their daily life know that not much seems possible. Our lives seem to be chock full of situations and personal tendencies that sweep away any semblance of presence. When we do manage a bit of presence, we typically last only a few seconds before losing it to some other force.

One common fallacy we perpetuate to ourselves as an excuse for not being present is that all that life throws at us and demands from us prevents us from being present. Certainly, the life of presence is an ongoing challenge. That challenge, though, is not truly from the circumstances of our life, but rather from our inner responses to life. It is our own long-established, personal ways of being, experiencing, thinking, feeling, and acting that shove aside our intentions to be present, to live in presence. We believe that life blocks presence. We may even believe that to be more present we need to withdraw from life, maybe go on a retreat.

The reality is different. What needs to change is not the external circumstances of our life, but our inner life. We give exclusivity and priority to the wrong things inside us. Yet presence does not mean giving up all our usual ways of experiencing, thinking and the rest. It means adopting another way of being, one that does not replace our current inner experience, but wraps it, and us, within the loving arms of a wider, more objective, and more centered awareness.

Wider awareness means not so narrowly focused on a small part of our current experience. Objective means not subjective, not so narrowly focused on ourselves. And centered means actually being the one who is doing what we are doing and experiencing what we are experiencing.

Except for the extremes, we do not need to work directly on changing what we think and feel. Instead we work directly on presence. The inner context provided by presence changes us indirectly in subtle and, over time, not so subtle ways. Presence enables us to grow, to evolve naturally. We slowly shed our problems rather than ripping them away. Maturity is not something we attain once and for all; it is a life-long process whose further limits bring us into the sacred. How mature is God?

In the coming weeks we will work with some of the many challenges to presence. We will look at challenges as the ways in which specific qualities of presence are called forth by their opposite tendencies in our usual way of being. In this way, we intend to extend presence into more of our day.

For this week, please work at being present during your day and notice what blocks that, what either keeps you from entering presence or makes it evaporate.

9.1 Hurry and Worry versus Calm Presence
(The Challenge of Presence 1)

Time is our most valuable asset, though we often make it our prison, like when we hurry or worry. When we are late or want to get something over with, we hurry. We could move quickly without being inwardly rushed or anxious, but instead we hurry, both inwardly and outwardly. Inwardly, hurrying makes everything a blur. Outwardly, hurrying makes us tense and mistake-prone.

If some potential problem looms in our future, we worry. We could take whatever actions are possible to prevent unwanted future occurrences without worrying. If no such actions are possible, worrying will not help anyway. Nevertheless, we fall into anguish, apprehension, and fear, or at least an uneasiness about what might be lurking out there, waiting to meet us as we are pushed along by time.

Besides their inherent unpleasantness, hurrying and worrying kill our precious time, waste our time. Instead of living in the eternal now of calm presence, we collapse into clock time where the present moment shrivels into nothingness. In the eternal now, experience is rich, it has depth and vivid color. In clock time, the present is gone almost before it arrives, impoverishing experience, keeping us barely on the surface, depriving us of a place to be and air to breathe.

This very moment is the point of contention between the forces, between living presence in the eternal now and dying descent into the fleeting instant of time. In calm presence, we feel the broadening of this moment, we feel its eternal quality. In calm presence, time is the opening into our future. We can be here in this moment.

In clock time, however, we shrink, along with our moment, each tick marking our loss. So much that comes to us from time pulls us into its ebbing tide. Can we stand up and be, while the waters of time swirl around us, while its siren beauties call?

Of course, we are constrained to respect time by our body, our family, our planet, which are, in part, products of time. So we do what we need to do to take care of the future. But we can do that from calm presence. We do not need to be a slave of time. And there is the future beyond our needs, the future that evolves, that we serve and create. We cannot serve that future if we are pushed along by time, if we live only in time, because we cannot see it, or conceive it. But from calm presence we can.

When we notice ourselves hurrying, what can we do about that? The most obvious thing would be to slow down and relax. But when we are in a hurry, slowing down may be exactly what we cannot do. But that applies externally. Inwardly, perhaps we can slow down, even while we outwardly rush forward. The effort is not to stop hurrying, but to move inwardly into calm presence while we hurry, if we must. For that, we pay attention to our body. We raise the level of our contact with our body. We enter our body. We sense our body. That contact enables us inwardly to move with our body, rather than allowing our hurrying body to drag us along. We are here in our body, moving as necessary, without the extra tensions. Engaging purposefully in that movement takes the emotional edge off the hurrying. We find ourselves calming down, resting in presence, even in the whirlwind of action and time.

When we notice ourselves worrying, what can we do about that? Sometimes nothing. If our anxiety is deep or strong, we ruminate obsessively on the situation, and our emotions contract into that one dimension. Even if our worrying is mild, we may not be able to just turn it off at will. Instead of trying to stop the anxiety, we shift our attention toward establishing ourselves in calm presence. We come into body contact, sensing our whole body. We relax into our body. We let our body absorb the worry, letting it dissipate. As that occurs, we relax our emotions. We move into the wholeness of presence. And here we are, dealing as best we can with the worrisome situation, but now from a place of calm presence.

The deeper our presence, the more we recognize the eternal beauty of now. Can we live in that? Can we notice what pulls us out into time? For this week, please take up the challenge of calm presence versus hurry and worry.

9.2 Presence versus Inertia

(The Challenge of Presence 2)

Sometimes we feel like a couch potato, even if not on a couch. We feel our weight and would rather not have to move it. Often this causes us to feel lethargic inwardly as well as outwardly, so this state can be a challenge to presence. In that lethargic trough we tend to live on autopilot, just drifting with our ruminating thoughts and self-elaborating daydreams.

Sometimes our inward inertia is of the moving type, known as momentum, like when we are in a rut, or acting by long habit. We may commute to work, arrive there, and then realize we hardly noticed anything along the way. We may eat our meal, finish it, and then realize we hardly tasted the food. This momentum of half-awareness, keeps us in its semi-conscious state with little or no presence.

It takes energy to move us out of static inertia or to

change the direction of our momentum. This applies inwardly as much as it does outwardly. To be more present, we need to break through that static inertia or shift out of our inner rut. But that is not so easy, since when we are immersed in that place, we have no impulse to rise out of it.

Because of this power of momentum and inertia, we must look elsewhere for an opening. In particular, we look to the transition between activities, or even where there is a small change in our activity. Examples include looking away from the computer screen, getting up from sitting, moving from one room to another, at the end of a train of thoughts, upon awakening in the morning, at the start of a commercial break in the show, at the start of a conversation, at the start of a meal, or at the start of anything. These and similar moments are breakpoints in our day, gaps that leave an opening for us, for our presence to enter. When we come to those breakpoints, we have a chance to reset our being, to begin again, to be here, to be more than just a passenger in our life, to be the one who lives it. The breakpoints are the timeless moments between one segment of time and the next. Their timeless nature has an affinity with the timelessness of presence, which makes transitional moments ripe for the entry of presence.

One particular advantage of starting an activity with presence is that you then have a chance to carry presence into the rest of that activity. Indeed, when starting something new that will take at least a few minutes, we can take a moment to establish ourselves in presence, then set our intention to be present during the whole of that activity and not to succumb to its momentum. Instead, we set up a new momentum of being present, intentionally, moment to moment, as we do the things we do.

For this week, please look to the gaps between and

within your activities as moments to re-establish your presence. In those gap moments, come into contact with your whole body, your thoughts, and emotions. Be there yourself, as the one who is present, the one who is doing whatever you are doing.

9.3 Responsible Presence versus Unreliability
(The Challenge of Presence 3)

It is not easy to be fully present and not do what you should do. We cannot face our own unreliability head on and for good reason. When we are here, we see, we see the reality before us and within us, including our actions and motivations. It is much easier to shirk our responsibilities, our duties, our promises, when we are hiding from ourselves, when we are not here.

Unreliability takes many forms, from simply forgetting, being distracted, not paying attention, not caring enough to follow through, to laziness, resentment, or intentionally reneging, lying, or cheating. None of these go well with presence. Generally, they wither in the light of presence.

On the other hand, being responsible, doing what we need to do, and following through on promises all arise naturally from presence. In presence we act from ourselves, from conscience. We are there whenever we do something, or not do something. We are behind and in what we do. When we act responsibly, we can infuse our actions with presence. When we act irresponsibly, we want to hide.

Having a purpose can be the core around which we build our life. More immediately, having a purpose for a given moment can be the core around which we build our presence.

Many of us do not recognize any particular overarching purpose to our life. However, day-to-day and moment-to-moment we do have purposes: responsibilities, duties, tasks, fulfilling promises, doing what needs doing. Each such instance is a purpose. These immediate purposes certainly can create our presence.

There is a positive feedback between purpose and presence. When we act with purpose, we become that purpose, we create ourselves as our purpose. Conversely, the necessity of fulfilling some responsibility or commitment, creates us. We have somewhere to go, something to do, someone to be. These purposes that create us can be on any scale. They can be minor domestic tasks, like washing the dishes or shopping for food. They can be major, like fulfilling some life goal. They can also be inner purposes like relaxing our difficult emotions, being kind, maintaining and enhancing our moment-to-moment presence, or practicing and deepening our work of meditation and prayer. Acting with purpose is an act of will. And we are our will.

We face continual temptations to be irresponsible and unreliable, to take the easy way out. But to shirk our purposes is to shirk our self. It weakens our contact with our own higher nature. To be unreliable means not to be able to rely on ourselves, it means letting our self slip into absence, the opposite of presence.

Shirking duties and commitments allows disorder. If we fail to clean and tidy our home, it descends toward chaos. Responsible, reliable action creates order. Presence creates order in our inner world, whereas lack of presence allows chaos to disrupt our inner world. We have a responsibility to ourselves, to our family and society, and to the Sacred to practice presence, to be present, to have that inner order. And the highest expression of order is love. So responsibility leads to presence, which leads to peace and through peace to love.

For this week, please notice the relationship between purpose and presence. Notice the inner difference between walking with purpose and wandering aimlessly. This is not to say that relaxation is wrong or unnecessary; indeed it is a legitimate purpose itself. But it is to say that there is value in seeing how acting with or without purpose affects us inwardly. Some say that there is a cosmic purpose behind the universe, that that purpose is God, that we all have some role to play in fulfilling it, and that when we act with purpose we align ourselves with the Sacred.

9.4 All-In Presence versus Scattered Absence

(The Challenge of Presence 4)

We all have the ability to focus our attention, perhaps our most important capacity. Yet we generally do not see it as important. Like the proverbial fish in water, we do not usually notice our attention itself. It seems nebulous, a behind-the-scenes facilitator, part of the furniture. When we need it, it appears effortlessly, that is unless that need is prolonged. In that case, we may notice our attention or lack of it, notice its limitations, its tendency to wander if left to its own or to vanish altogether.

Let's look a little deeper. We think of attention as an it, as something we have, like a car that we steer. But the reality is much more intimate and perhaps surprising. I am my attention. You are your attention. Attention is our will, is who and what we are. Many of us spend years looking for ourselves. We need look no further than our attention, for it embodies us, encapsulates us. Attention is not something we have; it is what we are. When our attention is strong, we are strong. When our attention is steady, we are steady. When our attention is weak, scattered, or non-existent, so are we. To be ourselves in any given moment, we need only be our attention. To be more ourselves, we need only gather our resources to be robustly in our thereby strengthened attention.

And of course, attention is the core of presence. Without attention, without us, there is no presence. That makes the difference between presence and absence. So the effort to be more robustly present is the effort to be fully in our attention, to stand with the whole of ourselves as our attention. To the extent we stay here, in and as our attention, we do not become scattered; we stay unified and present.

The countervailing force is the easy and unintentional leaking away and dispersal of attention. From being in a state of unified attention, we lose focus, either because we tire or because some distraction intervenes. Soon enough we are slipping into a state where we are half riding some thought-train, half pretending to be engaged in whatever our body is doing, and half worried about something that might happen. That is being scattered. This kind of unintentional, half-aware mode of being could be euphemistically called multi-tasking, whereas it is in reality a disorganized mode of pseudo-tasking, of unconnected mental processes. Little of real value gets done or experienced. But it is easy to fall into, even from a state of centered presence.

This is not to say that random trains of thought are a problem. Indeed, if they are loosely pointed toward some question, issue, or concern, random thoughts can generate creative solutions. And they will be with us all our lives. The vast majority of our random thoughts, though, are not pointed toward to some question and do not result in anything creative. They just serve some necessary mental function, like our breathing and heartbeat serve our body. But random thoughts do not disturb robust presence, they recede to the background while we stay here in the foreground of our being.

To stay in presence then requires a strong focus, an all-in approach to living in this moment, to being here, in our attention, now. It is not a matter of holding ourselves together to prevent the scattering of our parts. Like herding cats, that would fail. Instead we set up such a strong field of attention that it attracts and entrains all our disparate capacities into our unified presence. Here I am, doing what I am doing.

For this week, notice the tendency to slip into distractions, into being scattered. Contrast that with all-in presence, where you jump into yourself with both feet, where you are here fully and now. Practice rising out of being scattered, out of being absent and into presence. Inevitably, we soon fall back into being scattered, so we practice rising up again and again.

9.5 Engaged Presence versus Indifference
(The Challenge of Presence 5)

We are each passionate about something, and some of us are passionate about many things. A simple way to look at what it means to be passionate is to say full emotional engagement. This is the opposite of indifference, but not of equanimity. The latter means having a basis in peace, having your world view and the tenor of your emotional life rooted in inner peace, a rich soil for engagement. From that peace and in the right circumstances, wholesome, constructive passions spring up, changing our life and touching those around us. Such passions include what we truly care about, what we truly enjoy, and what gives us true fulfillment. In contrast, the soil of indifference is infertile.

Emotional engagement drives presence. When we care, our intention, our attention, our will is behind the caring, is the source of the caring. That will brings our thoughts into alignment with our emotion. It brings our actions into alignment with our thoughts and emotions. Having our will, our self, engaged to the point of unifying our body, heart, and mind is the very definition of presence.

Notice that this all starts with our will, with what matters to us. Sometimes, though, random events can trigger difficult emotional reactions that in turn infect our thoughts and draw us toward abandoning ourselves to the emotion. That is not presence, because it flows the wrong way around, with programmed reactions driving our actions while we avert our eyes. That is the opposite of engaged presence.

Life has many chores, many duties, such as taking care of our body, our home, our jobs. Though we must do all this, we may not be passionate about it, we may not be engaged by it, we may be indifferent. Then come the daydreams, the boredom, the resentment. We inwardly ignore these indifferent parts of our life; we fail to live them fully.

The challenge and joy of presence can offer hope in that emotional desert. The work of presence brings us alive. The work of presence transforms us. That simple fact elicits our emotional engagement in that moment, in the great life project of transformation. And that makes us passionate. We care about our life and the inner quality of being ourselves, being here and in contact, being kind and compassionate, being awake and alive, being in joy and in peace.

The inner work of engaged presence is to open our

heart to this unique moment in our life, to live it, to be ourselves in it, to care about whatever we happen to be doing or experiencing now. We dispel the drought of indifference with the waters of engagement. This does not require us to pick which moments are worthy of engaging with; the practice is to treat every moment as worthy and to open to it. Presence is not a dry, cerebral or body-mind state; we also need heart to come alive.

For this week, please practice engaged presence.

9.6 Grasping versus Just Being
(The Challenge of Presence 6)

The central teaching of the Buddha concerns dukkha, or suffering, sometimes translated as dissatisfaction, and its cause, desire. To transcend our suffering, we need to transcend desire, which is possible through a process of inner work. The nuances are manifold. For example, our body must eat to maintain its life. The maintenance of life is more than a desire, it is an imperative built into us. If we lose that life force, that "desire" to live, we die. That may end our suffering, but not in the way we had hoped. But what about that second helping of ice cream? What about eating that next delicious morsel after our stomach is full? The upshot is that the end of suffering comes through freedom from unnecessary desires.

What belongs to the class of necessary desires? Perhaps not so much: just what we need to maintain the health of our body and our family. But what about the desire for a better job, a promotion at our current job, or an increase in our business? Those things certainly serve to maintain our family. What about the desire for a nice home for our family or nice clothes to maintain our status in our profession? Those things also help maintain our body and our family. Maybe I need a car, a phone, and much else besides to maintain my body and my family. Living in our society today, our desires multiply and there is no clear line where the necessary crosses into the merely desirable. If we tried to analyze our desires and let go of the unnecessary ones, we would never reach an end.

Fortunately, there is another approach, simpler and more fruitful than cataloging our multitudinous and ever-morphing desires. That approach is to pacify the heart and mind of desire, to dissolve all our grasping in the clear waters of equanimity. With its cousin wisdom, equanimity filters the necessary from the grasping. We do what we need to do, with a heart at peace. And that leaves us free to continue into doing what we could do by way of creativity or service, even beyond the needs of body and family.

How can we pacify our heart and mind? How can we develop equanimity? The classic and highly effective approach is through meditation. We see our thoughts, our emotions, our sensations, our desires, our minor aches and pains and our reaction to them, and we let it all come and go. We just sit and see, alert and awake. If we notice ourselves wanting something, we just see the wanting as wanting and let it be. We do not let it distract us into the object of our wanting. The wanting passes on its own. If we notice aversion, disliking or not wanting something, we just see the aversion as aversion and let it be. It passes. If we notice ourselves falling into a train of thought, we just see the thoughts as thoughts without engaging with them and their meaning, and we let them be. They pass. This practice trains us in equanimity, the heart and mind of peace, of being at peace. We abide in awareness itself. Desires lose their hold on us and leave us in peace. As we relax into contentment, our dissatisfactions abate. This enables us to see more clearly what we need to do and what we should do, and our life can flourish thereby.

Grasping for something or grasping to be rid of something, either way grasping disturbs our peace, takes us out of just being. Our presence collapses into the thing that we want or don't want. We lose ourselves in that wanting or aversion. Only when we find our way into the place beyond grasping and aversion, can we just be, present and at peace. How, beyond the meditation cushion? We relax into our body. Presence in our body gives us a foothold in the peace outside the turmoil of attracted or even desperate emotions and compliant thoughts.

Desires take us out of the present toward the imagined future satisfaction of the desire. That satisfaction proves all too fleeting. So we work to stay in contact with our body, which is always now. In the now, in the peace of just being here, dissatisfaction evaporates. This is the push and pull between desire and equanimity, dissatisfaction and peace.

For this week, please practice just being.

9.7 Task Presence versus Distractions

(The Challenge of Presence 7)

We all know how it happens. We are working along on something, when suddenly a tangential thought or other distraction comes out of the blue. Without even noticing what is happening, we take off in a different direction, following the interloper wherever it leads us and leaving behind what we were working on. The result is lost productivity and time. We lose not just the time we were tangenting away into the universe of imagination, half-aware, but also the time it takes to fully return to the task. The latter includes reassembling the necessary inner machinery and context, putting that all back into our working memory.

This propensity to go off on inner tangents is even worse if we are multi-tasking. One of the multiple tasks may suddenly take over all our inner resources, and that task might not be the main one we were intending to accomplish. Or because each of the multiple tasks has less hold on us than a single task would, the multiple tasks are even more prone to disruption by distraction. Instead of multi-tasking, we could practice single-tasking, doing one thing at a time. That does improve the situation, but even so we remain vulnerable to distraction.

Presence can help. Without presence, distractions more easily steal our attention, inducing us to drop our task. Presence enables a greater focus on the task at hand. Not only is our attention stronger in presence, but even more importantly it is grounded, it has a root, a source, namely us, our I. In presence, I am my attention, I am behind and in my attention. I am where my attention is. This strong and rooted attention is less easily broken, diverted, or coopted.

Presence also enables more and broader self-awareness, so that we see what happens in our thoughts, we sense what our body is doing, we feel our task, and we notice the changes. In presence, we see the tangential thoughts in their moment and we are free to choose not to go with them. If we fail to notice the distractions as they arise, we have little freedom in front of them; they take us unawares. Presence defends us against distraction, making us more able to stay with what we choose and intend to do.

Nevertheless, attention does have its limits. When we engage in a protracted task session, we come to a point where our energy dissipates and our attention weakens, making us more vulnerable to the allure of distractions. When we recognize this occurring we could redouble our effort, bringing more energy to bear, or we could simply take a break to let our energy for attention replenish itself.

Distractions not only delay or completely derail the completion of our task, but they also can delay or even prevent us from starting the task. That looks like procrastination: doing something else first. This particularly takes hold of us if the task, as so many are, is one we would rather not do, but still necessary. Presence helps us set aside our preferences in the face of necessity. We just do what needs doing regardless, while our dislike melts into the peace of presence.

For this week, please practice presence in tasks you undertake.

9.8 Presence versus Thinking About Presence

(The Challenge of Presence 8)

We might sometimes think "I am a person who practices presence," or "I practice mindfulness," or "I am usually mindful," or "I work on myself," or "I am on the path of liberation and love." Such thoughts may even be true to some extent. But they have a pernicious side. They give us a dubious sense of satisfaction with the current state of our inner work, with its quality and quantity. This undercuts any drive to deepen or strengthen our inner life further. At best, we are treading the spiritual waters. How can we start swimming again?

We need to see our situation clearly and without blinders, to dispel the illusion of always-on presence. We can ask ourselves and observe ourselves to assess how much of our day we are truly present. Are we always in contact with our whole body, for example, sensing our whole inner body? Do we live in body sensation as our base of awareness?

When we are present, how stable is it? How stable are we? How long do we last? How long do we stay here and now? How long before we come back into presence after losing it? How broad is our awareness? Are we in contact with the wholeness of our current experience, and with the telling details?

To see truly into these questions requires us, among other things, to beware of the fact that moments of presence imprint themselves on our memory more strongly than moments of non-presence. So when we look back on our day, we mostly recall the moments of presence and are led to believe that it was all presence. A more sober consideration may reveal that presence only covered a small part of our day. The clarity that comes from looking carefully at our life is a powerful way to strengthen our wish to be.

Another way to reinvigorate our inner work is to take in the wonder of presence. When we are here, fully here, what does that feel like? Is our life richer, more vivid in those moments compared to others? Are we more at ease, more free of inner conflicts and tensions, more comfortable in our own skin, more content? What is the quality of the way we relate to other people in moments of presence compared to those of non-presence? Do we live and act more in accord with our true values?

In these and other ways we can distinguish experientially between presence and non-presence. This show us, for example, that thinking about presence is not enough. Thoughts of the Sacred are not the Sacred. Thoughts and ideas, no matter how sublime, belong to the surface of our being and cannot substitute for the reality they sometimes point toward.

However, thoughts can remind us to work at presence. Whenever we notice that we are thinking about presence, or reading or hearing or speaking about it, that can cue us to actually come back into our body, into awareness of our mind and heart, into ourselves. We can make it our practice to turn toward presence whenever the subject of presence comes up, in whatever way it comes up. Then we move from pretense to reality, from thought to inward action.

For this week, instead of letting thoughts of presence distract you from the real thing, let those thoughts trigger your return to actual presence, your return to yourself. Here I am.

9.9 Humble Presence versus Self-First
(The Challenge of Presence 9)

"Blessed are the pure in heart, for they shall see God."

Of all the possible human qualities, one that stands as an absolute requirement for entering the deeper realms of the spirit is humility. The usual notions of what it means to be humble, however, do not make it attractive, a quality that we would seek. But humility is not necessarily the bowed head and downcast eyes, the lowered voice, the meekly accepting and never questioning, the always giving and giving way, shaped to be unnoticed and unthanked. The humble person may or may not act in those ways. Nor can the humble person be characterized outwardly, for example by a lowly economic station in life.

The humble person can be characterized inwardly by the lack of feeling separate from the world, from other people. Humility is spiritually synonymous with oneness. If there is no subject, then there is no object. If there is no me, then there is no you, separate from me. Instead we open to this unbounded unity, this oneness of everything, this eternal moment and endless space, this consciousness that embraces all.

In presence we live as the true "I am." This is not our ordinary I, nor our ordinary am. Our usual I is the one we think. Our mind says "I am going to do this," or "I like that," or "they love me," or "nobody loves me," or "I am a success," or "I am a failure." This I and me is the one we build up from childhood. It is a mental and emotional construct that we believe in, a construct we defend and seek to build up even more. It is a mini-tyrant, with many facets, and even turns on itself with self-judgment. Every time we think "I" or "me," we reinforce this false but deeply ingrained and long-familiar notion of who we are. True humility comes from relaxing, seeing through, and dropping this false I, that considers itself separate from other people and everything else.

Piercing that illusion opens us toward the true "I am." The true I has no center and is centered everywhere. In our true I, we are not separate. We are unique, just as God is unique, but we are not separate. Our I is our will, emanating from and connected to the Great Will, the One Will, the Love and the Purpose behind everything.

Am is our being, our energies, for example our awareness, our consciousness. Moving into humility, beyond separateness, we open to the infinite, boundless field of consciousness. We live in that, are one with that. Our being encompasses the universe. We are not separate from all that. The consciousness that we already participate in, does not stop at our brain or our skin. It pervades all. In this sense, the universe is our body.

In humility we can say "I am" and have it be a statement of love. For love, which comes from beyond consciousness, seeps through the vastness of consciousness and touches us intimately, surrounding us with its warm embrace. This I am is who and what we are.

Contrast that with the self-centered, self-first, egoistic way of living in our pretense I am, constructed of the thinnest material, namely thought, emotion, and memory. Only our belief in it, in being that mental image, gives it the power it has over us and keeps us in its paltry orbit, unable to see the vast sky of consciousness that lies right here, hidden in plain sight. The paradox is that to have it all, to be it all, we must stop being what we thought we were and be what we are, we must move into no-thingness, beyond thought and reactive emotion.

For this week, look at who you are in the light of humility. See that you are not the thought "I."

10.0 Spirituality at Work
(Introduction)

We seek an effective spiritual path that does not cleave our life into two domains, the spiritual and the material. In truth, there is only one domain, only one life. And it is ours to live as well as we choose. The real split in our life is between when we live in presence and when we live in non-presence. We know the issues of work-life balance, which primarily concern time allocation. But we do not need to maintain a balance between our inner, spiritual life and our outer material life, because they can coexist, they can occupy the same moments. Outwardly, we do what we do. Inwardly, we could live in presence. It is not a question of trading off one for the other, but a question of the level of quality of both, for our inner work can raise the quality of our outer engagement, and vice versa. One is in time, while the other is in eternity, and both are now. So in this series, we look at how our inner spirituality can work in tandem with our outer life, in particular with our job or career, where we spend so much of our time.

Jobs require attention. We pay with our attention and action, and our employer or client pays us monetarily. Attention, though, is not only a core element of our external work, it also plays a crucial role in our inner, spiritual work. More generally, our will, of which attention is but one manifestation, occupies the core of everything we do, including both our job and our inner work. So rather than leading a split life, an inner life and an outer life, a spiritual life and a job, a job and a family, we begin to see and live one seamless life, where everything we do affects everything else, where we ourselves are the one constant in the ever-changing stream of our life. How we act at work can help or hinder our spiritual development, and our spiritual development can support how we perform at work. Our spiritual path becomes our life and our life becomes our path. We need not, nor can we, clearly distinguish between the two.

When you sit down to meditate, is that a purely spiritual endeavor? Perhaps that is your intention, and to be the most deeply effective, that needs to your intention. Yet, meditation strengthens your attention, your will, your clarity and peace of mind and heart. All these qualities also serve you in your job. Thus, meditation has a positive side effect: it enhances your job performance.

Similarly, other spiritual practices such as the work of presence, attention and kindness, respecting our conscience, noticing the creative impulse, and so on, notably develop our soul while at the same time positively impacting our outer activities including our job. Furthermore, we can engage in these types of practices in parallel with our job activities, in mutual reinforcement.

In this inner work series, we experiment with ways to incorporate our inner work into our job. Not every working moment requires our total attention; we may have some spare attention to use for our simultaneous inner work. Later though, this distinction, this need to divide attention becomes subsumed into one, more powerful attention that incorporates all of what's happening, all of what we're doing, both inwardly and outwardly. That way our inner work can enable us to bring more attention to our job, and more attention means more quality. Even the distinction between inner and outer can vanish into the one reality that we live. But at first we need that distinction as we learn the methods of effective spiritual inner work.

For this week, notice your attitude toward your job. Is your job time somehow time that you have sold, time devoid of your true interests, lost time that matters less to you than your other time? And even if you love your job, do you use that time to help build your soul? Can you, through your inner work, reclaim the time of your job, while enhancing both?

10.1 Presence at Work

(Spirituality at Work: Part 1)

"...my challenge is to try to live as well when I'm not working as when I'm working. ... I'm much more of a whole person when I'm working. I'm more collected, I'm more connected, I'm more there...That's why I feel better when I'm working,

because I have to be."
Bill Murray, quoted by Ann Hornaday in her Washington Post article, 12/6/2012

The spiritual practice of presence, rightly carried out, does not interfere with our job or anything else we might do. On the contrary it enhances what we do. It brings us into greater contact with our senses, greater awareness of our thoughts and emotions, stronger perception of the people around us, more attention, and more intention in whatever we do. In short, in presence we become more ourselves.

Now it is true, especially in the earlier stages of our practice of presence, that we should refrain from trying it during critical activities, such as driving a car, performing surgery, walking i-beams on a tall building under construction, and so on. This is because at first, we see the work of presence as calling for a dividing of our attention between what we are doing outwardly and our inner state. Later, our inner and outer merge into one robust presence fully engaged in whatever we do.

How can we actually practice presence? Though there is much more to it, presence begins with body awareness. We can always have this as a clear and objective benchmark of presence: no body awareness, no presence, more body awareness, more presence. In our approach to presence, body awareness means sensing our body.

To practice sensing, begin by directing all your attention into your right hand. Be aware of your hand directly, from within it. Keep your attention there for a few minutes. Then notice the difference between your experience of your right hand and your left hand. Your right hand may feel more alive, warmer, more vivid. If so, this is due to the presence of the sensitive energy in your right hand, brought and awakened there by your sustained attention. This is sensing the right hand. With this taste, you can then practice sensing each hand, foot, arm and leg, and then all four limbs at once. Then without focusing on particular inner organs so as not to interfere with their instinctive functioning, sense your torso and head, and finally your whole body. This practice of sensing can be carried into your day, so that you sense while you go about your daily activities.

After extensive practice and once you have gained some facility with sensing your whole body, you might move toward a more complete practice of presence, always based in sensing your body, but also incorporating everything else within your consciousness, including emotions, thoughts, and sensory experience. This type of practice is mindfulness practice, wherein we open to the fullness of immediate experience.

The core of presence, though, is our I, the direct experience that I am here, that I am aware of this moment, that I am doing what I am doing. Presence brings the innate pleasure of the bare fact that we exist. Here I am. This is not just awareness, mindfulness, but the ongoing recognition that there is someone who is aware, that I am here and aware of all this, that I am the one who is aware, the one who does what I do. Our I connects our body, our world, with the deeper spirit within and beyond us. With and through our I, we can finally be.

So how does this fit into our workday? First, we want to set up our day by practicing sensing and full presence in a quiet sitting meditation before we go to work. But what then? Is presence compatible with our life, with our job? Because we are more alive when we are present, it is certainly compatible with our life. Because we are more there and responsible and on task when we are present, it is compatible with most jobs.

The practice of presence does not have a set external form. It does not require a particular body posture or facial expression or tone of voice. It does not require inactivity, nor activity. It does not require tension or intensity. Thus, when you practice presence, it should not be noticeable to other people, except perhaps in the fact that you pay better attention, in a relaxed way. We do not make a show of it.

At work, we can start small, in the less demanding moments. We come into our body, sensing. We come into our self. We pay attention to the full experience of this moment. Then we can start branching out from the less demanding moments to the more demanding ones. Can we be present, fully there in our body, in our mind, in our heart, in our self? Can we be present, in a meeting, in a conversation, in a task we undertake?

Then unintentionally we fall back into non-presence: lost in a train of thoughts or images, doing things automatically by habit, with little awareness or contact with what we are doing, and with emotional reactions coloring our inner world. And then a moment comes when we wake up and notice our preceding state of non-presence. We come back into contact with our body, with our self. Thoughts go on, but we don't go with them. We are here. We remember ourselves. We sense our body to strengthen the foundation and staying power of our presence. And then it all goes and we fall back into non-presence. And then something wakes us up and we start again. Such cycles may repeat many times a day, up and down and up. All the while, outwardly we are doing our job and interacting with people. Inwardly, we are coming back to and standing in presence.

For this week, practice presence at work.

10.2 Excellence

(Spirituality at Work: Part 2)

The path of excellence calls us to perform at the very highest standard possible for us. When our performance reaches objective excellence, or perfection, the result is not only outwardly stunning but also inwardly transformative. That peak expands our possibilities and undermines our self-limiting assumptions. When we know that we can do something not just well, but perfectly, it changes us. When our practice of excellence starts bringing results that show glimmers of perfection, it draws us forward with a great attraction.

One could say that true perfection, of any kind, is the exclusive domain of the Divine. And that any perfection in this world of space and time is but a shadow of the true perfection. If this is the case, then being drawn toward perfection, whether in our own actions or to those of others, is the same as being drawn toward the Divine. Easily recognizable instances can be found, for example, in some of the great music and art of world, music and art that seem Divinely inspired. So our pursuit of excellence is not essentially separate from our pursuit of the Divine. The path of excellence is the path of the spirit. And the same qualities serve both: attention, insight, conscience, responsibility, energy, effort, discipline, and personal standards.

What better place is there to practice excellence than where so many of us spend so much of our time: at our place of work? Some people love or at least respect their jobs enough to give their utmost effort toward excellence. Such people are always looking for ways to improve, always alert to what they are doing at work, how they are doing it, and how well they are doing it. Such people develop high levels of expertise and skill while also, and not incidentally, developing their being.

Some people dislike their jobs, feel stuck in them, and dread going to work. Many others, perhaps most, have a more neutral attitude toward their jobs, neither hating nor loving them, just doing them as a necessity. And we may oscillate among all the different attitudes about our job, from loving it and giving it our all, to hating it and giving the minimum we can get away with. In all these cases, the practice of excellence offers us an opportunity to rise above our attitudes and desires, to bring more to our work. By doing so, we receive more. Suddenly we can become interested in our work, interested in how we can make more of it, bring more to it.

One way we grow both in abilities and being is through challenges. In the path of excellence we challenge ourselves to perform our job with ever greater quality and/or quantity, with what the job needs from us, and if possible with more than it demands from us. Even if our efforts are not recognized by our clients, customers, coworkers, or supervisors, we persist regardless, we do it for ourselves and for those who benefit from our work.

No overarching formula can be given for excellence, because it depends on the details of each situation. Thus it calls on our experience, knowledge, skills, and creativity, on our willingness to look to see what is needed, to see what is possible, and to do what it takes to improve. Continuous improvement is a widely-adopted business management practice. And we would do well to adopt and adapt that concept to our own personal efforts at work.

In the end, the results of our work go to those who benefit from it directly, to our company or organization, to our own finances and, just as importantly, to our being. Again, the closer we come to perfection, to closer we come to the Divine.

For this week, practice excellence in your work.

10.3 Ethics

(Spirituality at Work: Part 3)

There is nothing inherently un-spiritual or unethical about earning our living; our spiritual nature being neither tainted nor compromised by working. On the contrary, earning our living is the way of nature and is required of most of us. No work, no eat. But the manner in which we earn our living can and often does present us with ethical dilemmas.

Just as there are many situations that tempt us toward unethical behavior, there are many reasons to act ethically, actually a whole hierarchy of reasons. One kind of reason comes as we understand the truth of the law of karma, or "as you sow, so shall you reap." Unethical actions have unwanted repercussions. We do not know why this law holds or what mechanism makes it work. Yet by observation of our own and others' lives, we can see karma in action. Then part of life wisdom consists of avoiding the creation of negative karma and seeking the creation of positive karma, in all we do or say, including at our job.

Another reason to act ethically: our reputation as an honorable person has a very positive value when it comes to earning our living and for our acceptance by and standing in our community. The best way to establish and protect that reputation is always to act ethically. By working ethically and with excellence, our reputation builds itself, without us necessarily engaging in self-promotion.

A third reason flows from love and compassion. "Love your neighbor as yourself." The more connected we are with ourselves, the more connected we become with other people. Unethical actions directly hurt someone. The more connected we are with other people, the less we are able intentionally to hurt anyone. Compassion forbids it. Our spiritual practice deepens those connections and raises the level of our ethics.

A fourth reason concerns the benefits of a clear conscience. Raising the level of our ethics deepens our being. For our spiritual pursuit to blossom, a clear conscience is both a necessity and our guide. Conscience is a major channel between us and the Sacred. We cannot approach the Creator while wishing to hide our transgressions nor while hoping for the cleansing action of purgatory. Yet only the pure in heart can enter the abode of the Divine. If in our lifetime, we are to make any personal progress on the spiritual path, we cannot afford to pollute the channel of conscience with bad and hurtful acts, we need to align ourselves with the Will of the Sacred. How high we can and should set our standard is for each of us to discover.

Our lives can be complex and especially so our jobs, with many competing and conflicting goals, requirements, and forces. How we navigate all this partly defines us as human beings. Our challenge consists of the lack of a clear, pre-defined answer for every ethical dilemma. It certainly can help to ask a trusted friend for advice. But in the end, we cannot put the responsibility for our choices onto anyone else. This forces us to look within ourselves for the answer.

And the source of that answer is our conscience; it is that in us which knows the right thing to do in any situation. The more we pay attention to and act in accordance with our conscience, which comes at first as an intuition of rightness or wrongness, the more our conscience will show us the way. Of course, we always do the sanity check of staying on the right side of ordinary moral norms and legality. But so many situations remain ambiguous, not discriminated by morality or laws, that we need a deeper source to guide us, namely our conscience. This is not to say that our conscience is somehow outside or other than us. It is simply a deeper part of us, closer to who we really are.

For this week, notice any ethical gray areas that arise and look to your native intuition of right and wrong, your conscience, for guidance.

10.4 Responsibility

(Spirituality at Work: Part 4)

Someone we might describe as a person of substance is likely a person with significant being. One way to define being is as the capacity to be responsible. Thus, from time to time, we have people of great being who become leaders of nations or major corporations. But clearly not all leaders have great being: they may have the responsibilities, but not the capacity. Yet some have both. And it goes the other way also: people who receive great responsibility may rise to it and, in doing so, develop their being. These may grow in tandem, such as when the entrepreneur and founder of a successful new company is able to lead its growth, while his or her being grows apace. Beyond domain knowledge, people skills, and personal charisma, being is the hidden quality that makes for greatness in a leader, conferring creativity, foresight, and the capacity to be responsible.

The complexities of life offer us many responsibilities:

to our body, our family, our profession, our community, and to the Sacred. Responsibility means doing what is necessary and appropriate in each context. How do we know what's necessary? We know what commitments we have made and can readily see those as necessary. We can see our current situation and by our intuition of conscience know what is necessary and appropriate. By seeing, accepting, and fulfilling our responsibilities, we grow our being. This is the essential connection between our outer work in the world and our inner work of the soul.

The question that so often confronts us is whether we will actually do what we need to do or shirk and let things slide. It is not always easy to fulfill our responsibilities. Here our being plays its role in enabling us to persevere in the face of difficulties, which take so many different forms. The outer difficulties are the most obvious: competing demands on our time, our personal shortcomings, and an uncooperative environment challenge us. Inwardly, we have our emotional ups and downs, our changing interests, our laziness, and our tendency to retreat in the face of problems. All of it makes wonderful fodder for the growth of our being. Meeting our responsibilities, even when we would much rather do otherwise, presents us with the choice points that change us in our core.

The push and pull of responsibilities show the interplay of being and will. While being gives us a place to stand in peace and from which to act with vigor, it is our will that chooses, commits, and acts. Fulfilling responsibilities is an act of will. And all will derives from the One Will of the Creator. Thus, responsibilities offer us a way toward becoming a vehicle of the Sacred.

None of this means we should take on more than we can handle, nor that we should take on a responsibility just to have something to do. We choose carefully and direct our life thereby to the extent we can, rather than falling into responsibilities by accident or default. We need to choose and commit. Once we have done that, we fulfill our commitments. Our word is our bond and the strength it gives us is the strength of our being.

The simple, practical things matter: doing what we say we'll do, staying on task to completion, meeting deadlines, being organized, taking care of the details while keeping an eye on the big picture. This is our path toward living well, toward self-trust and confidence, and toward being considered trustworthy and reliable by those around us. And because not all of our time is filled with responsibilities, this is a path that leaves us with the clarity of mind and lightness of heart to enjoy our life, both at work and at play.

For this week, look again at your approach to your responsibilities.

10.5 Relationships

(Spirituality at Work: Part 5)

Our business relationships can be honest and heart-to-heart, while still contributing to our success. True interpersonal relationships are neither utilitarian nor manipulative. We relate as I and Thou. We relate to the person as a person, not as an object who can be useful to us. For example, networking for purely utilitarian purposes can have its drawbacks. In relationships, everything depends on our intentions. If we are out to use someone, to get from them what we can, or to ingratiate ourselves with the hope of winning favor, we fall short of the mark. Such an approach leaves our heart a little colder. In attempting to use someone else, we end up using ourselves, and paying for it by insulting our conscience. If we gossip, blame, or backstab, stepping on others on our road to success, we lose something precious.

One special and sometimes troubled type of relationship is between bosses and those who report to them. These cannot be peer-to-peer relationships, since we need either to follow or to give orders. Still, our general approach of relating to everyone with courtesy and respect also applies to how we relate to those above and below us on the org chart. Only it is not up to us to set the tone of the relationship with those above us, because there we are in the role of follower and must take our cues accordingly. People who are treated with respect tend to reciprocate. Remembering that can help in the difficult cases.

But respect is not just a matter of lip service. To be true it must also be an inner respect. Entertaining disrespectful thoughts and emotions, even when they do not spill over into outward actions, can poison any relationship. Here is the inner work of business relationships: to be open-hearted, courteous, and respectful inwardly as well as outwardly. That does not mean we give away the store. It does not mean we are weak in negotiations. It simply means that we do what we do with respect in our actions, speech, mind, and heart. The deeper we see into others and into ourselves, the more respect we have. It comes as a natural response to the reality of our being.

We aim to let every encounter with another person remind us to be present, even in professional and business contexts. Here I am with this other being, this other child of God. This person feels their personhood inwardly just as I do. This person is conscious, just as I am. This person has hopes and dreams, cares and concerns, just as I do. Being present with another person is an expression of love; it is a way of honoring the reality of their being, as well as our own. Despite and beneath all my thoughts and emotions, I am here with you.

How to do that? First by noticing how we treat other people in our mind and heart. When we see negative or demeaning thoughts, resentment, dislike, rejection, hatred, indifference, or greed within us, we see our inner state for what it is. Then we have the possibility of choosing to let that go, not to dwell in that realm. We refuse to go on nurturing negative thoughts about people. We choose instead to move into presence, into just being in this interaction with the people around us. Later, and with practice, the mere proximity of other people can awaken us to presence, to being with them, and to being open to and creating opportunities to do positive things for them, without seeking anything in return.

For this week, notice your attitudes to the people you work with and to those you interact with in your business dealings. Do you need to make any changes there, inner or outer?

10.6 Communication Presence

(Spirituality at Work: Part 6)

How well do we communicate? Through our multitude of interactions each day, we communicate along various channels: in person through words we say, our tone of voice, facial expression, gesture and posture, and remotely by writing, by speaking by phone, radio, or video, live or recorded, and so on. How does all that communication relate to our spiritual inner work? There are two aspects of that relationship. First, to what degree are we present when we communicate? Second, to what degree is the content of our communication in keeping with our principles, such as kindness, honesty, productivity, and so forth?

Our brains have mechanisms that make it very easy for us to talk on and on with little or no presence or intention behind what we say. We may talk to kill time, to fill up the silence, or to draw attention to ourselves, even when we have nothing of substance to say. Simple greetings and inquiries have their importance. But what about all the rest of our talking? Does it matter? What function does it serve? We rightly feel that talking does bring us closer to people. But superficial talking only brings us superficially closer. Shared experience can go deeper in that regard. To the extent we are present, really being there with and experiencing the other person, our conversation takes on a different quality: it comes from a place of togetherness, of consciousness shared, even if only for those moments.

For many of us, communication is a primary part of how we earn our living. We can't just be silent, we can't just be there: we are required to speak. And we are required to listen. In both cases, presence matters. When we are present, the words we say have a different weight by the mere fact or rather the force of our presence. When we are present we can also focus more on listening; we are less distracted with planning our response or with our inner reactions to what we hear. We are more interested in what other people have to say.

Beyond that, presence changes the content of our communication. In presence, we are more aware of what we are saying and hearing, of its meaning, of its impact. In presence, we are more in contact with our mind and heart, and even more importantly with our conscience. So we make fewer mistakes. We say what we mean when appropriate. We have a better chance of getting our message across, a better chance of supporting others and not hurting them with what we say, and a better chance of hearing and understanding others in what they say and do not say. Presence gives us the flexibility and balance to surf the waves of communication as they happen.

In presence, we are there in that moment to stand behind what we say, to mean what we say. We come into our self in presence, so that we can speak from ourselves; we can be the one who is saying what we say. We can be the one who is hearing what we hear. Otherwise, words slip out of our mouth unintentionally. Otherwise, what others say to us passes us by with little notice.

Presence begins with attention. Communication presence means bringing more attention to the act of communicating, to saying what we say and to hearing what we hear. Communication presence means communicating with quality, with excellence, to speak well, with clarity and kindness, and to hear well.

For this week, practice communication presence: Particularly in your work. Bring more intention and attention to what you say. Bring more intention and attention to listening. Be the one who is speaking when you speak and the one who listening when you listen.

10.7 Service

(Spirituality at Work: Part 7)

Why do we work? The obvious, primary reason lies in the necessity and dignity of earning our living. But there is much more to it. For one, we seek work that will utilize and develop our particular abilities and inclinations, work that will enable us to become our selves. We are each unique, a quality we inherit from the Divine. Our personal uniqueness is to be honored; it is Sacred. We cannot be someone else; we can only hope and strive to become our self. For each of us to flower, we must work, we must engage in life in our own unique way. For some that means working in the home as a care giver or homemaker. For others it means working outside the home. We may be concerned with the question of whether this or that job or career is right for me. That is a fine concern, as long as it does not paralyze us. Seeking the perfect job may prevent us from finding or accepting a good one, a job that suits us, that will enable us to take some steps along our path.

Yet there is still more. We seek work that gives us satisfaction. And the most fundamental satisfaction comes from being of service to other people. Fortunately, our economic system insures that our work is of service. Otherwise, no one would pay us to do what we do. So nearly all work is service. We could even define work as serving, as producing something useful or valuable to someone. The meaning of our work is the service we provide through it. So nearly all work is meaningful. The exceptions to work being service or meaningful are if what we do exploits, deceives, or harms others. Such work cannot be considered service to others and its meaning is a negative one. Service benefits other people.

For our spiritual path, the service side of work is its saving grace. To the extent we feel we are serving, we are partially protected from our work merely increasing our egoism, our self-centeredness. Service is an expression of love and love undermines egoism.

Take the notion of success. If I consider myself to be successful in my career, in my work, then that very success can easily inflate my self-importance. If that success comes with increased responsibilities or power, my self-importance may also increase, to the detriment of my spiritual possibilities. If I consider myself to be unsuccessful or to be a failure, then that can easily inflate my self-pity, self-hatred, envy, or resentment. Thus failure can also increase our egoism in the way of negative self-importance.

However, doing our work as service removes the issue of considering myself to be a success or a failure. The foremost question then is simply am I serving well? The focus is on our actual work and those it serves. The focus is off our self-image and how our work impacts it. We just seek to serve well. We seek to use our talents to benefit our fellow human beings, life on the Earth, and the Earth itself.

Along with our outer work, our inner work is also a form of service. Through meditation, prayer, and presence we serve the Sacred as well as our higher self. Our spiritual path is the way of service. This view of our inner work takes it out of the realm of egoism: it is not just for us. This deeper, non-self-centered reason to practice, puts our inner work on a sound footing. Motivation matters in the spiritual path. There is no higher motive than that of serving.

The motivation of service also helps us in our job. Keeping service foremost transforms our approach to our work. It is not just about what we can get out of it. It is also about what we can give through it.

For this week, look at how your outer work serves others. See whether that viewpoint can help you through any negative attitudes you might have about your work and those you work with. See whether serving helps you open your heart to your work.

11.0 Time and the Timeless
Introduction

We live in time and, less obviously, we also live in the timeless. To the extent we are out of touch with the timeless, we are slaves of time. Our heart beats, the clock ticks and we feel our time, and with it our life, slipping past us. One response is the attempt to fill our time with experience and activity, to make the most of our time. We dread wasting time, because we know our time is limited. We suffer from the fact that only one event can pass through the gate of time in any given moment, that we cannot be in two places at the same time, and that, notwithstanding so-called multi-tasking, we cannot do two separate things at the same time. This continually forces us to choose what we will do in each moment, or to make the choice once and live by habit, or to react unconsciously to whatever time brings us.

But we also can live a parallel life that is not in space and time, an inner life, a more or less conscious life. This is not a separate life from our life in time; we live one seamless life. But it has layers that intermingle. It has, for example, the layer of time as well as layers of the timeless. Our body and all other physical objects are trapped in time. Our consciousness and our will are not trapped in time, but belong to the timeless. Our mind and heart lie at the interface between time and the timeless. The Sacred resides in the timeless, but enters time.

Our life in space and time distracts us from and masks our life in the timeless. We may notice our thoughts, but ignore the unchanging, cognizant stillness behind them. We may notice our body, but ignore the I that we are, the source of our attention and our decisions.

In the coming weeks, we will explore in some depth the nature of our life in time, the nature of the timeless and our place in that, and how time and the timeless relate to our spiritual inner work.

For this week, notice how your attitudes towards life and toward particular situations are shaped by your view of time. Would these attitudes be different if you had more contact with the timeless?

11.1 Linear Time
(Time and the Timeless: Part 1)

Our life moves inexorably forward in time. At some moments we orient toward the past, in remembering, in appreciating what we value there, forgetting what matters little to us, and ruminating on the rest. Certainly our personal past affects us by the skills we acquired, the knowledge we attained, the wisdom we continue to distill from experience, and the unconscious tendencies that drive us to be the way we are and act the way we do.

The future is very different, as the domain of events that are almost certain to occur, events that are probable, and events that are possible. The march of time inevitably carries the force of disorder and decay, the law of entropy. Yet despite the certainty of our eventual death, and perhaps because of it, despite the uncertainty of its timing, and despite our fear of death, it is our life's work and our fate as living beings to go against entropy, to create order, to create beauty, in the face of this absolute but unknown limit on our personal time. The fact that we will die, coupled with the fact that this world and other people will live on, pushes us toward concern with our legacy, with whether we will leave this world a better place by our having lived in it. In this way, the limit on our time brings out the best in us.

Indeed, much of what we do now is for the future, both near and far. The act of cooking always looks forward to the meal to be eaten. Washing the dishes prepares them for the next meal. We start our journeys to reach our destination. We work for the paycheck to come. We save for our future. We acquire an education in part to open new possibilities for our future. Shopping serves the future in which we will use what we buy. We take good care of our children so they may have a promising future. We try to live well, in part because what we do ripples out into our society and across time. We care for our descendants by caring for our planet, so future generations of humans, animals, and plants may thrive.

Every act of service serves the future. Because of its openness, its undetermined nature, we are able to make the future, for better or for worse. Living consciously, we create our future intentionally by what we do now; we make decisions and schedules, set goals and deadlines, we prepare. We organize our present to create our future. Our positive actions feed back to us as our future unfolds. But in living by habit, living unconsciously, we abdicate our role in time, our role in crafting our future, and allow our future to be made for us by chance and by unintentional reaction and repetition. This tends not to turn out as we might have wished.

Much of our emotional life revolves around the past or the future. For the past, we have anger, regret, resentment, disappointment, sorrow, grief, satisfaction, pride and appreciation. For the future, we have fear and hope, hurry, worry and anxiety, anticipation and expectation.

Yet all our necessary orientation toward the future and

all remembering of the past impoverishes the fleeting now, this singular moment in time. Our present shrinks to a small bubble through which the future streams into the past. Our spiritual inner work, the work of presence, is all about expanding that bubble. Presence brings the timeless into time and changes our perception of time thereby. No longer does time seem to rush by or push us along. We stand agile and adaptable in the midst of the stream of time, anchored in our self. We experience time not as some implacable force, but as a series of events on various scales, as the domain of actualizing possibilities, the domain of our embodied life. The deeper our presence, the larger our present moment and the larger the scale of events we can notice and take part in. Here again service enters, since the quality of our presence affects the scale of the future we can serve.

For this week, notice some of the endless ways that time affects you. Notice also how your perception of time changes in moments of intentional presence.

11.2 Eternal Being

(Time and the Timeless: Part 2)

Time and timelessness are not mutually exclusive: they are different layers of our one reality. One of the layers within the timeless we call eternity. We will investigate other realms of the timeless later in this inner work series. For now we will focus on our experience of and understanding of one part of eternity.

The fact that time and eternity are not mutually exclusive means we do not need somehow to stop time in order to taste eternity. Time never stops. But our experience, our awareness can shift and expand out from being wholly in the stream of events, by turning toward the timeless, in particular toward eternity.

The most direct and repeatable way to taste eternity is in quiet meditation. After some time of sitting and just being, our thoughts begin to slow down, to stand out in relief. We begin to see between them, into the gaps. We begin to enter those gaps between thoughts. We discover a zone of stillness and peace behind our thoughts, a timeless zone of pure awareness, pure cognizance, without boundaries.

This is our consciousness, the conscious energy. In consciousness not much seems to happen: we just are. Consciousness belongs to eternity, not time. All the movements of thought, emotion, and body take place in time, while our awareness sits in eternity, in the timeless. Those thoughts that do enter the zone of consciousness have a different quality than our ordinary thinking. They come quietly, shedding the words that carry them to reveal pure meaning. Conscious thinking works at the level of meaning and concept, not at the level of words. While conscious thinking consists of interacting bearers of meaning, platonic forms, the primary experience of consciousness is of the cognizant, peaceful, and all-pervasive substance at the root of our mind.

Consciousness or pure awareness is not subject to time. This layer of experience surrounds and penetrates the stream of events in time, yet remains unchanged. Looking into your own past, you may recognize something unchanging, namely your basic awareness. The consciousness, the pure awareness through which you experienced your life ten years ago or yesterday is the very same as the one you have right now. Certainly the content of awareness, the stream of sensory impressions, thoughts, and emotions changes continually, but the consciousness that receives all that does not change. This fundamental awareness we have today is the same we had as children. This essence of our being is eternal and unchanging. All these events and experiences that have happened passed through our awareness, while our awareness itself remained the same. In this inner place, we are now where we have always been.

How is it that we miss this fact? All the experiential, endless content of our life masks the pure awareness that underlies it. It's like watching a movie at the cinema and forgetting that there is a white screen behind it. We lose touch with our being. We lose touch with the timeless part of us that belongs to eternity.

But it need not be that way. We can learn first to recognize our consciousness, our pure awareness for what it is. We gain a taste for it: Particularly in quiet meditation. And then, with practice, with the practice of presence, we can learn to be, we can learn to live more of our life from that place of inner peace, that place that is not in time, that place that is always here and now, always available to us. It may be masked by the stream of events that overlays it, but it is not hidden. It is accessible. It is right here within us. It is our home.

For this week, explore the zone of inner peace, the pure consciousness within you. Taste it, even if only in small doses. At times during the day, notice that inner peace, that pure awareness that is always with you, waiting for you to turn to it, to put it on like a favorite and comfortable piece of clothing.

11.3 Eternal Light

(Time and the Timeless: Part 3)

Beyond peace there is joy. Beyond stillness there is light. Beyond time there is the timeless. Though consciousness, that vast and boundless hall of peace, seems to be the ultimate, it is not. Just as consciousness is outside of time, so the higher realms are outside of consciousness, though not beyond possible experience.

The analogy with consciousness or pure awareness being beyond time, beyond thought, shows us the way. If we look within time and sensory experience, we do not see the pure awareness. If we look deeper within ourselves, beyond our senses and mind contents, we start to taste that pure awareness. Likewise, if look within awareness, we do not see beyond it. Instead, we seek a different direction, a different dimension, a way through the depths of silence, a way outside of our inner vision. Deep meditation and inner exploration can reveal it.

There is a fundamental difference between passivity and receptivity. One type of meditation is passive or nearly passive: the meditation of non-doing. We just sit and let everything be as it is in us. We relax our need to control and let all the thoughts, emotions, and perceptions come and go. We do not go with them. We do not act on them. We do not follow or intentionally think our thoughts. We just sit here in the middle of ourselves, relaxing into ourselves, into this moment. This type of meditation can and does lead to profound inner states. Once our thinking mind settles, we can rest in consciousness, in inner peace. Continuing on this way of non-doing, the higher realms may open to us spontaneously. This is an important kind of practice, with great value. But it is not the only practice for opening to the depths.

Receptivity means inwardly, intentionally turning toward the higher. This is not passive or non-doing. Nor is it active or forceful. It requires a balance of the active and the passive. The active aspect turns us toward the higher. The passive aspect keeps us open to receive from the higher. In practicing receptive meditation, we deal directly with the two forces, these two modes of action, the two ways of will. We are to some extent passive, but we are not just waiting as in the non-doing type of meditation. Instead, we engage just enough active intention to turn our inner world, our interest and attention toward the higher realm, toward finding that direction, toward opening to it.

There is a saying to the effect that we cannot enter heaven with our boots on. The passive aspect of this type of inner work is the equivalent of removing our boots. We cannot act on the higher, we can only allow the higher to act on us. Yet we can put ourselves there, we can knock on that door. We can stand before the door, we can open ourselves to receive the higher energy, the higher influence, but we cannot open the door. The purity of intention in our search makes it possible for that door to open. We do our part and allow the Sacred to do Its.

The higher realms are the spiritual realms and are Sacred. So another way of approaching this higher world beyond time and beyond consciousness is through prayer. Here we do not mean the petitionary prayer of asking for something, no matter how selfless the ask is, be it for personal health or world peace. The kind of prayer that is most effective at connecting us with the Sacred, aims only at that.

Through the centuries, people have devised and practiced many forms of this. A common example is the inner repetition of a sacred phrase or one of God's names. The fact that we do not consciously know a priori the direction toward the Sacred is why this type of prayer is so valuable. Sitting in the kind of meditation which we might call silent prayer or contemplation, the inner repetition lights our way and gives us a direction. Since we do not know the way, we take the phrase, the name, or the Sacred melody to serve as our guide or even as a vehicle to take us toward the Sacred.

Communal prayer is another way that at its height can help us find and open to the Sacred. The pure intention of all the members combine in the synergy of communal worship. Such prayer can lift the whole community at once. It lifts us toward the Sacred. It lifts us into the timeless.

For this week, practice opening to the timeless realm just beyond consciousness, the realm of the eternal and Sacred Light.

11.4 Timeless Patterns

(Time and the Timeless: Part 4)

Patterns surround us: the spatial patterns we recognize as the objects, life, Earth and cosmos persisting and moving around us, and the temporal patterns such as the regularities of heartbeat and breath, day and night, the seasons, speech and music. For our spiritual work, several kinds and levels of pattern matter.

Our body's spatial pattern is fixed in its flexible materiality. We do not need to hold our body together by our will. In its material nature it has a will of its own, by which it maintains its spatial pattern, as well as its many processes, its temporal patterns of respiration, circulation, digestion, sleep, and the rest.

But our inner, spiritual body is very different: it requires our will to nurture it and give it shape. Its substance is immaterial; it is made of inner, spiritual energies, principally the sensitive energy. When we sense our body, we impose a spatial pattern on this inner energy.

That inner body pattern lies at the interface between time and the timeless. Its source in our will is not in time. But its place in our body is in time and suffers interruption and dissipation thereby. So our potential inner body requires continual reinforcement by our attention and intention, by our acts of sensing to give it form, of energy breathing to build it up, and of presence to raise its quality.

In this we see the paradigm of pattern-making. By our creative imagination and our will, the pattern emerges from beyond time and space to organize what is in time and space. Take a simpler example relating to our spiritual work: we decide to meditate daily, to set aside time each day for formal sitting meditation. Or we decide to engage in prayer each day, perhaps the formal prayers of our religion. Or both meditation and prayer. By our decision, by this act of will, we create this positive habit, an action that recurs on a daily basis, an action that slowly deepens our inner life, nurtures our soul, enhances our perceptions, heals our psychological wounds, loosens the chains that bind our spirit, and contributes to the spiritual well-being of our planet.

Now though that habit manifests in time and space, and though it may reside in part in our physical brain, its origin lies in our will. Our will is immaterial and free, unconstrained by time and space. While its manifestations depend on our body, in itself will is beyond body and mind.

Between our will and our repeated actions, there is a pattern, in some cases a habit. Will is not an energy and our activities are material. The guiding patterns between our will and our activities are made of inner energies. That is why good habits are hard to form and bad habits are hard to break. We need to organize or disorganize the relevant brain circuits. But to do that we need to create or disrupt the patterns of energy flows. This takes the sustained action of our will on our energies. It applies not only to physical habits but also to patterns of thought and emotion.

Our spiritual practice trains us to do just that. In meditation, presence, and contemplative prayer, our attention and intention, our will acts on our energies. This is not a physical action in time and space. We can sit still, doing nothing materially, yet still engage in this inner work of the spirit. Or we can practice sensing and presence while in movement, with those inner actions being independent of whether we are moving or not. Such practice gradually opens our perceptions to the timeless, because that is where it takes place, in the realms of will and energies.

For this week, notice how your inner work has its place beyond the material world of bodies and things.

11.5 Timeless Acts

(Time and the Timeless: Part 5)

Where do decisions come from and how do they occur? The general pattern is that we consider our options, think about them, think of their ramifications, see how we feel about them, and then we commit ourselves to one option. The last step, the moment of commitment is the moment of decision, the rest being preparatory. That pattern can vary, such as when we decide something and then come up with reasons to justify that decision. However, in every case, though we may not recognize it as such, there is a moment of decision. The decision itself is an act of will, an act of our will, and comes from our core self, from beyond our mind. Although it plays out in time and space, the decision is made in the realm of will, beyond time and space, and so it is timeless.

Sometimes we wobble: we decide one thing and do another, we commit and then fail to carry through. These pseudo-decisions do not come from our core, do not carry the persistent weight of a true decision. Instead we may be driven to such false decisions by our emotional reactions to a situation, by old habits of body, thought and personality. For a decision to stick, to be effective over time, it must come from our core, from who we are, from the center of our will. In the moment of making the decision, we bring the whole of ourselves to bear. We feel: I am deciding this. By our full presence, by our full participation in the act of deciding, we make it a special moment, a timeless moment, one that we will remember and follow through on.

Another timeless act, another act of will, occurs whenever we pay attention. Attention is one of the powers of our will. And because it can occur so often during our day, it is the easiest way to begin to understand will in ourselves. For example, right now you are paying attention to these words. As you do that, you could also pay attention to your attention, to seeing what attention does, to looking for where your attention comes from. Attention is different than thoughts, emotions, or sensory impressions, because we can put our attention on any of these. Attention is different than awareness or consciousness, because attention can focus our awareness, focus our consciousness. Like decisions, attention comes from the realm of will, beyond time and space, but manifesting in time and space. Attention is part of our will: Part of who we really are. Where your attention is, is where you are. Directing our attention is an act of will. Paying attention or sustaining attention is an act of will, a timeless act.

Several kinds of practices relate to attention. First, is simply practicing paying attention, sustaining attention. This is not like watching a TV show or movie, where our attention is drawn without our actively doing anything. TV does not engage our will, we are just passive. But in other situations, where we intentionally keep our attention on something, we develop our attention, we develop our will.

Second is looking for the source of our attention. Where does our attention come from? This is not something to think about, but something to look for directly, something to see about. The practice of following our attention back along itself toward its source gradually teaches us about will and about a direction beyond space and time.

Third is being our attention. Join forces with your attention. Become your attention. Be the one who is looking, the one who is paying attention, for example, the one who is reading these words. This practice helps us become ourselves, become our will, become our I.

The second and third of these practices require experimentation on our part. If we have not worked in these ways, it may not be immediately obvious what they mean, what they entail. So we try as best we can, try variations, keeping at it until something starts to come back to us from the effort, some understanding deepens.

Choosing can be an act of will, akin to decision. But it is not always so. Often our choices are just one preference winning out over competing preferences, or our choice may be driven by some emotion like fear, anger, or greed, or by our body, like with gluttony or lust. These are not choices, rather they are the abdication of choice, wherein we become a little less than human, allowing ourselves to be controlled by our habits of thought and emotion, by reactions, by appetites. To be a true choice it must be relatively free, inwardly free. A free choice is informed by our conscience, the part of us that is connected to wisdom, the part of us that sees the truth. A free choice responds to what is right or best or necessary in a given situation, not with stock answers, not with pre-established patterns of body, emotion, or thought.

The difference is not always obvious. We may choose to eat that second piece of cake. Or we may inwardly shirk choosing, give up and let our body choose for us. Outwardly there is no difference: the cake gets eaten either way. Inwardly, though, we know there is a difference, even if we do not want to look at that difference. If we really choose, then it is somewhat easier to be present during the action we have chosen, somewhat easier, for example, to taste and enjoy the cake in peace, rather than gobble it down in a gluttonous rush. In the first case, we eat the cake; in the second, the cake eats us.

In meditation, we see our thoughts float by, embodying the passage of time, whereas we remain anchored in the spacious consciousness through which our thoughts pass. This is the interface, the shoreline between time and the timeless. Will comes from beyond consciousness, from a deeper level of the timeless, the realm of will. When we reach with our will from the timeless into time, we establish a moment of what the Greeks called kairos, a moment of destiny creation. Each act of will is a creative act. Through acts of will, we create our life.

In the context of spiritual practice, we find another example in prayer. In the depths of prayer, we reach out, our will reaches out, toward the Divine. We reach deep into and beyond ourselves; we open our very core to the Sacred. These are all acts of will. And because our will ultimately derives from and is of a piece with the Divine Will, these acts of prayer have the potency to transform us and to serve the greater Wholeness. When we reach toward and open to the Sacred, we are working to reconnect our individual will to that greater Wholeness, which our will embodies in this material world.

For this week, notice and develop your timeless acts of will.

12.0 Being Yourself
Introduction

What does it mean to be yourself? After all, who else could we be, if not ourselves? Yet the question remains, somehow resonating with us. At times we feel less ourselves, like when we are thrown off by an uncomfortable situation, by feeling unsure of ourselves or inadequate or anxious and not fully in control. At such moments we feel awkward, perhaps even ashamed; we are not at home in our own skin. These and many other types of difficult moments point to times when we might almost rather not be ourselves, if being ourselves means behaving and experiencing in those unpleasant ways. But to be more accurate, we should say that in those moments we are not fully ourselves. And that domain is where our inner work, our spiritual practice can help, help us be fully ourselves.

To be ourselves means to be who we are, in our core. Again, though, who are we? Who am I? That question itself can and does form the foundation of an entire spiritual path. One effective approach to it starts by elimination, by seeing that much of what we think we are is not who we are, is not essential to the person that is us. This is dropping some of the veils of illusion so often referenced in spiritual literature.

Our illusions about ourselves are of two major types.

First are the erroneous beliefs we have about how we act, about our place in the world, our personal status — in short, our self-image. We do not see ourselves objectively, as others see us. But our inner work of presence gradually dispels these illusions, as we begin to see and understand ourselves more clearly. This happens as a natural and important by-product of work on presence. It can at times be difficult, making it seem that we are regressing in our personal qualities. But that is a false impression resulting from the dropping of veils, from actually seeing and understanding ourselves more accurately, more objectively. It is a positive sign.

The other kinds of self-illusions run deeper. These involve believing that we are what we are not. Specifically, we believe our thoughts are who we are or at least speak for us, represent us. We believe we are our body. We believe we are our emotions. And finally, we believe we are the center of our personality, our ego. This last is an illusion about an illusion.

Dispelling these deeply ingrained and unquestioned illusions requires developing new perceptions. For example, if we can see beyond our thoughts, into the cognizant stillness of consciousness, we have a chance of entering consciousness, whereupon we see clearly that our thoughts generate themselves, arising and passing through our mind without our intention behind them. Thus our thoughts are not who we are, nor do they necessarily speak for us. This does not mean that we should ignore our thoughts. On the contrary, we want to be fully aware of them, to see what information they offer us, and to ensure that we are not unwittingly falling prey to them, to our implicit attitude that we are our thoughts. Like the situation with thoughts, each of the other kinds of illusory self-images, woven by our emotions, our body, our personality, our ego, and our roles in the world, calls for its own approach toward freedom.

In this series, we take on the major types of illusions about who we are and go further, not by rejecting but by accepting. By being each of our parts consciously, we become whole, we become ourselves. We embrace it all, inhabiting every aspect of ourselves, reclaiming our parts under the all-inclusive umbrella of who we really are: the one who lives in and makes use of our many abilities and talents. We learn that wholeness and healing come through respecting ourselves, not through rejecting our unloved parts. And we learn to live from the whole and not be driven by our destructive, unhealthy emotions and urges, not falling into a narrow view of who we are. This is the way of liberation, the freedom to be ourselves.

For this week, engage with the question: who am I? Look to see who or what you believe you are, in practice, in your day-to-day reality. Do I buy an attitude that I am my emotions, or my thoughts, or my body, or my personality? What could it mean to be fully myself?

12.1 Being Your Body

(Being Yourself: Part 1)

Being relaxed is intimately connected with being ourselves, being comfortable with who we are, in our own skin. Though relaxing can begin in the mind or emotions, those connect with our body. So by relaxing our body, we also may relax our mind and emotions. And by relaxing into our body, we feel more at home, more ourselves. Being in our body is the place to start on being in ourselves.

But aren't we always in our body? Well – no! We are where our attention is. Our attention can be broad, like a wide lens, encompassing our body as well as whatever else we are paying attention to. Our usual situation, though, is either that our attention is taken by something and does not include our body in its view or that our attention is so scattered as to be non-existent. If our attention doesn't exist, we don't exist. If our attention is lost in something external to us, or even in a thought or emotion, then still we do not exist, because all of that is external to who we are. But as soon as we include our body, our whole body within our attention, we move a step closer to who we are, because our body is always in the here and now.

Simply having attention on our body is a positive beginning. The next steps, as stated above, are to relax our body and then to relax into our body. We are not just paying attention to our body as if from a distance, as if we are in our head or our mind and our body is out there, down there. Rather we enter our body, we become our body.

This practice applies regardless of the condition of our body. If it's healthy and pain free, we may tend to ignore it. If our body has some discomfort or pain, this certainly makes us acutely aware of our body, but here we also tend not to be in it: we reject that painful part. We flee the pain, inwardly shrinking from it, not wanting to experience it. Our practice instead is, while taking whatever medical treatment or other steps are necessary and appropriate to heal our body, we fully enter our body, including the painful areas. We do not reject any part or any sensation of pain. We let the pain bring us more fully into our body. We relax, accept, and embrace our whole body as it is. Sometimes it may even happen that this acceptance, and yes love, can help alleviate the pain, or at least diminish the emotional pain that gets layered on top of the physical pain.

Yet there is more, in regard to how to do this. We can

be in our body more robustly through gathering and organizing a certain inner energy, the sensitive energy, the energy of sensation. Our experience of our body can be much more than of blood, flesh, and bone in action. Through the practice of sensing, we start to form an inner body made primarily of the sensitive energy, an inner body where we can be even more fully at home. We are not only our body. And we are not only our inner body. But being in them provides a place for our true self to reside. Here I am in my body, in my sensation body.

How to do that? It takes persistent, long-term effort to put and keep some of our attention in our body. The more we do that, the more natural it becomes for us to be at home in our body. So for example, we begin by sitting quietly and putting all our attention into our right hand. We experience our hand from within it, in a visceral, immediate way, not by thinking about or visualizing our hand. And we hold our attention in the hand. After a few minutes, we note the difference in our current experience of our right hand and left. Our right may seem warm, full of life, full of energy. By contrast our left may seem empty and flat. This is due to the presence of the sensitive energy in the right hand, drawn there by our attention. We continue this for a few minutes each with our right foot, then the left foot, and then the left hand, followed by sensing the whole right arm, then the right leg, then the left leg, then the left arm, then all four limbs at once, and finally our whole body, including our torso and head. We do not try to sense particular internal organs, so as not to interfere with their instinctive function. Rather we sense our torso as a whole, our entire body as whole.

Sensing our whole body puts us on the path toward forming a robust and enduring inner body. The more we practice sensing, the stronger our inner body, and the longer it lasts before dissolving whenever our attention and intention lapse. So we persist, coming back to sensing again and again. Having an inner body and abiding in it, even for a few moments, is a great luxury and a step toward the formation of our soul. With practice, we become able to be in our sensation, in our sensitive energy body as we go about our day. We find this enhances our participation in life. By being in our body, we can be in our life. We are more there, in a real way, in whatever we do, including in our interactions with people.

But not only that: being in our inner body gives us a foothold in a higher world, albeit one that should be natural for us. This is a world where we are more in contact with our life, less prone to being taken over by difficult emotions. And being in that world of sensitive presence, gives us a foundation to begin to understand the nature of higher levels of the spirit and to begin to reach toward being in them. At each step along this way, we become more fully ourselves, more uniquely ourselves.

For this week, please practice being your body.

12.2 Being Your Mind

(Being Yourself: Part 2)

Descartes' most famous line goes: "I think, therefore I am." This can be true, when our I directs our thoughts. But the overwhelming majority of our thoughts arise without the participation of our I: they come by chains of association, bouncing off other thoughts or in response to some sensory perception or event. We do not generally think our thoughts; they think us. Our automatically arising, self-generated, associatively activated thoughts run our mind. Though we cannot stop our thoughts anyhow, we do give them free reign to run our mind and pretty much run our life, precisely because we believe Descartes' dictum is always true, when in fact it is only infrequently true. Whenever we notice thoughts passing through our mind, we believe we are thinking them, we believe they speak for us, we believe they represent us. We even operate on the assumption that we are our thoughts, that because our thoughts are the most intimate thing we recognize in ourselves, then our thoughts must be the essence of who and what we are. This implicit, unchallenged assumption, distorts our life by putting our entire self-image on a false foundation.

  I vividly remember when I first saw this clearly. Someone was speaking about noticing their mind rehearsing how they would act in a particular upcoming moment. This struck me with great force, because I was aware that my own mind did the same. For the first time I glimpsed the charade and saw that my thoughts are not me, that I am not my thoughts, and that they usually operate without my intention behind them. This was a shock, a revolution in my view of myself. But it would be a good many years before that realization resulted in an effective change of attitude, one that affords freedom in front of thoughts. For that though, something more was required than a negative, something more than simply seeing that I am not my thoughts.

  What we also need is a positive, a new perception. If I am not my thoughts, then what am I? A good place to start is by being our body: Particularly our sensation body. From there we can work on being our mind, the mind that is before thoughts, the mind that does not depend on thoughts, the mind as a cognitive space through which thoughts and mental images appear and are perceived. We can glimpse this pre-thought mind in quiet meditation. We sit there just staying in the moment, seeing whatever comes to us. What does come up is thoughts, multiple trains of thought, branching onto associative tangents, circling around, vying for our attention.

Gradually, very gradually, as we sit there the thoughts slow down. Gaps open between them. What is in between the thoughts? The gaps seem to be just empty space. Sitting with this, we begin to realize that the empty space is our mind itself, is not just between our thoughts, and is vast. Our thoughts pass like small clouds through the endless sky of our mind. We open into and enter that spacious mind. We become our spacious mind. In the process, we relax more deeply than we had imagined possible. We discover true peace and equanimity. We spread our inner wings and can breathe.

From our mind we can see. This means perceiving, cognizing without the intermediary of thoughts commenting, categorizing and interpreting what we see. We just see directly, without filters. This is not some esoteric magic reserved for the special few. We all have moments of direct seeing, every day. We just need to start noticing those moments, noticing how they are qualitatively different than the perceptions that get interfered with and redirected by our thoughts. Once this becomes clear to us, thoughts no longer spoil our direct seeing. The thoughts may be there, but like small clouds they do not obscure the vast, cognitive sky of our mind. Our thoughts no longer define our mind, rather our mind contains and sees them.

For this week, be your mind.

12.3 Being Your Heart
(Being Yourself: Part 3)

From relaxing deeply by releasing our muscular tensions, letting our thoughts go where they will without going with them, and allowing our emotional stress to subside, many benefits follow. Among those benefits is a very different and more natural emotional tone, namely equanimity, the appreciation and joy of living, and a warm-hearted, fellow-feeling for people. This allows us to reclaim our heart, our natural heart, from all the destructive emotions.

Because we live so often at the mercy of destructive emotions like hatred and anger, jealousy and envy, greed, worry, resentment, frustration, and the rest, we lose ourselves. We vanish in the face of these emotional states. We are not living our life at those moments, our emotions are living for us. Every perception gets filtered by the emotion. Every thought feeds the emotion. Our body dumps stress molecules into our bloodstream. Our breathing changes to support the emotion. Our posture adapts to express the emotion. And we are not there. We do not exist in those moments. Only the emotion does.

When we notice one of these destructive emotions get triggered in us and begin gathering steam, a short window of choice opens up. If we ignore it, if we fail to choose, the default option has us falling headlong into the emotional storm, be it mild or severe.

But that window of choice presents another possibility: we have a chance to change our attitude toward the situation. Sometimes that's all it takes. We simply say to ourselves "I'm not going with this now," and it stops. But more often that kind of direct confrontation with our inner state does not work, because a real change of attitude requires forgiveness, tolerance, letting go, courage, fortitude, acceptance, or love. These qualities come to us from a higher world. Yet in the throes of a destructive emotion, we are mired in a lower world, generally precluding any contact with the higher. So our attempts to think our way out of it or change our attitude prove ineffective because they come from the same level as the emotion, and we slip deeper into its grip.

What we can do then is try to work around the edges, to come at the storm obliquely. All emotion has both psychological and physiological components. Even when our psychology is fully committed to the emotion, our body may offer a constructive avenue to ameliorate it. One approach to this consists of relaxing our body: Particularly our chest and our face, and sometimes also our shoulders or abdomen. Keeping at this relaxing of our body, our thoughts may follow suit. Soon enough the strength of the emotional storm may start to wane. Then by moving into some activity that engages us fully, we might shift our attention enough to free ourselves from the destructive emotion. Any wholesome activity may work, but one that particularly feeds our inner life is the practice of sensing our body, full body awareness, being centered in our whole body.

Sometimes we have the opposite problem, rather than a storm we have a flat, indifferent state of our heart. One approach would be to re-label that indifference or boredom as peace and allow it to penetrate more deeply into our emotional core. That can raise our state to true peace, which in turn enables other higher emotions to come through.

Some emotional states can be debilitating, chronic, and intractable. In those cases, we seek help from mental health professionals.

But if we can be there in our center, seeing all the emotions and other perceptions pass through our presence, we can learn to let them come and let them go without attempting to keep them or push them away, which generally does not work anyhow. This is the practice of equanimity, which is peace.

Equanimity is to our emotions what the silence underlying our mind is to our thoughts. A peaceful heart has room for the emotional storms to arise and pass by. On one level we may be in the turmoil of a strong and destructive emotion, while on another our inner peace remains undisturbed. Yet equanimity is not indifference. The latter blocks any warmth, whereas equanimity opens us to a warm-hearted appreciation of our life and of the people around us. Equanimity lets us be in our emotional heart, lets us be our heart, and lets us just be.

A peaceful heart, a silent mind, and awareness of our whole (sensation) body form the complete foundation for presence, for full participation in our life. For this week, practice being your heart.

12.4 Being Your Personality

(Being Yourself: Part 4)

All our patterns of behavior, inner and outer, including our thoughts, emotions, and our ways of interacting with people, taken as a whole form what we call our personality. Sometimes we may try to hide our real tendencies, to mask our personality. But the reality is that our personality itself is a mask, hiding our true I both from ourselves and from others. Our personality enthralls us, so convincing is it that this is who I am. Yet it is a distraction from our self, from the one who rightly could perceive and act and live our life. Instead we give power to our personality, to our familiar patterns of body, thought, and emotion. We let our personality run our life because we do not look any deeper to see beyond it. We do not even have a conception that there is anything deeper in us. It seems our personality is who we are.

Though we take all our patterns as a whole and call it personality, it is not a whole; it is just a bunch of parts, ways of thinking, feeling, and acting that are so familiar to us that we assume this amorphous collection is who we are. It spins an image, a self-image, which we label with our name and substitute for our real self. Some of these parts have ideals, while others wallow in base motivations. Many even conflict with each other: some parts love to eat, but others feel better when not overweight. So here we are living as our personality, as a mass of pre-programmed patterns, reactions, and contradictions. Its complexity hides its pre-determined nature. Nothing really new enters: this is how we have been, how we are now, and how we will be. That may be comforting, but it is also limiting.

One part of our personality is a story machine. It loves stories. It loves to hear stories, hence the popularity of movies, TV, and novels. It also loves to make up stories and tell them: Particularly to ourselves. We have the story of our life, continuously unfolding. Our personality tells us the story of who it thinks we are, recounting our history, narrating our present, and foretelling our probable future. We hear this story over and over and believe it. We want to improve it. After all, it is our very own story. If we can improve the story, we improve ourselves. But we are not any story. We are not the presumed protagonist in the story of our life as told by our personality. That story stands between us and our life.

Another part of our personality is the judge and commentator, evaluating everything and everyone, including ourselves. We hear these judgments and believe we are the judge. We hear our inner comments and believe we are the commentator. But again, this is just the judging, commenting, ruminating machine of our personality. It is not who we are. This machine filters our perceptions and stands between us and our life.

So what then? How to find freedom in the midst of all this? First, we cannot rid ourselves of our personality, nor can we effectively reform it. Freedom on this level does not mean removing or changing our personality, it simply means not being taken by it, not having it drive our life, not believing it is who we are. Furthermore, our personality is a powerful mechanism, with a great deal of knowledge about our world built into it. The question is: does it use us or do we use it?

If we fight it head on, we will not only lose the battle, we will also lose part of ourselves. In the end, we can only just be ourselves, we just allow our personality to produce its thoughts, emotions, reactions, speech, and actions, we allow it to spin our image, to tell us our story, to judge, comment, and ruminate. We relax and let it be and let ourselves be. We do not need to be wary of our personality, our image. But what we do need is to be awake, to be the one who notices, who sees all these happenings inside and outside of us. Then, when necessary, we are able to choose our actions rather than allowing them to be chosen for us by our personality patterns.

In the inner silence, beneath our thoughts and emotions, we can abide untouched by personality. Meditation shows us this still place in ourselves. Soaking in that, we become it. Afterward, as our personality returns full-force, we can be in it, we can be it, but without being only that. We have our thoughts. We have our emotions. We have our usual ways of acting. And all the while, we also have the stillness within us. All this coexists, but on different levels. On one level we are our personality, we are our self-image. At the same time, on a deeper level, we are the stillness within. This solves the problem of personality. We are it, but not only it. We can be our self, if we can be our whole self, which includes both the shallow and the deep, the mask and the one who wears it. We do not seek to destroy or overcome the shallow in us. Instead, we embrace it, we embrace ourselves with the compassionate arms of stillness.

For this week, be your personality and be the cognizant stillness behind it.

12.5 Being Your Relationships
(Being Yourself: Part 5)

Our many relationships seem to define who we are and rightly so, because what we are does not stop at our skin. Through our social intelligence, we all deal with variable relationships of many kinds, fleeting or long-term, superficial or intimate. We treat these as being between us and someone else, between two discreet people. This is our ordinary world of separateness, governed by the rules of morality, etiquette, and courtesy. But there are deeper levels to every relationship.

Space is one unbroken continuum. It opens to everything, yet maintains its own characteristics. It bends without breaking (the exception of black holes not withstanding). We may erect walls or build a box to divide up space. But that does not really divide space; it just makes barriers to movement. Notice, though, that the walls are no barrier to certain things, such as radio waves or gravity. Similarly, we have our own inner barriers that seem to define who we are, that divide us from the world beyond our skin, that separate us from other people. Again though, at more refined levels these inner barriers vanish and lose their effectiveness.

There is sameness, there is uniqueness, and there is

unity, three qualities at three different levels. Sameness enters at the level of the conscious energy. If we are quiet enough inside, we touch the place in ourselves that is the same in others, the quiet, cognizant stillness in them. This is not just similar and it is not just a copy in the sense of having the same characteristics. The stillness in each of us is part of the great continuum of consciousness that not only is the substance of our mind, but lies beneath all that exists. We all share in this cognizant stillness, just as we all live in and share the air we breathe. It means that, at a fundamental level, my awareness is the same as your awareness, that we share the same awareness. This is our pure awareness, prior to thought and emotion, prior to categorizing, interpreting, and acting. We all see with the same awareness. By being in our own inner stillness, we can notice it in others, notice that we share it. This profoundly affects our ways of relating.

Uniqueness enters at the level of the creative energy, the world of sacred light, but really concerns will, the uniqueness of our will, the uniqueness of our individual I. Every person is unique, in the way that God is unique. If each of us has the Divine nature within us, then we each inherit that Divine quality of uniqueness. If we are open to it, uniqueness makes people endlessly fascinating, because we can never know the full depths of any person, not even ourselves. We respect each other as unique beings with unique will. That respect shows our inherent equality, which is a manifestation of the fact that we all, in our will, derive from the Divine Will. We relate to each other as I and Thou, as two equal beings, equally children of the Creator. Outwardly we are not equal, we may be rich or poor, fast or slow, beautiful or homely, educated or not. But for our inherent value, none of that matters: we are all equal and equally unique. And because we are fully ourselves, we no longer need to keep other people at arm's length to maintain our own identity. Our barriers to each other grow porous.

Beyond sameness and uniqueness, there is unity. This also concerns will. A sports team, a tight knit organization, or a close family is one whose members share the same will, in a limited context. A team that is functioning well acts as unit, toward the same goal. Each member plays their allotted role, putting his or her unique talents to work for the whole. Each supports the others, empowering the whole. In doing so, each one contributes to and shares in the will of the team. Notice that each one is free and freely enters the will of the team. In fact, there is greater freedom in the greater will, because each is released from purely self-centered concerns, released from self-will. The less self-will, the greater the purity, and the more completely one enters the greater will. All of this is a reflection, though a pale one, of how we come toward unity with each other in the Divine Will. Our uniqueness testifies that we all share in That. But our self-centered egoism diverts our share of the Divine Will. For full participation, full purity is required. The closer we come to that purity, the closer we come to the Sacred, and the closer we come to other people, to our inherent unity.

All the levels of relationship matter, whether based on separateness, as most are, or on sameness, uniqueness, or unity. Feeling free in our relationships, we can be fully ourselves. For this week, honor your relationships and be them.

12.6 Being Your Job
(Being Yourself: Part 6)

There is great dignity in working, in being useful. The

act of doing something that benefits others confers one of the profound satisfactions of life and gives us meaning. The reason it is so essentially gratifying to be productive in service lies deep within us, in our spiritual nature.

We can describe the Divine as a mountain of purpose, one that far transcends our understanding. All work, by definition, has a purpose. Our small scale purposes may not seem to relate to the Divine Purpose, but they do. Purpose is purpose. And it requires acts of will to fulfill any purpose. Will and purpose are closely intertwined: every conscious act of will has a purpose. Any purpose in tune with our conscience, such as wholesome and beneficial work, aligns our actions with the Divine purpose, aligns us with the sacred. So to perform our necessary and our chosen duties to our body, our family, our society, and our planet defines us and connects us with the purpose of our life. We may not know that purpose explicitly, but clearly such duties form a part of our life's purpose. Our work, our job, and in some cases our avocations, be they paid or unpaid, in our home or outside it, give us the essence satisfaction of fulfilling, at least in part, our true purpose.

Of course, the closer our work aligns with and draws upon our natural gifts, our skills, and our interests, the more satisfying it may be and the more it helps us develop our individuality. But we become ourselves, in part, through our work and through choosing to do what we are doing, whether or not it aligns with our nature or our desires. Work, for most, is a necessity, a way of earning our living, paying for our life. Yet there's also an element of choice, not only in the kind of work we do, but in our moment-to-moment choosing to be here doing what we are doing.

This is part of presence in action and transforms even the most mundane tasks. That choice is an act of will, an act of our will. We choose to do what are doing here and now. Even if it is a humdrum and necessary chore or one that is imposed on us, we can still get behind it and choose it. We need not let our inner world in such moments be dominated by our dislike of a situation. Even if we are doing something we do not want to be doing, as long as we actually are doing it, we can choose to do it with both feet, with the whole of ourselves, fully engaged in this moment. In this way, we turn our ordinary work and our daily chores into actions that simultaneously feed both our outer world and our soul.

Inwardly we are free, free to choose to do whatever we are doing. In that freedom comes relief from resentment, boredom, grumbling, escapism, daydreaming, and being lost in thought and out of touch. Nevertheless, choosing to do what we are doing does not mean we must meekly give up hope of improving our lot in life or following our interests. We can, if we wish, work to change our circumstances, all the while choosing in each moment to do what we are doing at that moment. In so choosing, we bring presence to our work. We are here working. We become our work. We fill this moment with life.

Another aspect of doing our work is to do it well, with quality. We give each task the full and appropriate measure of effort and attention. We continually seek to improve what we do, to always get better at it, to be intelligent and heartful about it. Quality in the material world is a reflection of quality in the spiritual worlds. To the extent that we can be the vehicle for quality to enter this world, we serve as a bridge between the two, between the spiritual and the material. This is our intended role in the great harmony of the world. Any task performed with excellence feeds our soul, develops our individuality, and redounds with benefits that ripple well beyond our personal interests and satisfaction. True excellence reaches toward perfection, and perfection in a small task joins the perfecting of the spiritual nature of our world. Thus the dignity of work is unbounded in its very source.

For this week, be your job, be your work. Choose to do whatever you are doing, so you can fully be here doing it.

12.7 Being Your Presence
(Being Yourself: Part 7)

When we are not ourselves, if we are anything at all, what are we? We can mistakenly be almost anything, given our endless capacity for identification, for believing we are something other than who we are, believing it to such an extent that we become that thing for those moments. Instantaneously and without noticing it, we slip into identification. Prime examples include hot button thoughts, daydreams both pleasant and unpleasant, reactive emotions, and problematic bodily states. Any one of these, in their countless variations, can suddenly take center stage of our inner world and we collapse into it, we believe we are that thing.

Non-identification means not being lost in that way. We are present. We abide in the cognizant container of our perceptions, instead of losing our self in the perceived. To put it simply, we come back to ourselves. Any time we recognize that we are not in ourselves, that we are identified, we have already taken a step toward non-identification and presence. We can choose presence any time we remember to do so. Yet our presence proves unstable. It lasts for a moment and we fall off again, back into the mesmerizing stream of perceptions.

This is precisely where the practices of presence show

their value. As always, we begin with body awareness, with sensing our body. We go beyond the subject-object style of body awareness, where we are in our head and aware of our body which is out there. Instead, we enter our sensation, we enter our whole body, we become our whole body. This lends some stability to our presence, because our body is always in the real here and now. The stronger our sensation, the longer it tends to persist. Even we when fall back into being pushed and pulled by the stream of perceptions, sensation can awaken us spontaneously: we unexpectedly notice the sensation of our arm, which reminds us to sense our whole body and be here in this moment.

As powerful as sensing is as a practice of presence, it does not yield full presence. For that we need more. We add presence of mind and of heart. Rather than being carried off in our associative thought-stream, we become aware of the cognizant stillness beneath our thoughts, at the root of our mind, and we abide in that. We see our thoughts without being taken by them. Doing this from the platform of sensing our body gives us a place in ourselves to stand and be aware.

Presence of heart comes from abiding in the peace and equanimity at the root of all our emotions. Standing in body sensation and stillness of mind gives us a way into the peace of heart. We are here and at peace with being here. Just as beneath every thought there is the cognizant stillness of our mind, beneath every emotion, including the difficult ones, there is the peace and equanimity of our true heart. We need only look deeper into our heart, beyond our emotion du jour, to find our home of peace.

Each of these three practices supports the other and lends further stability to our presence. The practices of inner work need practice. Presence is not something we can choose once and expect to stay in it. It vanishes; we vanish. And so we choose presence again and again, continually. We are always losing ourselves, losing our presence, and thus we frequently have the opportunity to come back to ourselves, back to awareness based in body, mind, and heart, back to being here. It is a set of practices that require dedication and long-term persistence. Coming back to ourselves, again and again, is exactly what is needed. This inner work pays tremendous dividends in the quality of our life. Yes, there is that free and continual outpouring of grace from the beneficent Source of the world. But to receive it, we must at least be here. So we repeatedly, indefatigably step into presence.

Again though, there is more to presence, there is consciousness itself. Equanimity and stillness lead directly into the pure, unbounded, spacious awareness that underlies all our perceptions. And we abide in that, we become that, we become consciousness itself. Quiet meditation can give us the taste, which in turn can show us that the pure awareness, consciousness is always here. We live in it. But like the proverbial fish in water, we do not normally notice it. So we open our mind, our heart, our being. We let all the thoughts, sensations, and emotions roll on, while we turn toward the underlying spacious awareness, so close and intimate to us. We cherish the moments when we can live as that.

For this week, be present more, and be your presence. This means not just being fully aware, but inhabiting that awareness, being that awareness.

12.8 Being Your I
(Being Yourself: Part 8)

I can ask myself: who or what am I? Looking as carefully as I can into that question, I see that I am my will. I do not feel that I am my body, for I can sense my body and control many aspects of it. Sometimes though, for example when my body is in pain, it seems that I am my body. But I know it isn't so.

I do not feel that I am my emotions, for I perceive my emotions and sometimes they have a life of their own, out of my control and clearly not me. Sometimes though, for example when my emotions are very strong, it seems that I am my emotions, for I agree with and believe in them. But I know it isn't so.

I do not feel that I am my thoughts, for I perceive my thoughts and can to some extent control them, although like my emotions they seem to have a life of their own and go on without my direction. My thoughts can slow down or even stop momentarily and I am still here without them. Sometimes though, for example when my thoughts express opinions or worries, it seems that I am my thoughts, for I agree with and believe in them. But I know it isn't so.

What about my awareness itself? Am I my awareness? This comes closer to what seems true, yet not quite there. I have some control over my awareness. Through my attention I can direct my awareness, here or there. My awareness is like my body. It is like an inner body made of sensation and consciousness, responsive to my choices, serving a crucial function. Yet my awareness is not me. With practice I become able to be aware of my awareness. It is not who I am.

Who I am is the one who sees, the one who perceives, the one who chooses. This I is not something I can inwardly see or be aware of, for it is the one who is aware. No mirror can show my I to me. So all that is left is for me to be my I, to be my will, my intention, my deciding and choosing, my attention, to be the one who does what I do, the one who experiences my life, the one who lives my life.

But isn't that how we live all the time anyway? Not really. Generally we live in identification, assuming we are some strong emotion, or convincing thought, or bodily sensation, some desire or some repulsion. That seems to be who I am in those moments. But I am none of those things. I am I. There is no content in my I. It is pure will. True, higher emotions like love, compassion, joy, and equanimity can enter my being through my I, coming from a deeper place than my individual I. Still, I am not those higher emotions either. I am I.

This I is not mysterious. It comes through at times in all of us. We each have our own I. We are just out of touch with it and do not recognize it for what it is — nor for what it is not. We live on the surface of our being, not in and as our core, our I.

So a deep part of our self-development, both psychological and spiritual is truly to be ourselves, to be our I, and not anything else. The most easily recognizable approach to this is to start by being our attention, by being the one who pays attention, the one who directs and focuses our attention, the one who sees what our attention points toward.

Note that our ego is not our I. Our ego manifests as set of patterns of thought, emotion, and action which are self-referential, which create an image of a self that we believe we are. Ego feeds and serves itself, first and foremost. Our I by contrast is not a pattern, is not any set of thoughts, emotions, or actions, and is not self-serving. It is pure will. Of course, we let our I get fooled into believing we are our ego and there our troubles begin, as our ego takes control of our will and we live a self-centered, self-serving life.

For this week, practice being your attention, as the first aspect of being your I. Notice your attention. Get in it. Be the one directing it. Pay attention to some object and be the one seeing that object. Switch to another object and be the one making the switch. Be your attention and thereby be your I.

12.9 Being Your Conscience
(Being Yourself: Part 9)

We have in us an impulse to do the right thing. The source of that impulse is our conscience, in the core of our will. Conscience comes through our I, so that we intuitively recognize the right action to take. Although conscience generally accords with and is informed by our childhood training and the moral norms and laws of our society, it does not depend on childhood training, norms, rules, or laws. We know what is right and what is wrong and thereby we also obey the law.

Still, we sometimes confront situations where it is not clear what is right and what is wrong. Here we tread carefully. This lack of clarity can be due to our unwillingness to accept what we know to be true, driving us to put up a fog of self-obfuscation, dissembling, and justification. Whenever we notice our mind raising arguments that a certain course of action really is OK, that is usually a sign that it is really not OK and we are just trying to convince ourselves otherwise. We take care in such cases not to allow our preferences to cloud our judgment and obscure our conscience.

But it does happen that there are gray situations, where none of our options seems clearly superior in terms of right and wrong. Then we can look at other criteria like congruence with our life goals and effects on other people and the environment.

Conscience is the basis of integrity. We all know and respect people of integrity. We also know that integrity is perhaps the most valuable quality a person can have. The value of integrity is clear in our day-to-day life. We trust a person of integrity and tend to treat them well. Yet it is just as crucial in our spiritual life.

A clear conscience helps enable our contact with the spirit, whereas actions that go against our conscience and weigh on our heart put up barriers to that contact. Access to the deeper realms of the spirit require purity of motivation and a clear conscience. Without that we get bounced out of heaven.

But we have all done things that violate our conscience. Is there any hope? Some of those things stand out, causing us to feel remorse. Those actions we redress where possible by trying to make amends, such as apologies and/or compensation for the wrong we have done to others. Then we may be able to forgive ourselves. If not, the fires of remorse may gradually purify us. And most importantly, we resolve, going forward, to listen to our conscience and act accordingly. If we aspire to the spiritual heart of the world, we cannot afford to bury our conscience by ignoring it or acting against it. We can liberate ourselves from the burden of acts we know to be wrong. Conscience helps us toward freedom from our egoistic self-centeredness.

For some, the notion of karma, or as you sow so shall you reap, provides the extra motivation needed to do the right thing, knowing that if we do the wrong thing, undesirable results inevitably rebound on us. For others, love and compassion provide the needed motivation, knowing that harming others is like harming ourselves, and harming ourselves is off the table because our love and compassion also extend to ourselves.

Our transformation depends upon allowing our conscience to play a larger and larger role in our life. Conscience is not alien to who we are: it is who we are. Conscience is right here, just behind the core of our will, coming as our I. Obeying our conscience is not like obeying some other person or even society. It is obeying the truth, obeying ourselves, our higher self, informed by love. Sometimes this is difficult. We have some strong desire and our conscience weighs in against acting on that desire. What we choose to do in that case shows how well we are meeting the ongoing test of life and spirit. This is where the work of conscience becomes very practical and concrete. This is the work that truly can set us free.

The more we pay attention to and act in accord with our conscience, the more readily it comes to us. It becomes natural to us to be a person of conscience, to do the right thing. Even then though, it sometimes happens that a dilemma confronts us and a strong part of us wants to go against our conscience. But we do not. We find we cannot. And our work continues.

For this week, notice the promptings of your conscience and act accordingly. Imagine how different our world would be, if all people strove to live by conscience.

13.0 Mind and Thought
Introduction

Thoughts pass through our mind almost all the time. Logical and creative thinking is perhaps the principal feature that makes us truly different than other animals, while the totality of our thoughts define us as individuals. Our thoughts shape our life, shape who we are, what we do, and how we respond, for better or for worse. Yet despite their centrality, we hardly notice our thoughts as thoughts. We consider them to be our private inner voice that speaks for us and as us, a window into our very soul. We do not consider our thoughts to be separate from who we are. We do not question their role as the basis of our mind, our self. Indeed, we believe we are our thoughts. When a thought arises in our mind, our unexamined assumption is "that is what I think." Our very identity is submerged in, defined by, and embodied by our thoughts.

Often our thoughts are commenting on whatever is happening at the moment or even narrating our life. And of course, we presume that we are the commentator or narrator. Or our thoughts may be ruminating on some past event, telling us, embellishing, and interpreting the story. And of course, we presume that we are the story teller. Or our thoughts may be planning some future actions that we may undertake, but often do not. And of course, we presume we are the planner. Or our thoughts may be aimless, just wandering around our mind, as we wander with them. Or they wander in a specific direction, which we call daydreaming. And of course, we presume we are the wanderer and the dreamer.

Because of their range and flexibility, our thoughts give us the illusion of freedom. But the truth is that our thoughts are bound by their patterns and by memory. Their central pattern is that they refer to a non-existent self, our ego, that we believe we are. Our thoughts create our ego in the same way that a novelist creates a character. It's just words, but they paint a convincing image that we take to be the real thing, that we take to be who we are. We believe that we are the one that our thoughts reference all the time. Whenever the thought "I" arises, we take that to be who we are. But the thought "I" is just a thought. Our true I is not a thought and does not depend on thoughts to define or announce its reality. The I that is defined by our thoughts is that self-centered ego, an imposter and usurper.

A very important measure of inner freedom and spirituality is the degree to which we are free in front of our thoughts. Our attitude toward our thoughts, regardless of their specific content, affects our happiness or lack thereof, our relationships, and all that we do. Yet how much effort have we put toward examining this central issue of how we relate to our thoughts? Yes, we pursue an education and various interests which affect our thoughts, but those efforts affect the contents of our mind, the information embedded in our thoughts, not the meta-level issues regarding the place and role of our thought processes themselves.

In the coming weeks, we will explore our relationship with our thoughts and the mind in which they roam. For this week, please see if you can catch glimpses of your unvoiced attitudes toward your own thoughts.

13.1 Noticing Thoughts as Thoughts
(Mind and Thought: Part 1)

To see our thoughts as thoughts simply means to realize that the thought we are inwardly seeing or hearing is just a thought and nothing more than a thought. It is not who we are. It does not necessarily represent our views or values. It has no power over us, except the power we give it. We all know that we do not need to act on our thoughts. But beyond that, we do not need to believe or believe in our thoughts. We do not need to accept that our thoughts express anything significant about us. We are no more our thoughts than we are our breath or our pulse. But as long as we do not notice our thoughts, or notice only their meaning and get enthralled by that semantic stream, we are chained to them. Stepping back, we go beyond their meaning to see them with our mind's eye for what they are: just a series of mental words or images. This is what we mean by noticing our thoughts as thoughts, which is a major step toward inner freedom.

In trying to see our thoughts without getting lost in them, it helps to set aside time to sit quietly, get in contact with our body and its sensation, be there in our body, and then turn our attention to noticing our thought stream, with a light touch, so as not to disturb the thoughts too much. We notice an individual thought start, happen, and end. And then we notice the next one and the one after that. All the while we stay grounded in our body to keep us here in this moment and prevent us from floating away down that thought stream. If we do come to and realize that we have fallen into our thoughts instead of observing them, then we simply and without self-recriminations return to being in contact with our body and seeing our thoughts.

One of the big challenges in the practice of noticing thoughts as thoughts is the very wide range of our thoughts, in terms of type and subject matter. Inevitably and without warning, one comes along that grabs us firmly or lulls us to sleep and away we go. For example, when we are sitting in this meditation on thoughts, we will of course have thoughts, some of which might be like "why am I sitting here?" "Am I doing this right?" "How can I see my thoughts better?" "This is boring." Such thoughts often do not register as thoughts while we are observing. They seem to part of the observation process. But they, like all the others, are just thoughts.

Some time outside of formal sitting meditation, when you want to practice seeing your thoughts as thoughts, try this. Read something. And as you read pay attention to the sounds of the words you are reading as they make themselves known in your mind. With your inward ear, you can hear them like you would any other thought. But because this is intentional and structured, you may have a better chance of noticing them as thoughts. Even though these are not "your" thoughts, but those of the author you are reading, it is still good practice for recognizing thoughts as thoughts.

Alternatively, just stop whatever you are doing for one minute. Use that minute to notice your thoughts, without trying to change them in any way. Put your attention into your mind and see the thoughts coming and going of their own accord. Let them come and let them go. Just see what is there, moment to moment. This practice has a subtle, slow, but profound effect on us: it leads to inner freedom.

The more settled into our body and the more relaxed we are, the better our chances of seeing as thoughts the words and images passing through our mind. If we are inwardly rushed or in some state of agitation, anxiety, or other difficult emotion, we are unlikely to have enough free attention to notice our thoughts as thoughts. Instead we will just be swept along by them. Then thoughts come and go, while we believe them and take them at face value, if we notice them at all. In this state, which is our usual state, our thoughts shape us and run our life. And because our universe of thoughts is inconsistent, self-contradictory, reactive, random, and even chaotic, our life takes on similar flavors. There is no freedom in that.

Take the example of worry thoughts. Perhaps you have a situation that is both significant and uncertain. You worry about it. Your thoughts keep returning to the situation, ruminating on it. And because you believe in your thoughts, again and again you let the worry thoughts grab you. But if you see these worry thoughts as thoughts, you do not need to go with them. You can allow them to arise and pass by without getting caught up in the worry. Yes, you take these thoughts as information to consider and perhaps act on. You do what you can or need or choose to do about the situation. Beyond that, the worrying only wastes your time and energy and colors your life in a troubled hue. So seeing your thoughts as just thoughts, your worry as just worry, lightens your load and helps you toward inner freedom.

For this week, practice seeing your thoughts as thoughts.

13.2 Who Is Thinking?

(Mind and Thought: Part 2)

Sometimes I think, but mostly it thinks. "It" in this case refers to the automatic mind, the mental machinery that churns out thoughts based on reacting to sensory impressions of the moment, bouncing off accidently triggered memories of the past, responding to unconscious concerns and drives, or chaining off other automatic, self-generated thoughts. These automatic thoughts think themselves and dominate our mind, both in being the most prevalent type of thinking and in being the most influential, in a pre-conscious way. They acquire their influence from the simple fact that we claim them, or rather they claim us. They pretend to represent our views, to be our very own inner voice. And we accept that at face value.

This ongoing stream of automatic thinking is so prevalent, so ordinary, and we are so accustomed to it, that we just believe all these thoughts are ours, are the voice of our soul, and are truly coming from our core self. This despite the fact that a little direct and unbiased inward observation clearly shows that nearly all our thoughts are thinking themselves. The thought stream goes on and on, without any intentional thinking on our part, without the need for our participation. It never stops its inner talking, to us as passive spectators and believers.

One of the major functions of our mind is to make sense of our life and our world. So our thoughts form around the events, people, things, goals, difficulties and all the rest in our life. These attempts at sense-making include many automatic thinking processes such as putting what happens, putting the stuff of our life into the story of our life, into our ongoing narrative and commentary on our life. This occurs by itself, with little or no intention on our part. But it seems important, it seems to be about us personally, and it seems to be us, our I, that is doing it. While this sense-making is important and useful, and is often about us, it is mostly just the complex mechanism of our brain doing its own wonderful thing, without our I being the one who is doing it. It happens almost entirely automatically. At times, though, we do intentionally think about some aspect of our life. Then I am the one who is thinking. But usually our brain is thinking for us, automatically. And it draws us into this orbit of automatic story-telling, narrating, and commenting, which all together form an image that we take to be ourselves. This is our self-making mind.

Another reason the automatic nature of our thoughts

is so difficult for us to see is that the times we do think intentionally leave us with the impression that all our thoughts are intentional. Yes, we can and do drive our thoughts. We plan, we solve problems, we consider issues and much more, by intentionally thinking. In these cases we have a very different relationship with our thoughts. We are not just passive in front of them. We get their meaning, we evaluate them, and choose further directions for them. The quality of energy is different than the automatic energy that fuels our associative thinking. With intentional thinking, we use and direct the sensitive energy as the very stuff of our thoughts. We do the thinking. Our I thinks. No longer is it thinking.

But that does not last. At some point, usually unnoticeable and unremarked by us, we slip out of sensitive thinking and back into automatic thought. There is no readily discernable boundary between the two states. So while we still believe that we are thinking, as was the case a moment earlier, now it is thinking, not us. And off we go.

Another mode of sensitive thinking runs parallel to automatic thought, wherein we are in contact with the meaning of our thoughts, including those in the automatic stream. We see and recognize our thoughts as they go by, without intentionally changing them. We pursue this in the practice of presence, awareness of the whole, including the contents of our mind. We practice this in meditation. If we are particularly settled in our meditation, we might see one of the underlying layers of our thought-mind, a layer of free-floating snippets of thought, unconnected, not forming complete sentences, sometimes not even forming complete concepts, a kind of thought soup. No one is thinking those snippets; they are just the raw material from which thoughts form. Then some of these snippets coalesce into a whole thought and join the great ongoing stream of thought.

For this week look at your thoughts as they stream by. Ask yourself who is thinking these thoughts? Am I thinking these thoughts, or are they thinking themselves? Who does this thought think it is? Who do I think this thought is?

13.3 Beyond Thought: The Conscious Mind

(Mind and Thought: Part 3)

Freedom in front of our thoughts has pre-requisites. First, we need a place to stand from which to see our thoughts, so that we are less likely to be carried off by them. Contact with the sensation of our whole body can serve as that place. Second, as discussed in the previous parts of this inner work series, is noticing and recognizing our thoughts as thoughts. This brings the sensitive energy to bear in our mind. It enables contact with the meaning of our thoughts and with the fact that they are just thoughts, usually thinking themselves. Third, though, we need contact with a deeper part of our mind, beneath and beyond our thoughts, a zone that brings new modes of being, yet can become readily accessible.

That deeper part is our conscious mind. It opens to us in silence and stillness, through the conscious energy. It confers peace, joy, and appreciation for the wonder of life. A classical and effective way to learn about the conscious energy is through meditation: Particularly if it incorporates the three pre-requisites of freedom in front of thoughts.

We start by sitting quietly and relaxing into our body. Keeping our attention in our body, we come into contact with the sensation of having a body, into contact with our proprioception. Staying with that attention to our body, that body perception grows stronger and broader, becoming what we call the sensitive energy throughout our whole body. We are sensing our body. This gives us a platform, a place to stand in the present as we turn to the next phase of the meditation, which is watching our thoughts while staying in contact with our body.

We let our thoughts come and go, recognizing them as thoughts, as if they were going by on a screen like a news ticker. Thoughts are just thoughts. We do not need to engage with them just because they arise. We do not need to react to them, to fall into them, to be swept along by them. We sit in our sensation body and watch our thoughts come and go, come and go, on and on. We sit patiently, neither grasping any thought nor pushing it away. We let them be as they are, whatever they are. But we do let them take us or be us. We stay here and now in our body and stay with watching our thought stream. Whenever we reawaken, noticing that we have been lost in our thoughts, we just relax, reestablish our contact with our body sensation, and go back to watching our thoughts patiently.

Gradually our thoughts slow down and gaps open up between them. When we start to notice those gaps, we turn to noticing what is in those gaps. Nothing – it seems. So we look further into the gaps. And still we see nothing. But we do see our mind, empty in those gaps. The mind-space around our thoughts begins to reveal itself. This cognizant stillness, which we glimpse between thoughts, is the deeper layer of our mind, the conscious layer, the pure awareness prior to any content. Here is the realm of peace and freedom. It lies beneath and around our thoughts. We are immersed in it. This consciousness at the base layer of our awareness is there, not only beneath our thoughts, but beneath all our sensory perceptions.

The more we acquire a taste for that cognizant stillness in meditation, the more we become able to be in it, both in meditation and even while going about our daily life. This peace is here in our being. We do not manufacture it, we just need to open to it, by seeing beneath all that our senses display on top of this layer of consciousness. We learn to recognize the cognizant stillness. We learn that it is not truly hidden by our sensory impressions. It remains here and available. It just takes a shift in our attention, an opening of our attention to include both the cognizant stillness and the sensory stream of life. In this way, it becomes clear that our thoughts and sensory impressions are just little waves on the surface of a deep pool of consciousness.

Learning to live more of our life in contact with consciousness has subtle but powerful impacts on us. First, it brings peace to our heart. We are no longer so reactive to our thoughts and emotions, but are even more responsive and engaged in our life. We are less easily thrown off our presence by the events of our life. We are less concerned with defending and building our ego, our self-image. We are more in contact with the reality around us, including the people in our life. We are more readily able to do what needs to be done.

And on a deeper level, consciousness opens us toward the sacred spirit that lies beyond even consciousness. In the silence of consciousness, contemplative prayer moves a step closer to the Sacred.

For this week, explore the mind-space surrounding your thoughts. Taste the peace of consciousness.

13.4 Freeing Our Mind
(Mind and Thought: Part 4)

The more we can live in the open mind-space of consciousness, the fundamental pure awareness that is here with us always, beneath all our perceptions, the more freedom we enjoy. Inner freedom is the first freedom, because so many constraints are imposed on us by our habits of mind, by our reactions, by our desires, by grasping and rejecting. All this clutters and obscures our mind-space, encumbering us like so much baggage. Inner freedom releases the grip that our mind-baggage has on us.

The first steps, as discussed in the previous parts of this inner work series, are to see our thoughts for what they are, namely just thoughts, mostly self-generated and all without inherent power over us, and to get a taste of another way of living, of another possibility, namely the spacious mind of pure consciousness, prior to and beneath thoughts, emotions, and sensory perceptions. For the first step, we need to observe our thoughts objectively. For the second, we can turn to meditation.

Having made those steps and having seen that we have within us a deep, all-pervasive pool of peace, of cognizant stillness, we soon find ourselves falling back into passively riding along in our thought-stream, buffeted by our emotional reactions and desires. What then?

Seeing a truth once is not enough: we need to integrate that realization into our life. Like the practice of meditation, we can in our daily life, whenever we notice that we are identified with some thought-stream or reaction, return to being in contact with our sensation body and from there with the spacious mind of consciousness. Though we may want to be free, when in the grip of some compelling set of thoughts or emotions, we find it hard to imagine that a deep pool of peace and consciousness lies just beneath all that, and even harder to actually turn toward that peace.

Yet for every one of us, that peace of consciousness is there in every moment. It is part of our standard equipment as human beings. Just as we have our body always with us: Part of us, we also have the unformed elements of our soul. That ocean of peace is one of those unformed elements. We can just relax: first our body and then our mind. We relax back into awareness itself, into seeing, into being the one who sees all that we perceive. In that seeing, we are in consciousness, in the cognizant stillness whose nature is peace and wholeness. Nothing is missing and nothing is amiss. We feel complete and content. Equanimity pervades us through and through.

When totally under the influence of some persistent series of thoughts and emotions, the memory of freedom gained in meditation might jog us into wishing for that freedom in the present. Knowing that the cognizant stillness is here in us, presents us with an alternative to being pushed along by our thoughts and emotions, and gives us a place to turn toward. If we wish for it, know the direction, make the choice, and take the necessary inward action, we can slip beneath our thought-stream, slip out of its grip and into our spacious mind, a welcoming place that feels like home.

And then we fall back again into identification with the contents of our mind. So we repeat our movement into peace. This process recurs during our day just as it does in formal meditation. It is one of the practices we can fruitfully carry into our life. The more we do this, the more confidence it gives us that inner freedom is and is possible for us, and the more live it. Our inner constraints weaken and our inner mind-space opens up. We can breathe again and flow with our life.

For this week, work on freeing your mind, by stepping into your body and into the cognizant stillness beneath the contents of your mind. Your thoughts do not define you and need not limit you.

13.5 Beyond Mind

(Mind and Thought: Part 5)

The vast and all-encompassing field of consciousness is the basis of our mind. All experience seems to come through consciousness. And its inherent nature is cognizance, peace, and wholeness. It is seductively easy to believe that consciousness is the ultimate, is God, is the Divine. Many do believe exactly that. Whole teachings are based on that notion. But it is not true. The Sacred lies beyond consciousness, beyond the mind. An accurate reading of Buddhism, for example, shows that consciousness is not the ultimate.

But what really matters to us is what we come to ourselves, through our own deepening perceptions, not what someone tells us and not what we might read here or in Buddhist texts or anywhere else. The texts and teachings can be valuable pointers, but cannot substitute for our own inner explorations.

When we come into the field of pure consciousness, it is so remarkable, so welcoming, so blissful, that we just want to stay in it, or at least come back often. The more we live in consciousness, the more it transforms our life. And it is right that we should do so, to the extent we can. Yet if our inner work stops there, remains at that level, we are stopping short of the truly Sacred realms.

So how can we explore beyond consciousness? How can we open to that Sacred realm? Let's say our inner work: Particularly our practice of meditation, has reached the point where we are more or less conversant with consciousness, with how to recognize and enter the cognizant stillness beyond thought. And let's say we are sitting in meditation, in that expansive, boundless, and unobstructed field of pure consciousness. Now what?

Two classical categories of approaches recommend themselves: complete receptivity and receptivity mixed with an active element. Why receptivity? The Divine is higher than we are. We cannot make effective demands on the Sacred. Yes we can ask, but we cannot insist. Just as a single cell cannot control the whole body, we cannot manipulate the Divine. Our role is to serve life and seek the Sacred. In doing so we hope to become worthy enough, pure enough, for the Sacred to open its door to us. Joy is a byproduct of such a life.

So what do we do inwardly?

In meditation and contemplative prayer, the purely receptive approach is to do nothing, or more accurately, to not do anything. We just sit. We do not try to shape our inner experience in any way. We notice any impulse to go with a thought, to pay particular attention to something, or to change our inner state. But we let those impulses fade without acting on them. We just sit and wait and allow everything to be as it is. This silence of our will attunes us to the deepest silence, to the realm beyond space and time. In this practice of non-doing, we make ourselves available to the Sacred depths. It is not our part to make something happen, much less make any demands. We just sit and be. Gradually our thoughts subside on their own. If and when and to what degree the Sacred touches us, we will know. But that only happens in its own time and only if we are available.

The practice of non-doing can profitably alternate with a slightly more active approach of directed receptivity. It is as if we are aiming the dish-antenna of our being toward the Sacred. For this we might use a prayer or repetition that touches us. We let the inner sound of the prayer awaken our heart. We let the prayer serve as a place to stand a little closer to the Sacred.

Given that the Sacred is beyond consciousness, another approach is to look for a direction, a dimension outside of space and time, outside of consciousness. One direction to look is deeper within, for example back along the line of our attention, back toward the source of our attention, back into the recesses and source of will. It is as if we are accustomed only to look around us and never to look up. A whole new world may be waiting for us, if we only can bring ourselves to look up. But where is this direction of up? For that, we need to explore our inner world. What can be outside of consciousness?

For this week, remember that the mind, even at its most sublime and unbounded cognizant stillness, does not reach to the Divine. Look for an inner way toward the Sacred.

14.0 The Path of the Path

Introduction: Peaks, Valleys, and Plateaus

Like other aspects of our life, the spiritual path has its inevitable ups and downs, peaks, valleys, and plateaus. The state of our body varies from day to day and has a profound influence on the level of our inner work. The state of our emotions varies from day to day, with a greater influence on our inner work than our body has. The state of our spiritual hunger varies and matters even more than the rest. And the causes of these variations are not usually clear to us.

Then we have our external circumstances, which change all the time and certainly impact our spiritual life.

When we are with our spiritual friends, with a spiritual group, or with a spiritual community, it lends invaluable support to our inner work. And when we are not in those situations, our inner life depends even more on our own motivation and initiative. Our life circumstances make demands on us, sometimes more and sometimes less. Life presents us with opportunities, obstacles, and distractions. Events affect us and our ability to be present, to be kind. Even the weather affects us.

In these and other ways, our inner and outer circumstances can awaken us to the Sacred or close us off from That. So we are forced to give up any expectations of a smooth road up the spiritual mountain and instead take it as it comes. The single most important act, in terms of our progress on the spiritual path, is to resolve and continually renew our resolution to keep with our practice come what may. The seasons of our path, with the rebirth of spring, the growth of summer, the inward turn of fall, and treadmill of winter, come and go of their own accord, without a schedule. As we have seen, the causes are complex and often indecipherable. It taxes our wisdom to do more than just muddle through.

The resolution to continue our inner work, come what may, holds the key. When everything is rosy and we feel on top of the world, we also face the temptation to coast inwardly, to sit back and enjoy our state and our life and downplay our inner work. But do we engage in our spiritual practice in order to be happy or in order to serve our neighbor, our planet, and the Sacred? In serving the spirit, happiness often comes as a by-product of leading a right life. In primarily seeking happiness, we tend not to find it. The extent to which we stay committed to our inner work in the sunny moments, reveals our motivations to us.

In the down times, the valleys of our life, we may more

keenly feel the need for spiritual succor. So if we are able to muster the energy for our practice, we do. Truly though, our need is always there: it's just masked from us at times.

But it's not just that our life has peaks and valleys, our path itself does. As noted above, so many influences, inner and outer, affect our ability and our wish to practice. This is where experience, wisdom, and an unflagging commitment help. We notice what helps and what hinders our inner work and we bring our intelligence, creativity, determination, and love to bear. In the coming weeks we will look at how to manage our spiritual practice in the face of the peaks, valleys, and plateaus of our inner life.

During this week, please look at the ups, downs, and flatlands of your spiritual practice.

14.1 Handling Our Peaks

(The Path of the Path: Part 1)

Some people enter the spiritual path prompted by their own gradually increasing connection with the spirit. Others start because of a peak experience that affords them a glimpse of some aspect of the spirit. For those who are engaged in spiritual practice, results do come, sometimes in the form of an extraordinary, temporary perception of the spirit. Such peak experiences of the spirit affect us positively, profoundly, and sometimes permanently by reshaping our world view. Yet our attitude toward such experiences matters.

With the Sufis, we make a distinction between state and station. These terms refer to our inner condition, to the level of our experience. A state is temporary and our station is long-lasting. Our inner state fluctuates up and down throughout the day, but generally stays within a band that defines our station. Thus our station is our home, the level of our being. At whatever level we are, we may temporarily rise into the next higher level or fall into the next lower. But we come back home to our station, the stable zone of our being.

The spiritual path, our inner work is rightly directed at changing our station, at a lasting transformation of our level of being. The methods of the path accomplish this by training us to enter into and extend our stay in a state corresponding to the next higher level beyond our current station. The intention is eventually to make that next higher state our new station, to enable us to live in that new way. This takes long-term persistence.

Though temporary states can show us our possibilities, no single experience of a higher state, on its own, will change our station. This has definite consequences for how we approach the path. We are not seeking a temporary state, regardless of how sublime. There are methods for doing that, but they are like using drugs: fun, but useless or worse. So we do not chase states. We do however persist in our inner work. We try to live in slightly more and deeper presence. And we keep trying. Gradually the new way of living soaks into us, becomes part of us.

Very high experiences are remarkable and reset our view of reality and possibility. Yet such experiences also tend to feed our egoism in two ways. One is that we may become fixated on repeating that experience, on coming back to it. This is usually fruitless, because high level experiences are not in our control. Our personal readiness for deeper experience is necessary but not sufficient. The Sacred Spirit chooses if and when to touch us. That choice is not ours; we can only open ourselves toward it. We work toward the future, not toward the past.

The second ego fixation from high experiences is that we are now somehow special, different and better than other people who have not had that experience. This is a serious misconception. We are all equally children of the Creator or, if you prefer, of the universe, of life. We may differ in our form and abilities, but fundamentally we are the same: we are all human. We all matter equally. To feel that our personal experiences of the spirit make us better than others, to inflate our ego by using such experiences for bragging rights, bragging either to ourselves or to others, is a misappropriation, an abuse of those experiences. And it also makes deeper experience less likely to come to us. The grander our ego, the more of an obstacle it is to the spirit.

To return to where we started, the true value of peak spiritual experience is in showing us a glimpse of reality and our own possibilities, and thereby encouraging us to begin or persist in our spiritual inner work. As the Koren Zen Master Chinul taught, sudden enlightenment should be followed by gradual cultivation.

For this week, note your own peak experiences and how they have influenced your inner work. Are you making use of the motivation they provide?

14.2 Profiting From Our Valleys

(The Path of the Path: Part 2)

Sometimes we find ourselves in a spiritual desert. We lose our motivation for inner work. We lose our taste for and contact with the spirit. We lose our connection with faith. We may have energy, but not the deeper kind. Our inner work suffers both in quality and quantity. Because it takes effort just to maintain our place on the path, our being slips down the sacred mountain. We feel unable to engage in the practices of the way.

Whatever the cause for this inner desert, it presents both a challenge and an opportunity. The more arid our inner life, the more each small bit of inner work matters. When we have no motivation to practice, and nevertheless dig deeper to find even a trickle, that trickle springs from a pure source. This can mark a stage of our path where the ego motivations, such as becoming better than others, lose their allure. The path has shown us the emptiness of such dreams. Yet the pure spring of faith is there in us, perhaps mostly buried. And despite everything, we find the will to serve it.

The spiritual path is a way of self-creation, of soul-creation. Much of the action of the path can only come from us, from our willingness to act, our willingness to create ourselves from nothing. So we do what we can, even if only a small amount of presence, meditation, sensing, or prayer. We choose from ourselves to do that. Then we choose again tomorrow. And the next day. Slowly the weight lightens and the waters of the spirit begin to flow again. We take another step, then many steps, and we're back on the way.

When life puts us in a valley of inner difficulty, it is sometimes associated with or caused by outer difficulties. Again, this presents both an inner challenge and an opportunity. We do what we can and need to do about our outer situation. Yet our inner life need not be entirely at the mercy of our outer life. When life is not going as we might wish, can we remain free inwardly? Can we find the ocean of peace and equanimity that is always there in us?

The regular practice of meditation is one way. We learn

to just sit and be, without reacting to whatever thoughts and emotions arise in us. We let it all come and go. We let it all be as it is. But we do not let it take hold of us. We persevere in sitting in awareness. And awareness is the surface of peace. This type of meditation teaches us about peace, shows us the peace that surrounds us, shows us how to open to that peace, and trains us to rest in equanimity and awareness come what may. That is a perfect training for meeting life wholeheartedly and without being thrown off center by events.

Difficulties can prompt us to redouble our spiritual efforts. When times are tough, our ordinary supports get knocked out from under us. Things are different. Gaps open up in our usual world view. Change is more possible. We may naturally turn to prayer, to ask for healing, for resolution, for repair of our situation. This is right, to turn our suffering to account, to draw something constructive from it. In our more desperate moments, the practices of the spiritual path can anchor and comfort us, give us something to hold onto, and draw us nearer to our true self.

Nothing lasts forever, including the barren deserts and the down times. Can we persevere with our spiritual practice throughout the roller coaster of our life? Can we maintain a steady orientation toward the spirit regardless?

For this week, notice the degree to which you turn to the spirit in your moments of need.

14.3 Rising Above Our Plateaus

(The Path of the Path: Part 3)

What is the difference between being in a groove and being in a rut, with regard to our spiritual inner work? Let us say that one means gradually moving up the sacred mountain through the quality and quantity of our inner work, while the other means doing just enough to stay at the same level. Regularity of spiritual practice is a hallmark of a well-conducted inner life. But regularity sometimes leads to complacency.

As our inner work deepens, joy, love, conscience, and equanimity suffuse our life. This is wonderful and, for many who come to it, good enough. So after reaching that grand plateau, one can practice just enough to maintain the necessary inner tone. If that meets a person's goals and aspirations with regard to their inner life, then he or she has attained what they sought. This is completely honorable. The world certainly is a better place because of people who live in such a state. This is a groove, not a rut.

For others, however, the spiritual path has no upper bound. Their aspirations reach all the way to the Divine. For them, any spiritual plateau, no matter how sublime, is a rut, a temptation to be overcome.

How does this situation arise? Let us presume the person in question has a regular and effective spiritual practice. Perhaps it is primarily based on one or more daily periods of meditation, prayer, or other formal practice. After years of such practice, they reach the plateau of peace, love, and joy. Life is rich and flows smoothly. The natural and reasonable lesson is that they only need keep up their regular, daily practice to maintain this satisfying way of life, both inner and outer.

But something in their conscience nags at them. That something hints that greater perfection is always possible, that the peak of the spiritual mountain still lies far above, that Jacob's ladder has no top rung on which to rest. In response, we have only one option: more and deeper practice. This is not so easy, for it means going beyond what we know and are accustomed to. For example, it means making more efforts of presence throughout our day. But we get busy with our life. And besides, we had a good sitting this morning and we feel just fine. Certainly we all want happiness and it does tend to flow as a by-product of well-conducted inner work. But is our inner work about making ourselves feel good?

What is the purpose of our inner work? Whom do we serve by it? Only if the answers to both of these questions point beyond ourselves, do we have any prospect of actually doing what we need to do to rise above this sweet plateau. Do we have any sense that our inner work serves our neighbor, our society, our planet, or the Sacred? If so, that sense can give us the motivation to do more, to find ways to deepen our inner life.

Fortunately, it is not all up to us. There is grace. And in prayer we can ask for help, with our awakening, with our soul, with our service. But we must not wait for grace or for help. They come in their own time and manner. Meanwhile, we can take responsibility to do what we can from ourselves. In a balanced practice, doing what we can includes non-doing, letting go, and just being, along with the more active forms of inner work such as being in contact with our sensation body, active presence, being our I, fasting, and acts of kindness, as well the receptive forms such as meditation, prayer, and opening to higher energies.

If we find ourselves on a spiritual plateau, at whatever level, it behooves us to review and question where we are and whether we have arrived at where we want to stay. If we want to move forward, what will that take?

15.0 Deepening Our Inner Life
Introduction

The deeper we go into the spirit, the more radiant and beautiful our ordinary world becomes and the more meaningful our life is. This is not a change in our world, but rather a change in the clarity of our perceptions. The less distracted we are by our self-generating thoughts and reactive emotions, the more we can see the world, and see it as it is. The mere existence of this planet and all the life on it, including the people, is truly remarkable. Setting aside our jaded attitude toward life, we begin to appreciate it all so much more.

This does not mean that we self-impose an expectation of constant happiness, nor that we reject our thoughts and emotions. Rather, the deepening of our being gives us a different perspective, one that accepts everything, including ourselves, as is. We can still work to change, to improve, but without the self-rancor and rejection. We work toward our goals, we work to serve, not to escape ourselves.

Our spiritual practice can open our perceptions to the depth and beauty that surrounds us. But the vast array of practices presents a challenge: which ones should we take up? Some are more effective than others. Some are more suited to our unique individuality, our background of experience, and our current state of being. What we need and what is possible for us can and do change, year to year, day to day, and moment to moment. Having tried various practices and worked with them to the point of familiarity and some facility, we can rely on them as elements of our inner work tool box.

This is where we can profit from taking a scientific approach, using both theory and experiment. The useful theories include, for example, the schema of inner energies and the procedures of the various practices. Theories of the nature of the soul and the spiritual realms abound in religious and spiritual literature. From those, we take what speaks to us, what we relate to, what inspires us.

And then, guided by the theory, we use the practices as experiments, with ourselves as the experimental subject. We notice what works and what does not. What works best? We look for different ways to evaluate our practices. What does it mean for a practice to "work" for us? How can we recognize the effects of a practice? How long does it take to make a valid assessment of the usefulness of a practice for us? If we try a particular type of meditation once, is that enough to judge by? Is there something new we should try?

Closely associated with the experimentalist approach is the creative and exploratory approach. Are there aspects of our inner world which matter but which we have ignored? Are there new directions we need to explore inwardly? Are there adjustments we need to make to our practices, even going beyond how they were originally taught to us? One reason this matters is that much of what is most important about the spirit, about inner work, cannot be taught, cannot be put into words. Instead we need to discover the depth for ourselves, by seeking ways to go beyond our current understanding and experience, by looking inwardly in new directions, in ways we have not looked before.

While our inner experimentation and exploration need to be pragmatic, it profits us to heed the small hints, the tentative intuitions that point toward new possibilities. Is this just imagination and wishful thinking, or is there something real there? We give it a chance; we try it out for a while. Then we get pragmatic. Does it fit? Is it effective? Does it open something new and real to us? And is it worth our limited time and energy?

As we work our way along the path, the spirit calls us more vividly, re-awakening our longing to become what we could be, to live a more soulful life. Wherever we are in the great chain of being, wherever we are in our personal journey at this moment, that is the only and the right place to begin again to deepen our spiritual work. In this series on deepening our inner life, we will look at certain spiritual practices and approaches that we may find particularly useful.

For this week, please begin or reinvigorate that self-experimentation and exploration.

15.1 Silence

(Deeping Our Inner Life: Part 1)

The daily practice of meditation, for many people, is the foundation on which their entire spiritual path can be built. Meditation provides the energy and peace that allow presence to grow, joy and love to blossom. While there are many different styles of meditation, one characteristic shared by their deeper reaches is silence, both inner and outer.

The outer silence is relatively simple. We find a quiet space in which to meditate, even if that means wearing earplugs. We find a comfortable, erect way of sitting, which we can maintain for the duration, without moving or fidgeting and without falling asleep. It may take some weeks or months to find our *seat*, but eventually our body settles into the necessary posture. This provides the context of outer silence. Though outer silence is not absolutely necessary, it helps, for example by decreasing the number of stimuli that might set off trains of thought.

Inner silence is a different matter. As we sit there, we discover the endless and familiar churn of our thoughts, the unceasing inner voice which we take to be our own. There does not appear to be any room for inner silence, since every crevice of our cognitive space seems filled with thoughts or emotions or sensory perceptions, in an endless stream. At first blush, the answer might look as if we should intentionally and directly stop our thoughts. But a little experimentation quickly shows us the difficulty and near impossibility of that.

So we take a more subtle approach. We allow our thoughts, mental images, emotions, and sensory impressions to come and go, without trying to stop or control them. The key here is to notice them, continually, so that we do not fall prey, do not fall into the stream and get carried off by it. We just see our thoughts as thoughts, emotions as emotions. We see them for what they are, without judgment, without grasping for them or pushing them away, and without being taken in or away by them. This takes a good deal of practice, for we repeatedly find ourselves captivated by our thoughts and emotions. When we come to and notice this, we simply return to watching, again and again.

For this to work well, we need an inner place to stand and watch, a safe and stable base for viewing. That base is our body, our direct perception of our body. So we begin our meditation session by slowly scanning our body, by coming into inner contact with each part of our body and then with our whole body. Thinking about our arm or even knowing that we have an arm are quite different than being in the arm, being in contact with the arm, in this moment. So we practice staying in direct, visceral contact with each arm, then with each leg, then with all four limbs, and finally with our body as a whole.

Sitting here in our body and keeping that vivid contact as the background of our awareness, we also watch the parade of thoughts and emotions pass by, without interfering with them and without allowing them to interfere with our body contact, nor with our watching.

Gradually, something almost magical happens. The watching changes our relationship with our thoughts and emotions. We are no longer quite as enslaved by them. We are no longer quite as identified. Though part of our equipment, just as our body and breathing are, we see that our thoughts and emotions are not who we are, do not define us. A little more light of inner freedom dawns. We realize that we are the one who sees all this. We are the one who is aware of our thoughts and emotions and everything else. We are the one who can, if we so choose, think intentionally. Yet our typical running thoughts do not speak for us, they speak for themselves. They are not us. They are just long-ingrained patterns, combined with haphazard, accidental sensory impressions setting them off. They are just thoughts.

Furthermore, inner silence begins to reveal itself. Gaps of silence appear between our thoughts: at first brief gaps and then wider ones. Silence appears to surround us, to fill our inner space, with the thoughts and emotions passing through without disturbing the underlying silence. We rest in this natural home of silence, in this big sky of our silent mind, which is awareness itself. We sink into awareness, into just being. We soak in that silent awareness. And so we find relief in this inner peace, which then carries over beyond our meditation session into our day.

Eventually we become able to be in contact with inner silence even in the midst of outer events and the busyness of life. It gives a base of peace and equanimity to all we do. Out of that, joy comes, and love, and a new dimension of depth to our inner life.

For this week, please practice contact with silence.

15.2 Energy Breathing

(Deeping Our Inner Life: Part 2)

A sea of precious spiritual energies surrounds us. The air, for example, contains such energies, a fact attested to by most major spiritual traditions. The Hindu notion of *prana*, which means breath in Sanskrit, refers to the energies carried by the air. The Hindu word for soul, *atman*, also means breath in Sanskrit. The Latin *spiritus* means both breath and soul, and forms the root of related English words like spirituality, respire, inspire, and expire. Numerous other languages and traditions similarly affirm the close relationship between the air and soul energies, the air acting as a reservoir of energies: Arabic *ruh*, Hebrew *nefesh*, *ruakh*, *neshamah*, Greek *pneuma*, Chinese Taoist *ch'i*, the Christian Prayer of the Heart, Gregorian chant, the Sufi zikr, and the Yoga of *pranayama*. In ordinary, automatic breathing, however, only a tiny amount of these spiritual energies remain with us after we exhale.

Intentional energy breathing enables more of the energy to be drawn into us from the air and to stay with us, fueling our spiritual practice and strengthening our soul. In contrast with the practice of conscious breathing or breath awareness, in energy breathing we direct our attention to the energies in the air we breathe, rather than simply to the physical sensations associated with breathing. We intentionally draw the energy from the air into us, infusing our body with that energy. We can cast our attention as a "net" to capture the energy and carry it into us as we inhale. Alternatively, we can use attention as a "filter" placed in the nostrils to release the energy as the air enters the nose. The spiritual energy within the air around us is a special part of the atmosphere, the air of our inner world. We reach out, with our attention and intention, into this energy atmosphere and draw the energy into us with an inner breath, the inner side of our ordinary breath. As we exhale we hold our attention in our body, allowing the energy from the breath to find its own place within us.

This practice does not require any significant alteration to our breath, and should not make us dizzy, should not cause us to breathe at an abnormally fast or slow speed, nor deeper or shallower than usual. The difference between normal breathing and energy breathing does not lie on the physical level, but rather on the level of the energy body. We breathe at a normal pace and depth. But with fine attention to the air where it enters our nose, we consciously and intentionally bring the energy into our body.

As we work on becoming aware of and breathing this energy, we discover an unmistakable and wonderful flow of energy in our breath, strengthening our energy body. But this energy flow is never automatic; it requires intention and attention to separate the energy from the ordinary air. Spending time every day on this energy breathing practice proves invaluable in filling us with sensation and establishing our energy body, giving us a sturdy vessel for presence and for deepening our path.

At first your perceptions may not be refined enough to experience the energy in the air. In this case, use your imagination and practice as if shimmering particles of energy were entering you as you breathe. Allow the energy to spread throughout your body, joining the sensitive energy and strengthening your sensation. Work at this as part of your sitting meditation. If, after practicing energy breathing for some period each day for a week or two, you still find the energy flow elusive, please drop the exercise and consider returning to it again at another time. But bear in mind the many spiritual traditions affirming the presence of soul-related energies in the air. If this is possible for other people, it is also possible for you. As your other spiritual practices and perceptions deepen, your ability to contact and absorb the energies in the air will grow apace. Then this vast reservoir of energies will begin to strengthen your inner life and make it even more real.

15.3 Developing Our Sensation Body

(Deeping Our Inner Life: Part 3)

After practicing sensing our body piecemeal by sensing a hand or an arm or a leg, we can further deepen our inner life by turning toward the true power of the practice of sensing, which begins with whole-body sensing and moves toward a robust, fully-established, and persistent sensation body. The experience of whole-body sensing is qualitatively different than sensing a part of our body, because it brings wholeness and is complete. In its own way, whole-body sensing is perfect.

The quality of wholeness in whole-body sensing lends stability to our awareness by connecting with the quality of wholeness inherent in the next higher energy, the conscious energy. So when we sense our whole body, we feel complete, we can just be here and do what we do, without the nagging energy drains. A persistent body of sensitive energy not only helps us stay awake to the present moment, but raises us toward freedom from our neurotic tendencies, from our identification with our thoughts and emotions, from the story they continually tell us, a story we mistakenly take to be our very self.

When we are sensing our whole body, it seems filled with the sensitive energy. As we continue to work with this and strengthen it, it fills to such an extent that the sensitive energy takes the shape of our physical body and seems to form a body within our body: an inner body or sensation body. We can be in our sensation body. It feels comfortable and right. It feels like home, like we are at home in ourselves. We have a place, a special place. We have arrived.

To make this last, or at least to make it more frequent, takes persistent effort. But that effort does not need to be constant. We find moments where our sensation body is strong enough that we can just be in it for a time, without it dissipating.

What efforts are needed? First is sensing. We learn how to sense an arm or a leg by putting and holding our attention in it. Then we expand to sensing our whole body. We persist, coming back to having attention in our whole body, again and again.

With that, we intentionally move into our sensation body, we reside it. We shift from being nowhere or being in our physical body to being in our sensation body. We practice that again and again.

We notice that the amount and intensity of the sensitive energy in our sensation body is sometimes stronger and sometimes weaker. So we feed this growing sensation body. We feed it by energy breathing, by drawing from the air around us the sensitive energy, which is the primary substance of our sensation body. Indeed, being in our whole body facilitates energy breathing, because it gives us a platform, a place in a world that has an innate affinity with the energy in the air. Because we are now in our sensation body, we are no longer limited to breathing through our mouth or nose. We can breathe with our whole body, our whole sensation body. With our attention and intention, we draw the energy from the air through the entire surface of our sensation body. That energy fills us, strengthening this inner body. We put our attention out into the air, draw the energy in, and along with the movement of the energy we shift our attention inward to being in our sensation body and let the new energy settle there and be absorbed.

And so we continue to work. Stabilizing our sensation body takes persistent efforts, of attention, of intentionally residing in our sensation, of feeding it with the energy from the air. We return to it throughout our day, day after day. We make our sensation body our new inner home and we deepen our inner life thereby.

The development of the sensation body is not the whole of spirituality, but it is fundamental to our path and makes the deeper reaches of the spirit more accessible. Furthermore, our inner body also needs other forms of energy than what sensing and energy breathing can offer. For example, the energy of higher emotions feeds our soul in crucial ways. We will turn to that in the next part of this inner work series. But for this week, please work on developing your sensation body.

15.4 The Energy of Higher Emotions

(Deeping Our Inner Life: Part 4)

Through emotions we can be touched by something ineffable yet recognizable as being sacred. Such emotions include longing for the sacred, faith, love, joy, compassion, and awe, among others. At a slightly lower level, we have the higher emotions of brotherhood and sisterhood, friendship, sincere well-wishing, joy in another's joy, and more. The regular practice of prayer naturally, or even supernaturally, leads us to open to such higher emotions. This holds for any type of prayer, whether petitioning for something, contemplating the Divine, or more actively seeking to approach the Divine. All types share the requirement that to be real, the act of praying must include opening or attempting to open ourselves toward the Divine. This is inherently humbling and creates a gap in our ego, in our self-centered attitudes, a gap though which a real connection can arise. We know this has occurred when through that gap higher emotions flow into us.

The many ways of prayer, in their deeper manifestations, share this characteristic of opening toward the Sacred. What is the essence of that action of opening? We can compare it to a house, a house that we live in. It has a front door, which opens to the external world, through our outward facing senses. The interior of the house is our inner world of thoughts, emotions, and body sensations. This house also has a rarely-used back door. This back door opens to the Sacred. We may not even be aware that this back door exists. Like the front door, the back door opens inward, opens toward the inside of the house. The various forms of prayer concern that door to the Sacred and aim to have us find the door, unlock it, and either open the door from the inside or allow it be opened by the Sacred. This metaphor of a house with front and back doors comes close to how it really is in us.

When that door to the Sacred opens even a little, something wonderful comes into us. One form that takes is as higher emotion carried into us as a potent but rarefied energy.

That type of energy feeds our soul directly. It can combine with the sensitive energy we have prepared by working on our sensation body. Through that combination, the sensation body grows more robust.

The whole action also works to purify us. It takes a certain genuine longing and humility to open that door. The action helps reorient us, balance our view of life, so that we not only face the external through our front door, but also look toward the Sacred through the back door.

Higher emotions not only result from opening that door, but also provide the means to open it in the first place. Yet prayer is not about conjuring up or manufacturing some emotion. It is about relating ourselves to something even more real than we are, to our all-loving Creator.

This beautiful, amazing world embodies the work of a loving Hand. And behind every point of this façade, including behind us, lies a deeper world, closer to the Divine Source of All. We turn toward that unseen but felt Reality. With a bittersweet homesickness, we long for That. We discover a hole in our very core, a hole meant to be filled by the Sacred, a hole that shows us what we are missing, a hole that awakens that homesick longing. The mere awareness of this hole makes us want to be more than we are, to be kinder and real and complete. It makes us want to serve. And again it makes us homesick for our Source.

For this week, return to that place in yourself.

15.5 Fasting and Other Will Tasks

(Deeping Our Inner Life: Part 5)

Why fast? Some people fast for health reasons. But

what about fasting for spiritual reasons, fasting as a method of spiritual practice? Why is it effective? And what effects does it have? First, though, what is fasting? What counts as a fast? Here we find a wide variety which we classify into two main types; a narrowly targeted fast that involves giving up one thing, such as alcohol, for a set number of days, typically around 40, or a complete fast of not eating or drinking anything for a set number of hours, typically 24 or 36.

Either type of fast can serve to strengthen and purify our will, which is the primary spiritual benefit of fasting. We can say with truth and accuracy that more than anything else, we are our will. Our will defines us. Fasting is the work of will, by means of deciding to temporarily deny our body one of its needs or one of its pleasures. As such, fasting is a sacrifice. We give up something to serve the Sacred. Fasting serves the Sacred by strengthening and purifying our will and by directing our will acts toward the Sacred.

How should we conduct a complete fast? Its completeness makes it simple. We just give up eating or drinking anything for the allotted time. But our bodies are different and we need to adapt our inner work to our personal circumstances. For example, for me, drinking two glasses of plain water during a 36-hour fast seems to prevent inordinate stress on kidneys or other organs, while the limited amount of water does not seem to diminish the spiritual benefits of the action. By experimenting with different modes and lengths of fasting, you will soon find what works for you. Of course, if you have medical issues that could be exacerbated by fasting, consult a physician first.

For the narrow fast, we meet the question of what to target with our fast. This involves understanding ourselves well enough to choose something that is neither too easy nor too hard. If it has a practical benefit as well, that's a bonus but not a requirement. We could give up alcohol for 40 days, or sugar, or ice cream, or chewing gum. It should be something you take in fairly regularly or the fast would be pointless. It should be something that you are able to give up for the allotted time: stopping a pack-a-day smoking habit may be beyond our current capacity.

While fasts involve giving something up, we can also take on positive will tasks that involve doing something daily for 40 days, something we might not otherwise do, something that has a practical benefit for ourselves or others. We choose carefully, choose within our capacity to carry it through, set our start and end dates, make a commitment to ourselves, and then stick with it all the way through.

In both the narrow fasting and positive will tasks taken on for 40 days, we intend to carry it out to the letter, for the full, allotted time. Each morning we remind ourselves about our 40-day decision. Each evening we review our day to ensure we carried it out. However, it can happen that we fail on one occasion. If such a lapse does occur, we immediately move forward and continue with the fast or task. But we do everything in our power to carry through on our self-commitment. We take it seriously. This is who we are. I am my will. It's not a matter of being in control of our life or of gaining power. It's a question of what am I willing to give to be what I could be, to become fully myself and fulfill my personal destiny? Our will matters deeply, because this is who I am. By respecting our will, we respect ourselves. By respecting ourselves, we respect the Sacred.

15.6 Cultivating the Heart of Love

(Deeping Our Inner Life: Part 6)

Many emotions flow through us on any given day. Yet we know of master emotions, which, if we could cultivate them, would profoundly change our life for the better. Prime among these is love. One way is to start from below by paying attention to our moments of non-love. In that way, we notice our indifference toward others, our uncaring, negative attitudes, thoughts, and actions toward others. This seeing in itself diminishes the grip of non-love, but only if we see from a place of love, or at least self-acceptance. Any rejection just feeds and perpetuates our destructive patterns.

Yet there are also ways to start from above, from love itself and from its close companion, kindness. Every day we have moments that touch our heart. Some are unpredictable, though others come through regular contact with our loved ones. By whatever route these moments that touch us arise, we can use them, and indeed any other moment, as opportunities to cultivate the heart of love.

Say, for example, you are in a situation where you see other people, whether strangers or not. You could inwardly wish them well or inwardly ask for a blessing on each one individually. You could inwardly say "May you be happy." Or you could inwardly say "May the Lord bless you and protect you." Or you could use some other phrase that touches you.

While having such positive thoughts toward others is an important step, we can go a bit further. We can engage our heart. We can feel what we are thinking.   So we direct our attention toward the person and inwardly we say the phrase, while being aware of its meaning and letting our heart feel that meaning and emotionally embody our positive intent. It sounds like several different pieces, but they coalesce into a single act of loving well-wishing. This is a practice we can invoke anywhere, including in difficult moments with other people. It helps purify our heart of self-centeredness and of criticizing, judging and condemning, both others and ourselves. "Blessed are the pure in heart, for they shall see God."

Another step is to take our well-wishing and act on it: the way of kindness. We pay even more attention to how we interact with other people, to what we say and do, to the expression on our face, the tone of our voice, the gestures we make, the effect we are having. But it all begins in our core, in our attitude toward the person, in our thoughts and feelings. By practicing the heart of love in the midst of our interactions, we change the tenor of our relationships. For example, the practice of courtesy, in deed and in word, puts us in the frame of kindness.

Beyond that, how do we react when someone crosses us, such as a discourteous driver? Fear and anger may be our normal and immediate reactions, but we do not need to nurture them beyond their momentary usefulness in alerting us to the danger and preparing us to respond. Can we open our heart, even to that person who has crossed us, turn the other cheek? It is a hard thing, but love demands it of us. Love reveals that we are not separate, not even from that person. Love asks us to become still more able to give and to give way.

Beneath all our perceptions, beneath our senses and thoughts and feelings, is a pure awareness, our true consciousness. We all share the same consciousness, for it does not stop at the boundaries of our body. And beyond that shared sameness, we have our individual, unique will. Yet the individual will of every one of us comes from the one Source, and that

Source is the source of Love. We aspire to the great heart of love.

15.7 Being Who I Am
(Deeping Our Inner Life: Part 7)

Knowing yourself matters, but being yourself matters much more. And for both there are ever-deepening levels of meaning.

The usual interpretation of self-knowledge is objectively knowing our strengths, weaknesses, and personality traits in their manifestations through our body, heart, and mind. There can be no true end-point to the acquisition of such self-knowledge for two main reasons. First, our personality has too many possible modes of acting and reacting to exhaustively know them. We can always surprise or surpass ourselves. Second, we change continually. So what we thought we knew about ourselves yesterday may no longer be true today.

Nevertheless, clearly seeing ourselves as we are, without flinching or self-recriminations, provides great benefits, not least of which is, paradoxically, a type of confidence. If we already know the best and the worst about ourselves and accept the truth of that knowledge, then we can confidently move forward within our limitations or push ourselves to exceed our limits. The more we know ourselves the less we have to fear about what others might see in us. We know where we stand. This affords us the freedom to do what we need to do.

Knowing our personality, capabilities, habits, preferences, and limitations is like knowing our history, because they are the result of our genetic traits and life experience. But our history, our story, and our personality do not fully define who we are. There is much more to us than that.

We begin our work of being who we are, which is the true meaning of presence, by being in our body, being in contact with our body. We practice sensing, which not only entails awareness of our body, as taught for example in mindfulness meditation practice, but also entails enhancing our contact with our body by building up the sensitive energy. To be who we are with respect to our body, means inhabiting our body. I am here in the whole of my body. With determined practice of sensing, our awareness expands to include awareness of our thoughts as thoughts and our emotions as emotions. This body of sensation serves as a platform for our awareness. We inhabit our body, our mind, and our heart. We reclaim this endowment of ours from the zone of auto-piloted non-presence.

The next step has us noticing that beneath all that sensory awareness of body, thought, and emotion, there is a layer of quiet, cognitive stillness, the pure consciousness underlying our awareness of specifics. Our consciousness is the screen on which all the content of experience plays. But in itself consciousness is peace, a substantive continuum of cognitive energy that does not stop at the boundary of our body. So we practice being in our consciousness. This does takes some practice, because the blank screen of consciousness is not so easy to recognize. When you go to a movie, how much are you aware of the screen itself versus the images portrayed on the screen? This is exactly the difficulty we face in acquiring the taste of consciousness. But the more we have that the more equanimity and peace we enjoy in flow of our life.

Basing our presence in body sensation offers some stability, enabling us to abide in consciousness a little longer than would otherwise be possible. What happens is that from being in the pure seeing of consciousness, we get caught by some passing thought or emotion or sensory impression, which takes us away on the stream of impressions and breaks our contact with consciousness. If, however, we intentionally maintain our contact with body sensation, then we are not so easily swept away, and we can open to the peace of consciousness; we can for a time, be consciousness.

Yet the truth of who we are goes deeper even than consciousness. Each of us can say "I am my will." For example, I am my attention. Through attention we can select bits from the stream of experience and focus our awareness, our consciousness on them. Thus attention and more generally will are deeper than consciousness. So to come into who we truly are, we practice being our attention, being the source of our attention, being the one who directs our attention. This is an unmediated experience. I am here, directing my attention. I am the one who sees what my eyes bring into my awareness. I am the one who chooses what I choose, who does what I do. I am the one who experiences what I experience. I am the one who lives my life.

To shed a little more light on this, take the example of thinking. Usually, I am not thinking my thoughts: they are thinking themselves. Thoughts run of their own accord, automatically, in reaction and in patterns. But sometimes, I intentionally think about some subject, ponder something, make a plan, work on a problem. Intention is the key aspect, for it signals the presence of will. When I think intentionally, I am the one who is thinking. Only then is it true that I think. Otherwise my thoughts think, my mind thinks, but it is not I that am thinking, for at such moments I do not exist.

For this week, practice bringing yourself into existence, creating yourself moment-to-moment, by being who you are.

15.8 Inner Excellence

(Deeping Our Inner Life: Part 8)

We are so focused on being good at what we do outwardly that we largely ignore our inner state, except when it runs out of bounds and disrupts our outer life. But we can bring the same level of commitment to excellence in our inner world as we do in our outer world. Just as outer excellence begins in awareness of our surroundings and our actions, inner excellence begins in awareness of our inner state: Particularly our thoughts and emotions. And just as outer excellence is not compromised by events around us that we cannot control, inner excellence is not compromised by the content of our automatic thoughts and reactive emotions.

A fundamental difference exists between thoughts that come to us by association or reaction and the thoughts we think intentionally. All manner of untoward thoughts may arise in our mind, but as long as we do not buy into them as true or as what we believe or as a guide to action, then they can come and go without impacting our striving for perfection. But as soon as we intentionally think some thought, or buy into one that arises on its own, we become responsible for that thought, we own it. Intentional thoughts are acts and, as such, have consequences. We may not be able to control our associative or reactive thoughts, but by definition we can control our intentional ones. We are only responsible for what we can control.

There is a gray area here in our thoughts. Say you notice a series of thoughts or emotions of a judgmental, hateful, or even vengeful nature. Do you tacitly approve of those thoughts and emotions, while letting them run on? Do you allow your inner life to serve as an arena in which you inwardly act out in ways that you know you should not do in your outer life? Maybe you see this as a harmless outlet, a way to let off steam as it were. The question is: does this pollute your inner world? The alternative would be to disavow such thoughts and emotions, to turn your face, your attention away from them.

Responsibility produces excellence. And our personal guide to how to be responsible is our conscience. Thus, conscience is our ally in the path of inner excellence. Conscience illuminates our inner world, showing us what is true and what is not, even in the gray areas. Can we live with an inner standard of excellence? Can we live so that even our thoughts and emotions reflect who we wish to be? In our depth, we have the purity of our true nature. By striving for excellence and purity in our inner world, we align ourselves with conscience, with our true nature.

When we look at who we are, there need not be this mixed bag that includes aspects of which we might be ashamed. Can we extend the Golden Rule to apply inwardly as well as outwardly? Can we treat other people, even in our hidden thoughts and emotions, as they would wish to be treated? Can we treat ourselves with respect and kindness, even in our hidden thoughts and emotions? Can we meet the future by preparing it in the present, without buying into our overblown anxieties?

These issues are not only about moral and psychological norms; they are deeply spiritual questions. The higher realms of the spirit have gates of purity. Only when our being becomes relatively pure can we have any hope of entry there. This is a law of the spirit, just as there are laws of nature. It is a fact of how the spirit works. Purity matters. And the road toward purity begins with the effort of inner excellence.

For this week, work to bring excellence to your inner world.

15.9 Whole Presence
(Deeping Our Inner Life: Part 9)

The transition from non-presence to presence and back tells us a fundamental but nearly always overlooked fact about our life. We suddenly come-to. But from what? A moment before we were not here, we were not in contact with our surroundings, with our body, with ourselves. And now we are. For a precious few moments, we are here, alive in our awareness. And then the kicker: we fade back into non-presence. We do not notice that happening, because in non-presence we do not really notice anything. Sensory impressions come in, get handled by the automatic working of our body and mind, and do not touch us. We can rightly caricature this usual state of ours as a zombie-like existence, empty of real life. This is a fact.

Now we might protest: "I'm no zombie!" And that's true, a least for that moment of protest, while the affront to our self-view awakens us. But then we all-too-quickly drift back into autopilot.

Fortunately, we can do something about this situation: we can practice presence. Unfortunately, that takes persistence, a great deal of persistence, a lifetime of persistence. The spiritual traditions have developed and taught many methods for presence. All the methods though, if they truly promote presence, share the characteristic of training us to make and be in contact with our inner and outer sensory experience. But, while necessary, this is only half way to presence. The rest of the way requires us to be ourselves, to be in contact with our very self. This cannot be taught directly, but must be inferred from all our first-half practice of presence and discovered by our own introspection and exploration of our inner world.

We practice sensing our body, being in direct, visceral contact with our body and with the sensitive energy in our body, as much as possible during our day, during every day. We extend that to being in contact with all our senses: sight, sound, smell, taste, touch, and with our inner sense that enables us to be aware of emotion, thought, and mental images. This persistent grounding in our sensory experience, this mindfulness, keeps us in the present moment and enriches our life enormously.

Yet, the question still arises: who is aware of all this? We might say "I am." But then who or what am I? Here a different level of presence begins to open, one that is deeper than our sensory experience and the sensitive energy. We start to notice our inner home of pure awareness, of consciousness. This vast, boundless, cognitive stillness, the plenum and screen on which all our sensory experience gets displayed, feels like home. It is pure peace. We can rest in that.

And still the question arises: who is it that is aware of consciousness? Who is conscious? And we see that though consciousness is a deeper energy, a cognitive energy, it is not who we are. This is a subtle but important realization, for it leads to further heights of the spirit. It leads us first to realize and be the one who is doing what we do, the one who is experiencing our life. So, while grounding our practice of presence in contact with our body and senses, we extend that practice to being the one who is present. Gradually we learn to let our body remind us to sense and let our sensing remind us to be. We become ourselves.

This latter cannot become automatic, can never become

a mere habit. It directly involves our intention, our will to be. But what does happen is that when we are not ourselves we begin to miss being ourselves and that prompts us to return. The more we do that, the deeper and richer our inner life becomes. We can truly say "here I am." And along with mindfulness of our sensory experience, this completes our presence.

For this week remember that presence has two parts, contact with our senses and being our self, being the one who is in contact with our senses, the one who does what we do. Please practice whole presence.

15.10 Informed Initiative
(Deeping Our Inner Life: Part 10)

In many facets of life and society, we value initiative as a quality of creative and effective people. In our inner life, in our spiritual practice, initiative also matters in important ways, although it does not necessarily become visible to other people. Initiative generally is a manifestation of will. We put ourselves into what we start. The degree to which we do that impacts the effectiveness of our initiative.

For our inner work, a prime example is the initiative in any given moment to wake up and be present. In one sense, this is a moment of grace, with the initiative coming from beyond us, yet acting through our will. Our own initiative in awakening enters with what we do with that moment of grace. Suddenly I am here. Do I take this opportunity to practice, for example to practice presence? Do I gather my attention into my body and begin sensing? Do I practice conscious breathing or energy breathing, right now? If the situation is appropriate, do I practice kindness? Or do I let the moment fade, as I fade back into autopilot living? Awakening opens an opportunity, with many immediate possible follow-on choices. It is our initiative that can meet this moment and rise to its promise.

Yet our inner work initiative must be well informed. Without having learned various practices, we would not even know that they exist as possibilities. Without honest self-assessment, we would not know which practice to begin in that moment of awakening.

Inner work initiative also goes beyond the immediate opportunities of the moment. We can set a strategy. We can set a schedule, for example, for our formal meditation sittings. We can answer the questions of when, where, and for how long we will sit, of how to manage our life and time to make room for our sitting practice. This takes initiative to start and to maintain.

Sometimes we need to make a change: sit longer, engage in a different inner practice during the day, fast, learn a new practice, join a group, and so on. All such changes take initiative, informed, spiritual initiative. And changes are necessary. Our soul and spirit evolve and grow as our inner work takes root and ripens. The frontier of our personal evolution continually shifts as our practice proceeds or slips back. So we try different approaches, find what works, and go with that. Even one practice, such as sensing or meditation, deepens as we stay with it. And to support that deepening practice our style must change and keep pace. Informed by our self-knowledge, we adapt our practice to our unique possibilities, limitations, and need. Then we note the results and adjust, again and again. This all takes initiative.

Another type of initiative is that of the explorer who sets out discover new realms. So it is with our inner world. Within us, layer upon layer of inner energies and our own spirit await us, hidden from our current perceptions. Our ability to see, recognize, and work with what is truly there in us and beyond us needs to grow. The exploratory initiative, that has us seek new ways to look into our soul and spirit, makes that growth possible. This keeps our meditation practice, for example, from being an unchanging repetition. Repetition and persistence are absolutely necessary. But they are not sufficient. Our initiative carries a creative element that enlivens our inner work.

Finally there is the informed initiative underlying service. Our spiritual practice is not only about inner work, but also includes our service to our family and society. What service to undertake and how to perform that service requires informed initiative. Otherwise we stumble along with eyes half-closed.

For this week, re-engage your own initiative in your spiritual practice, informed by your experience, knowledge, and perceptions.

15.11 The Source of Will is the Source of All

(Deeping Our Inner Life: Part 11)

Everything, the universe, the multiverse, and us people, comes from one unfathomable Source. Physics tells us that Source is the Big Bang, which happened some 13.8 billion years ago. This view leaves us with no connection to the Source. It was long, long ago, and although we see remnants of it with our telescopes and satellites, it does not touch us personally, individually. Even though our bodies are made of stardust, we are on our own, disconnected from those far-distant roots.

This picture looks very different, however, if we consider the Big Bang to have been intentional, not just some inexplicable, mechanistic accident. If that consideration is true, then the One whose intention it was must still be here, and the will of that One is even now driving the whole accelerating expansion of the universe, and much else besides.

The mystery of will goes deep, deep enough to touch each of us directly, intimately. One way, from a rational, logical stance, to see how that can be is to suppose that the Will of the Source touches us all by operating through a higher dimension than space-time, a dimension that gives that Will access to every point in space-time, including within us personally. Imagine the fingers of a hand touching a flat surface. From the point of view of the surface, there are five separate circles. But from the point of view of the hand, there is one unity in which all five fingers are included. If we now add a further supposition that the degree of complexity of an entity determines the degree to which it can manifest will, then we humans, with our remarkably complex bodies, must have some strong capacity for will.

This is not to say that we all exercise our will all the time. Clearly we do not. The times we live on autopilot are most certainly times of lower degrees of will. But when we are more awake, more present, we have greater capacity to act from ourselves, from our will, rather than from reaction or habit.

The form of will that is easiest to recognize in ourselves is attention. We choose where to put our attention. In doing so, we drive our awareness and senses. Moving our attention is an act of will. Holding our attention on something is an ongoing act of will. Furthermore, our will defines us. At our most essential, we are will, we are our own will. All inner work, whether active, receptive, or synergic, involves will. Our work of presence: Particularly, can teach us who we are, that we are our will, that our will is I.

Yet we mistake our ego for our I. We have a lifetime of building and defending the personal illusion of my ego. We take our personality patterns of thought, emotion, and action, our skills, memory and experience, and we weave them together to form our self-image. That self-image is our ego. It is just an image, but one that we take to be our very person. It is an illusion of parts making to which we give a name, a name that implies a wholeness that is not really there, and that is what we believe we are. Yet our will, our I, goes well beyond our thinking and emotions and personality patterns. Our I is not defined or limited by any of that. It is pure will. We are pure will.

This becomes even more significant in the context of the Source, for the Source is will, the Will of World. The nature of will as being unconstrained by space and time makes it something of a mystery to us, different than anything else in our experience. The Will of the Source is a unity. All will belongs to that unity. We share in that unity in our own individual will. It is both uniquely ours and a ray of the great unity. Thus our personal will is directly connected to the Source, is the Source. But the illusion of our ego inserts itself, making us see the world as flat, and preventing us from opening to our true nature.

In deep meditation and contemplative prayer, we can relax deeply, let go deeply, to the point that we temporarily drop our posture of being our ego, of being our name, of being separate from everything and everyone. In that moment we can reconnect with the Source, we can become the Source, or rather the Source can become us. If that happens, then we are and the Source is, and there is no difference between the two.

Indeed there are not two, just One. Right here in our own core, our I is the Will of the World. And we recognize that same Will in everyone else.

The question remains: how to reconnect with the Source? First we need our quiescent and unified will, free from any attachments and identifications, at least for the period of deep meditation or prayer. Then two effective approaches open. In one, we wait. We remain in the stillness. Any thoughts or emotions just slide past. We make ourselves available to the Higher by waiting. In the other approach, we reach out and in, we reach toward to Sacred. We open our mind, heart, and soul toward the Sacred. We bring our entire being, our entire will into this one intention: to connect our will with the Divine Will, to enter the Greatness, to invite, to beg the Greatness to enter us. We do not know the direction. We do not know the signs. But yet we look, we try, we invite, and we plead. Here I am, for You.

For this week, open toward the Will of All.

15.12 Persistence: Doing What Matters

(Deeping Our Inner Life: Part 12)

At times we wonder whether there is a secret to progress in our inner life, in our spiritual life. Though progress is almost always slow, there nevertheless is a secret to it. But contrary to what we might expect it to be, say some advanced, hidden form of meditation, the secret is simple: persistence, staying engaged for the long haul. If we stay with our practice, with actual practice, through thick and thin, rain or shine, each drop of effort accumulates and winds up making a gradual but huge difference to our inner experience.

Some days our inner work comes easily. We have the energy. We have the need. Our emotions are not pulling us in another direction. So we work, although it takes little effort and does not feel like work. We practice presence and kindness. We pray. We meditate. We breathe consciously. We breathe energy. We let go of our identifications. To our abundance on those days, more is added. Here the temptation is not to bother with inner work, to ignore our need, to just cruise along enjoying the ride. Life is good, satisfying and fulfilling, as is. If it were a hand of poker, we would stand pat. Instead, on those sunny days of our life, we seek to go beyond the easy flow, we seek to intensify our efforts of presence and the rest. We seek to be, really be. And to do what is right, necessary and possible, inwardly and outwardly.

On some days we live under a dark cloud. We are tired or sick or in pain. We lack energy. We lack motivation. Our attention wanders. Things go wrong. Yet on such days even a little inner effort goes a long way. That seemingly small effort requires a real choice, a pure instance of will. The effort comes from us, from what is left when so much else is stripped away. It comes from seeing what does not matter and remembering what does.

Our inner work matters. Obviously it matters for us personally. It gives us joy. It makes our life more vivid. It brightens our relationships. It gives us more energy to think, to feel, to act, to create, and to experience. It frees us of so much baggage that drags us down, of our identification, of our negativity, of our rejection of ourselves and our life. It enables to be ourselves and live a full life. It feeds and develops our soul. All this and much more comes about through persistent inner work, through day-in and day-out, blue-collar inner work.

Importantly and remarkably, our inner work also

matters beyond our personal life. It is more than personal. Our inner work is needed. Through our practice we transform inner energies, raising their quality and quantity. We create a surplus beyond our personal needs, a surplus that goes to fill the needs of the earth, of the spirit of life around us, and even of the Divine. This is why we are here: to transform energies, to take in the raw material of food and air and sensory impressions, and from that to produce higher energies. The methods for doing so are precisely the methods of practical inner work: presence, prayer, meditation and kindness.

So our inner work matters to us personally, to our community, to the Earth, and to the Sacred. It serves both our own and the greater good. Thus it gives meaning to our life, real meaning, motivating meaning.

We want fulfillment. At some points we believe our fulfillment will come from having. Then at other points we believe fulfillment will come from doing. And in the end we find fulfillment in being, in being ourselves, and in serving thereby. To become ourselves, though, requires us to do something, namely our inner work.

For this week, raise the level of your persistence in your inner work. Work more each day, each moment.

16.0 Energy Practice
(Introduction)

We may hear about spiritual energies, but we cannot perceive them nor understand what they are unless we engage in actual spiritual practice, in particular practices designed to access, accumulate, generate, and transform the various energies. These energies shape our moment-to-moment experience, in every moment.

There are a number of qualities, types, or levels of inner energies. Each is quite different in character from the others, so different that training ourselves to perceive one level of energy does little to prepare us to recognize a higher level. We tend to keep looking in the same old way, assuming that all the stuff of the world is like the stuff we already know about. Yet the reality is not like that and invites exploration.

The energies of most interest to our inner work, to our spiritual practice, are the sensitive, the conscious, and the creative energies. The energy level below the sensitive is the automatic, which enables our default mode of living on autopilot, with little freedom and rote awareness. There are also energies above the creative, but our recognized contact with them is irregular and the bulk of spiritual inner work does not reach to those levels. Nevertheless, the highest energies, those of Love and the Transcendent, do affect us and form the fundamental substrate of existence: the loving, benign, yet powerful character of the Sacred.

In this series on energy practice, we will describe the characteristics of the various energies and introduce methods for perceiving and acting on or opening to them. Why does this matter? What difference do these energies make to us?

First, as already noted, energies shape our moment-to-moment experience, in every moment. The quality or level of energy predominating in any given moment determines the possible quality, breadth, and depth of our experience; it sets the size of the box we live in. The energies are the medium of experience itself. If we deplete a particular energy, that quality of experience evaporates until the energy is replenished. For example, our ability to pay prolonged, active attention diminishes after a while and we need a rest to replenish it. The quantity of energy also determines the possible intensity of experience. More inner energy yields a more vivid awareness, our senses come alive. So whether we know it or not, energies affect us directly and affect the quality of our life.

The second major reason to work on energy practice is that energies form the very substance of our soul. One purpose of spiritual inner work is to develop our soul. That development has two aspects. The first aspect is will, which concerns who we are and what we do. Will is a big and important subject, which we discuss elsewhere. The second important aspect of soul development involves collecting, producing, transforming, and organizing our inner energies into a coherent, permanent soul. This is a sacred quest that requires a lifetime of heartfelt dedication and intelligent effort. It concerns our very destiny, individually and collectively.

Which leads us to the third major reason why energy practice matters: through such practice we serve not just ourselves but also our fellow human beings, our planet, and the Sacred. The simplest part of this to see and understand is that our inner state affects the people around us, and vice versa. Someone who is agitated or angry, brings out the same in others. Someone who is calm, kind, and conscientious, brings that out in others. Those effects appear to act through the mechanism of our five senses. But our energy states affect other people directly. A person who is in a heightened state of awareness or has joy or love in their heart, without exhibiting outward signs, attracts a similar state in others. Walk into a room where people are meditating and your own awareness level is almost immediately raised: the conscious energy is at work. If raising the level of our own energies can have a positive impact on the people around us, then by extension, it can impact our planet and serve the Sacred.

For this week, please pay attention to how other people's energy states affect you.

16.1 Contact with Sensation

(Energy Practice: Part 1)

The sensitive energy, as its name implies, mediates our contact with our senses, with sight, hearing, touch, smell, taste, thoughts, and emotions. One way to work with the sensitive energy is indirectly, by focusing on awareness of sensory impressions. This, for example, is part of mindfulness practice, to be aware of the content of our senses. Our way, however, goes a significant step further by working on contacting and accumulating the sensitive energy itself. We do that primarily by engaging our body as the vessel for that work.

We begin with our proprioceptive sense, our perception of the inner state of our body, our perception of having a body, of having a right hand for example. If you like, try this. Focus your attention on your right hand. Be aware of the hand, of the inside of the hand, of the sensation of having a right hand, of the aliveness of your hand. Looking at, visualizing, or thinking about your right hand does not help in this. Go for a direct perception of the hand. Hold your attention in your hand for a minute or two. When you notice that your attention has wandered off, simply bring it back into the hand.

You may notice a certain something gradually accumulating in the hand. It has a slight vibration, warmth, or tingling. It brightens your awareness of your hand and makes it feel more substantial. It provides a place for your attention to occupy. Now notice the difference between your awareness of your right hand and your left hand. This difference shows the presence of more sensitive energy in your right hand than in your left at this moment.

Next you can repeat the exercise with your right foot, just putting and keeping your attention there and allowing the sensitive energy to awaken and accumulate. Next the left foot, then the left hand. Then the entire right arm, then right leg, then left leg, and finally your left arm.

This practice can open your perceptions to the sensitive energy, to the energy of sensation in your body. And in doing so, it opens you to what may be a new world for you, the world of inner energies. As such, it is a major step on the spiritual path, for it shows us that inward actions matter, literally. We begin our journey into the world of energies with sensation for two reasons: it is the easiest of the energies to perceive and it is the energy most responsive to our intention and inward action.

And we not only start this way, but we keep working with sensation in our body throughout our path, because the sensitive energies form the vessel of our soul. We may come to deeper levels of spiritual practice, but we continue working on all the inner levels to which we gain access, including the level of the sensitive energy. One way to look at this is that our soul encompasses several levels, all of which need care and feeding. Another way is that we need balance in our practice, balance among the levels: we keep our feet on the ground while our soul reaches toward heaven. Presence is always now. Our body is always now. So sensation is always now. The upshot is that work on sensation is important, is fundamental, and by itself takes us well down the road of our transformation toward a freer, richer life.

In future weeks, we will both broaden and deepen our work with sensation and with higher energies. For this week, we practice opening to the perception of the sensitive energy and sensing parts of our body.

16.2 Breathing Energy

(Energy Practice: Part 2)

Our body produces a certain amount of the sensitive energy in its normal, healthy functioning, enough to mediate our contact with our body, to have a sense of having a body. This is fine for ordinary purposes of living, but for spiritual purposes it is not enough. The practice of putting our attention into our body and being in contact with and sensing our body, as described in the previous part of this inner work series, does increase the production of the sensitive energy. But to build our soul, we need still more of the sensitive energy.

The time-honored way in several spiritual traditions consists of breathing in the energy. In the Hindu and Taoist traditions, the sensitive energy is called *prana* and *qi*, respectively. The breath is known as the avenue to increase our store of that energy. Other major spiritual traditions also approach this in various ways.

True energy breathing is a very specific practice: it means consciously and intentionally drawing the energy from the air into our body and retaining that energy. This differs fundamentally from ordinary breathing, where there is no awareness of the energy in and from the air and little or none is retained. It also differs fundamentally from conscious breathing, wherein we focus our attention on the sensations associated with breathing. Such conscious breathing practice, as taught in some forms of Buddhist meditation and as the way pranayama is typically taught in yoga, is an excellent practice for being present, but does not develop awareness of the energy in and from the air, nor retain it.

Sit quietly and bring your attention to your breathing, in particular to the sensations in and around your nostrils and upper lip as you breathe. Feel the air passing in and out. When your attention wanders and you notice that, gently bring your attention back to the breath awareness. Stay with this for ten minutes or however long it takes to reach a concentrated state, where your attention is not wandering away.

Now shift your attention from the body sensations of breathing to the air itself: Particularly on the inhalation, as the air comes into your nose. Use your attention as a kind of net. Put it out into the volume of air you will breathe in. Then as you inhale draw your attention back in, along with the air. While you exhale, let your attention rest on your nostrils and upper lip. Become aware of the particles of energy in the air you are breathing in. Set your intention to draw those particles of energy into your body. If you could see them, they would be shimmering particles of energy in the air. After you draw them into your nose, let the energy flow on its own, where it will, throughout your body.

Gradually, that energy builds up the sensation in your body, by joining the sensitive energy already there. Your sensation body grows stronger and your awareness of your body and your sensation grow more vivid. Note that this practice does not require you to hold your breath, nor to intentionally alter the normal, physical pattern of your breathing.

As you gain experience with the practice of breathing energy, you begin to notice that the energy you draw from the air does not enter only through your nose. You can breathe energy in through the entire surface of your body. This is whole body energy breathing through your skin. The advantage lies in the greater surface area allowing for more energy to be drawn in with each breath, as compared with only taking what's carried with the air you inhale. Taking this a step further, you notice that drawing the energy in does not need to be associated with the action or timing of your physical breathing. You can simply cast the net of your attention out into the space surrounding your body and pull it back in along with the energy from the air, without synchronizing with your breath. A step further still and you can draw an influx of energy from the air continuously, rather than in cycles like the breath. For that, instead of going out with your attention, keep it inside your body, but change your intention to an active need for the energy and to allowing it to flow into you. At each stage of this progression of energy breathing technique, more energy becomes available to you, to your soul.

We are surrounded by a sea of spiritual energies. True energy breathing is one major way of accessing a particular stratum of those energies, namely the sensitive energy carried by the air. Without this, we leave untapped a sacred resource for nourishing our soul. With it, we accelerate the growth of our soul.

Next week, we will explore how we might retain more of the energy we breathe and use it to nourish our soul. For this week, please practice the energy breathing itself.

16.3 Inhabiting the Sensitive Energy

(Energy Practice: Part 3)

The practice of breathing energy can dramatically increase the amount of sensitive energy passing into us, into our body. But without the necessary actions on our part, that energy will rapidly dissipate. The question can be framed as where does the incoming energy go: into our physical body or into our sensation body?

At first this distinction is subtle because our sensation body is thin and weak, effectively just a sprinkling of sensitive energy in parts of our physical body. Our body awareness remains almost exclusively awareness of our physical body. Although our sensitive energy serves as the medium of that awareness, the quantity of sensitive energy present at this stage is not enough to become much of an object of awareness itself. As long as our body awareness is primarily physical, any excess sensitive energy we generate by attention, by sensing, by breathing energy, or by other practices, tends to dissipate back to the norm of mediating ordinary contact with our physical body.

So the practice needed consists of turning toward the possibility of a body made of the sensitive energy. We do that by inhabiting our sensitive energy, by being here, in our body, in the sensitive energy. This goes beyond putting our attention into our body. When we put our attention on something, including part of our body, there is typically a division between us and the object of our attention. It is as if we are in our head and what we are attending to is out there. We are not inhabiting it. I am here in my head as the observer and my right hand is out there as the observed.

To inhabit our sensitive energy, we begin by sensing our entire body. For that, the practice of breathing energy does help. It enables us to fill our whole body with more and more sensation. In doing so, the sensitive energy itself becomes the object of our attention. We become aware of this energy as a whole, contiguous with our physical body. From there, we shift our feeling of where we are. Instead of being in our physical body, which happens to be full of the sensitive energy, we feel ourselves to be in our sensation, which happens to have the shape of and be in our physical body. At that point we can begin to consider that energy to be a body in its own right, a sensation body.

Then we bring our intention to bear and occupy our sensation body, more and more robustly. We direct our attention into all the sensitive energy throughout our whole body. We encompass and embrace the whole, including ourselves, with our attention. We are in our sensation body. We reside in it. We stay in it. We continue to feed it by breathing energy. Only now, when the energy comes to us, we are there throughout our sensation body to receive the incoming energy. We give it a place to land. By raising our will-to-be and turning that will, our will, to the job of inhabiting our sensation, we provide the scaffold to stabilize our sensation body. The energy has a shape, that of our physical body. And we have a place, our energy body, our developing soul. We are intentionally basing our presence in our sensation body, in this moment. And in the next.

For this week, practice inhabiting your sensation body.

16.4 Sensitive Energy in Body, Mind, and Heart
(Energy Practice: Part 4)

The sensitive energy mediates all our sensory perceptions. In the past few weeks, we have worked on the sensitive energy in our body, which we can call sensation. Now we include the sensitive energy in our thoughts and emotions, which together with sensation provides a more complete wholeness.

Our thoughts relate us to time and our emotions to values. Clearly, we would be far less than human without our thoughts and emotions. However, with both thoughts and emotions our ordinary mode of experience runs on autopilot, on the automatic energy. Our thoughts think themselves and our emotions emote reactively. In this mode, we hardly exist, incorrectly assuming that we are those self-generated thoughts and reactive emotions.

The sensitive energy, being the next energy up the scale from the automatic, can lift us out of such identification, out of the half-asleep functioning that impoverishes our life. The sensitive energy puts us in contact with our body and does the same with our other parts. The sensitive energy in our mind puts us in contact with our thoughts, so that we recognize thoughts as they occur, we know their meaning, and we see our thoughts as thoughts. We are not underneath them, subject to them, lost in them, as we are when on autopilot. The sensitive energy in our emotions puts us in contact with our emotions, so that we know that we are feeling, we know what we are feeling, and we see our emotions as emotions. We are not just lost in and driven by them, as we are when on autopilot.

With sensitive contact with our thoughts, we can just allow our thoughts to think themselves, without believing in them, without believing that they necessarily represent our views, without needing to do what our thoughts tell us to do. We just know our thoughts and let them be. Resisting unwanted or troubling thoughts just gives them more energy and prolongs them. Instead we give our thinking mind free reign and let thoughts subside on their own. Then our thoughts do not trouble us.

All this becomes possible when we pay attention to our thoughts and thereby raise the sensitive energy in our mind. We just watch our thoughts, moment-to-moment. We watch them come and go, change and change again. We know them as thoughts, as just thoughts. Because we see our thoughts, we realize that we are not our thoughts. We let them arise and we let them vanish. We realize that our thoughts do not speak for us, nor control us. We do not need to act on them.

The sensitive energy in our mind, brought by our ongoing attention to our thoughts, enables us to know our thoughts as thoughts. We do not get lost in the content of our thoughts. Rather we see the process of automatic thinking, how one thought leads to another, on and on. The sensitive energy also enables us to drive our thoughts in a particular direction, for example, to consider some issue or problem, or to make a plan. This is intentional, sensitive thinking. Only then can we say that we are thinking, otherwise our thoughts are thinking themselves. We could even say that when we are thinking our thoughts are made of sensitive energy. Sensitive contact with our thoughts broadens our presence by bringing our mental capacity back into the fold of our being.

Paying attention to our emotions raises sensitive energy that enables our contact with our emotions. If we then allow ourselves to feel whatever we are feeling, to accept our feelings without rejecting them, then our discordant, troubling, and difficult emotions have more of a chance to subside on their own, as long as we do not nurture or get behind them. Like thoughts, resisting our difficult emotions just gives them more energy and prolongs them. And also like thoughts, our emotions need not dictate our actions. Sensitive contact with our emotions gives us more freedom to choose our actions, rather than automatically reacting or falling under the spell of some emotion. We feel what we feel without feeding it. Resisting our difficult emotions, trying to ignore them, trying to sweep them under an inner rug, trying to drown them in alcohol or unnecessary eating, just gives them more life. Full awareness through sensitive contact with our actual emotions helps heal the difficult ones and helps prevent us from acting on them in ways we might later regret. But more than that, sensitive contact with our emotions broadens our presence by bringing our emotions back into the fold of our being. Letting our difficult emotions fall away on their own, in the light of sensitive awareness, makes room for more positive emotions, like the natural joy of living.

Whole body sensing can lead to whole presence contact, wherein we sense our whole presence, including our head and our chest. We do not try to have more sensitive energy in our head or chest than in other parts. We work to develop a smooth and equal supply of sensitive energy in all our parts, a sensitive presence of the whole. But the sensitive energy in our head becomes sensitive energy in our mind, helping enable us to sense our thoughts, to know our thoughts as thoughts. And the sensitive energy in our chest becomes sensitive energy in our emotional center, helping enable us to sense our emotions, to feel our feelings as feelings. In this holistic approach, we sense our body, we know our thoughts, and we feel our feelings. In doing so, we begin to make our three parts into one whole, we begin to be more ourselves. We begin to be more.

For this week, practice awakening the sensitive energy in your body, your mind, and your heart, and all three together.

16.5 Conserving Inner Energy
(Energy Practice: Part 5)

All the wonderful spiritual methods for increasing our inner energies appeal to us intrinsically: energy breathing, meditation, contemplative or ecstatic prayer, and others. Many actions not usually considered part of spiritual inner work can also increase our energies, such as creative actions, music, dance, writing poetry, skiing, hiking, mountain climbing and other sports, and so on. As we gain experience with inner work, we come to recognize the quantity and quality of our inner energies in any given moment. That perception matters because it opens the door to noticing which of our actions increase our energies or raise their quality and which actions waste our energies or lower their quality. Managing our inner work, our inner life, is intimately bound up with managing our energies. Methods to increase our inner energy form one side of energy practice. Another side concerns not wasting our energies. It matters little if we gain an ability to draw energies in, to raise our energy level, if we then just let it dribble away uselessly. As long as we have holes in our bucket, filling that bucket does little good.

The intuitive perception of our energy level enables us to judge our life, our actions with respect to their effect on our energies. Though this is different for each of us, there are some guidelines we can use as starting points for noticing our own energy flows.

Overindulging our bodily appetites tends to waste our energies. For example, overeating may use up some of the energy that we would otherwise have available for our inner work. Not eating enough can also diminish our energy production. We each need to find the balance that works for us personally. The same can be said for how much sleep we get. For necessities like eating and sleeping we seek the appropriate level for our own body. Moderation works here.

Some habits we seek to eliminate altogether. That goes for all recreational drugs, including marijuana, cocaine, psychedelics, uppers, downers, and the rest. They might boost our energies temporarily, but then they leave us inwardly flat for a prolonged period. We end up lower than where we started and possibly dependent on or even addicted to the drug. Recreational drugs are not compatible with spiritual inner work. Tobacco is another habit we need to eliminate altogether, for it not only harms our body but also harms our soul by wasting our inner energies.

Other physical habits, like drinking alcohol, fall into a middle ground where the right approach is either to eliminate it or at most to drink moderately. Too much alcohol disorganizes and depletes our energies; a spiritual seeker should never get drunk. Generally, the less alcohol we drink, the better off both our body and spirit are. If we use alcohol to escape unwanted feelings, that can be a problem. However, if we use it socially, moderately, and occasionally to relax with friends, there may be little harm to our body or spirit. We can each judge how it affects us personally and then act accordingly.

Generally, we watch our urges and impulses, the type that drive our bodily addictions and overindulgences. We can watch without letting those urges and impulses control us. Nevertheless, we avoid becoming too fastidious or puritanical, for that would block our spiritual life by feeding our self-centered egoism. We seek the middle way.

Mental and emotional habits can also be major wasters of our inner energy. Strong, destructive emotions can deplete our energies quickly. Obsessive and enthralling patterns of thought also deplete our energies. Daydreams, images, negative scenarios and ruminating can take over our mind. But how can we manage this? Resisting unwanted or troubling thoughts just gives them more energy and prolongs them. Instead we give them free rein and let them subside on their own. Only we do so by putting them in the foreground of awareness. Then we can let the thoughts roll past without letting them take us for a ride. We watch without letting the thoughts move us. *These thoughts do not necessarily speak for me, nor need I allow them to dictate my actions.* That way our thoughts do not trouble us. All this becomes possible when we pay attention to our thoughts.

As for emotions, if we allow ourselves to feel whatever we are feeling, without rejecting our feelings, then our discordant, troubling, and difficult emotions have more of a chance to subside. Like thoughts, resisting our difficult emotions just gives them more energy and prolongs them. And also like thoughts, our emotions need not dictate our actions. We feel what we are feeling, but we do not allow our emotions to control us; we do not allow our emotional reactions to take us for a ride. We reclaim our heart as our own. We do not allow the waves of reactions to life's events to overshadow us.

We judge all that we do in terms of how it affects our inner work. If it diminishes our ability to be present and if it is not necessary, then we know what we need to do or not do in order to help our steps along the path. When we fail, we immediately get up and start again. We also understand that our efforts of self-control in one area can lead to temptation in another area, like pressing on a balloon. We watch for that. We watch for the attitude of "I've been so good at that, I might as well allow myself a little extra indulgence in this."

We all have holes in the bucket of our being and we cannot plug them all at once. So we work to get one thing right, and from there move on to the next, always remembering why we are making these efforts of self-control and always remembering that this effort of not wasting energy is not an end in itself. Conserving our energies is a means toward supporting and enhancing our positive inner work, our practices of prayer, meditation, presence, and kindness, our work of raising our energy level, and our acts of service and creativity.

One measure of being is the degree of togetherness. Practicing presence holds us together. So without trying to ration our energies, the very act of presence conserves them and even increases our supply. So presence affords us another avenue of work in the arena of inner energy conservation, in addition to the self-control avenue.

For this week, please work on not wasting your inner energies.

16.6 Consciousness: The Metacognitive Energy

(Energy Practice: Part 6)

Consciousness is often misunderstood by mistaking the sensitive energy for the conscious energy. There are two major reasons for this confusion. First, the sensitive energy is much easier to know, understand, and control. We notice our sensory perceptions: that we are able to see, hear, taste, smell, sense our body, and be aware of the contents of our mind. When looking into ourselves, these perceptions are the most obvious ones and we assume that this is what consciousness is. But that is only partially the case and brings us to the second reason for confusion about consciousness: that the sensitive energy and the conscious energy nearly always appear to be mixed in us. The sensitive energy mediates our perceptions, bringing that information to consciousness, providing the contents of consciousness. So consciousness is involved in our ordinary perceptions, but gets hidden behind the more obvious sensitive energy.

The situation is similar to watching a movie at a theater. The screen itself is like consciousness. All the images on the screen are like the sensitive energy. When we watch a movie at a theater we are rarely aware of the screen as a screen. Rather we are engrossed in the images, the sounds, and the story, just as we are in our daily life. The sensitive energy effectively masks the conscious energy.

Fortunately, we can train ourselves to look behind the scene of our senses, thoughts, and emotions to the source of awareness, to pure consciousness. One effective means toward that is the meditation style sometimes called choiceless awareness. It can also be called non-doing or just sitting. In this meditation it is always best to begin with some preparatory practice that grounds us in the moment, in our body. So we might practice sensing our body or awareness of the sensations associated with our breathing, or counting breaths while being aware of the sensations associated with them. After becoming focused by this preparation, we can let go of those efforts and just be. We notice whatever comes for what it is: our thoughts as thoughts, our bodily sensations as sensations, and all our sensory perceptions as sensory perceptions. We do not try to shape our experience by running after or pushing away any particular thoughts or other perceptions. We just sit and be, letting everything, letting all the constantly changing contents of our awareness come and go without our interference. This non-judging, non-doing, choiceless approach to our immediate experience gradually allows us to become that in us which sees the whole parade passing.

If we are sitting comfortably in a quiet place with our eyes closed, our thoughts will gradually slow down, as will our sensory experience. Gaps will open up between thoughts. Empty gaps. Sitting in those gaps, it appears that nothing is there in them. Nothing. And indeed no thing is there, no content to latch onto. But after all the content of our experience temporarily recedes into the background, we notice that these gaps of nothing are still filled with our awareness, our consciousness. This basic silence in our mind, at the root of our mind, is cognizant, a cognizant stillness. We come to rest in its peace, not lost in the contents of our mind. We have relaxed into just being, into our consciousness. This continuum of simple awareness is the conscious energy.

Practicing this type of meditation, so that again and again we soak in the peace of consciousness, we become familiar with it. We acquire its taste. Then we can start to recognize it in the busy midst of life. We see that beneath the whirl of our senses and thoughts, beneath our actions and emotions, that cognizant stillness is still there, is always there. All our senses, thoughts, and emotions no longer mask consciousness. We have seen the screen behind the movie of our life, and we can be that screen. We find it possible to base ourselves in the cognizant stillness, even as we go about our daily activities. This transforms our experience and our life. We are rooted in consciousness, in the metacognitive energy that gives awareness of our sensory awareness. We have peace in our mind and equanimity in our heart. We can just be ourselves.

Because pure consciousness is so wonderful, so transformative, it is misunderstood in yet another way: that of assuming that consciousness is the highest energy, the ultimate, even the Divine. That assumption is not valid. Nevertheless, if we could come to live in consciousness, our life certainly would have entered a deep transformation.

For this week, please practice entering the cognizant stillness within you.

16.7 Sacred Light Energy

(Energy Practice: Part 7)

The deeper our search, the more spiritual it becomes. Working with the sensitive energy is not so different than practicing a musical instrument, playing a sport, doing our chores or performing a job. It is work. After an initial familiarization, the necessary effort is fairly clear and within our power. At the level of the conscious energy, an element of receptivity enters, as well as a more subtle perception. We need to allow ourselves to enter the realm of cognizant stillness. The effort is more indirect and not as readily at our command.

With the energy of the Sacred Light, we enter fully into the realm of the spirit. Here we are supplicants. We can represent the effort as comprising three stages, from more active to more receptive. The first stage concerns finding the direction of the sacred, a direction deeper into our inner world. The second stage concerns pointing ourselves in that direction. And the third stage concerns opening to that sacred realm.

Finding the direction toward the Sacred Light is akin to finding the direction toward the conscious energy. The latter search required us to learn how to look deeper, how to look beyond all our ongoing experience, how to recognize something that at first appeared to be nothing, to be insubstantial, which later we found to be more substantial, to be the background of all experience. That search for the conscious energy refined our perceptions and taught us to look in new ways and new categories.

Moving toward the Sacred Light is similar. Only this time we need to go beyond consciousness itself. How can that be? Consciousness surrounds us inwardly and outwardly. It seems to define the totality of our experience in every moment. Yet there is more. And it can be a major purpose, indeed the purpose, of a life well-lived to find the direction toward the Sacred Light, to open to it, to become a vessel for the energy of the Sacred Light, and thus enable that energy to flow into this natural world of our life together on this planet. Lord knows we need it.

So how do we find our inner way beyond consciousness? Prayer can help. But it needs to be prayer that touches us, touches our soul, consuming our mind and heart. Perhaps there is a phrase of prayer or a sacred name that touches us in that way. We can repeat that inwardly or in a chant and let it carry us deeper.

The way beyond consciousness is the way of depth. Because consciousness is the source of all our ordinary perceptions, we cannot look beyond it by looking in any outer direction. We look deeper into ourselves, behind our thoughts, behind our mind, behind our very awareness itself.

Is there a compass that shows us when we are nearer the right direction? For consciousness that compass was peace. For the energy of the Sacred Light, that compass consists of the light energy that streams through the cracks in our wall of separation from the sacred. We can be touched by this in prayer, in supplication to the Spirit. But many other moments also offer a taste: the grandeur of nature, a special moment of music, the eyes of someone we love, a transcendent work of art, literature, or speech, or whatever else may touch us in that way. The point is to recognize such moments for what they are, an opening to the spirit, and to realize that we need not wait for such moments to arise haphazardly but rather we can work toward opening to the sacred intentionally.

Once we begin to have an inkling of the inner direction

toward the Sacred, we sit down in meditation or contemplative prayer and point ourselves, our soul toward that direction. Our will is not bound by consciousness or any other energy. So our will, our intention, our attention, our heartfelt longing, can point us toward the depth within, the depth beyond consciousness.

Having pointed our inner face beyond consciousness, we then open ourselves, our will, our soul, our heart, to the Sacred. That opening takes place at our very core. We relax back into ourselves, turn toward the Sacred, and empty our heart in a gesture of supplication. Then something unmistakable may flow down to us: cascades of the energy of Sacred Light.

Though it is sublime, sacred, and in the neighborhood of the Divine, the energy of the Sacred Light is not in itself Divine. There is More.

For this week, please practice finding the direction beyond consciousness, pointing your inner face toward the Sacred, and opening to the energy of the Sacred Light.

16.8 Love

(Energy Practice: Part 8)

The dissolution of our inner barriers opens us to love. And we all have true moments of love. The question for our spiritual practice is how we can enter love as our normal state of being. Toward that, the practice of love addresses both our defensive barriers and the reality of love.

First, the barriers. Foremost among them is our self-centered egoism. The base nature of egoism is to create a false distinction between self and other. Ego is an assumption that I am here, while everything and everyone else is out there, separate from me. Ego builds a wall and claims that it, that we, exist inside that wall. True seeing, though, reveals that it is just a wall with nothing substantial inside. Indeed, the wall itself is ephemeral, built as it is out of our thoughts of who we are, out of our patterns, our history, our hopes and dreams, and the stories we tell ourselves about ourselves. Even the thought I is part of this illusion, for it is just another thought, one that refers to what we assume is inside the wall. But there is nothing inside that wall. Nevertheless, the illusion masks a reality: we have a real I, our individuality, but it does not depend on the wall of ego, and has an unbounded nature. When we think of ourselves, we think of our ego and its patterns. So we end up looking in the wrong place for who we are.

The wall of ego is a pattern of energies. When those energies, when our mind, begins to quiet down, the assumed existence of our ego and its flimsy nature stand out in relief. When our mind fully quiets down, that assumption, that ego of ours, evaporates, at least temporarily. This begins for us when we enter the peace of the conscious energy. When our thoughts and emotions settle down, we enter a greater wholeness, one that transcends us, transcends our ego, which for those moments has receded into its true state of non-existence. That wholeness includes all things, all life, all people. All the differences are seen as surface phenomena. Underneath is the unity: not the unity of interconnected parts, but the unity in which each part is the whole. All the fundamental boundaries we believed in are not actually there. The boundaries are superficial and evaporate to reveal our unity.

There are levels to the unity. At the level of the conscious energy, we are unified within ourselves and we are individuals sharing in the one seamless field of consciousness. We all partake of the same consciousness. At the level of the

Sacred Light, our dual nature comes forward. Here we are individuals and at the same time we all serve the Sacred and are transparent to the One Will. At the level of Love, the unity is complete. We are one. No longer is it me seeing you. No longer is it you seeing me. No longer is it the two of us. It is just us, just seeing. That way of being, that way of seeing, is Love.

The energy of sensation puts us in contact with our senses. The energy of consciousness puts us in contact with awareness itself. Living in that cognizant stillness, we spend less energy maintaining and defending our illusory ego. The energy of the Sacred Light puts us in contact with the unimaginable joy and perfection emanating from the Source of All. And the energy of Love ushers us beyond our boundaries into the fundamental unity of all.

Inner peace allows our ego to subside. The Sacred opens our heart. And Love awakens our natural humility. Not only are we not better or worse than others, and not only are we not different, we are not even separate.

For this week, seek Love and let Love find you.

16.9 The Transcendent Energy

(Energy Practice: Part 9)

> *Wisdom says I am nothing.*
> *Love says I am everything.*
> *God says I am you.*
> *Among these three, our life flows.*
> (reworked from Nisargadatta Maharaj)

Although we cannot see It, touch It, or in any other way sense It, we nevertheless have a deep, usually buried, intuition that there is indeed an Ultimate Source, that this remarkable universe is not an accident, that our lives have an objective meaning and purpose beyond our personal, subjective ones, and that our true identity is somehow directly connected with that Source. That intuition has another name: faith. To what extent do we allow faith to come into us, to affect how we are and what we do? On the face of it, faith seems unnecessary. It appears we can live quite well without it. But if we do let it in, faith brings a whole new dimension to our day-to-day life.

We can agree that faith in the Ultimate Source is irrational. We may, however, disagree on what that means. Usually people take irrational to mean sub-rational, a view resulting from a disturbance of the mind, from a less than thoughtful position. But we take the irrationality of faith to be supra-rational, more than logical, and resulting from a truth beyond the mind, beyond thought. This can be difficult because we are so accustomed to having things make sense, in terms of logical thought. Faith bypasses thought. It certainly affects thought, but does not depend on it. So the leap of faith is in part giving up our inherent resistance to anything not reasoned and logical, our inherent dependence on and overestimation of our thinking mind.

Faith is a higher emotion. Unlike our usual emotions, which generally arise in self-centered reaction to some situation, higher emotions derive from higher perceptions. These bypass both our thoughts and our ordinary senses. So faith is there underneath as an invisible force drawing us toward the Sacred. This can manifest in various ways. One way is that we feel a need to undertake spiritual practice, which further strengthens our faith by opening our perceptions, our connection with the Sacred. The Ultimate Source does not reveal Itself at our initiative: it goes the other way around. But spiritual practice makes us more available to It. Meditation and prayer raise our level, raise the quality of our perceptions and our energy. Both help prepare us to be receptive to what flows from above.

Other kinds of actions also make us more available to the Source. These include creative acts like making music or art, or any other activities that engage the whole of ourselves, in which we lose our usual self-centeredness and open to a greater reality that transcends us. When we disappear in the midst of a creative act, something higher can appear in our place. Maybe this is just a moment, but it is a golden moment of purity, a moment that connects the Ultimate Source with this material world, through us.

Which brings us to a remarkable aspect of the Source, namely that we ourselves, in our deepest essence, are emanations of that Source. Our separation from It consists of the intervening layers of perceptions that obscure and distract. Behind all that we see, behind all our senses, there is the Source. Behind who we think we are, behind our very presence, there is the Source. Hidden within our neighbor, there is the Source. The higher purpose and method of prayer is to allow God to pray through us, as us, to let go of our separate identity and allow the Source to assume Its true place in us.

The Transcendent Source is the Mountain of Purpose, the Will of the World, that continuously creates this universe and all of us. Faith takes us beyond thinking of God as a nice theory to actively and receptively working to open ourselves to the reality of the Source.

17.0 Transcendence
(Introduction)

The work of spirituality calls us to transcend our limitations, some of which are more or less known to us, while others elude us entirely. Those known to us may include our physical limitations, what our body can and cannot do, what it needs and what it wants, what it likes and what it hates, its demands and its habits. We also know some of the limitations of our emotional life, like how we tend to get angry or anxious when the relevant psychological buttons get pressed, how we react so predictably to minor occurrences. We recognize some of the limitations of our minds, like how our thoughts tend to circle around a personally-charged event and our tendency to judge others much more harshly than we judge ourselves. And in all of this we have little or no choice: it all just happens, and though we may see it happening, it all limits how we live.

Other limitations, though no less real, remain hidden from us. We may not realize that the whole arena of our emotional life is flat and reactive and that an entirely different level is possible for us, a level of higher emotions, such as an underlying tone of peace and equanimity, or a way of relating based in love. We may not realize that all of the thoughts and mental images arising in our mind comprise only its surface layer, hiding depths of perception, hiding our true identity, and distracting us from living in presence.

I may not realize the subjectivity of my world view, that everything revolves around me, that I mainly think and care only about what affects me and how it affects me. Obviously, some of that is necessary for survival, but transcendence can take us to a much broader view, one that incorporates a wider universe without shortchanging our personal needs. Love is not only about our attitude toward others, but also toward ourselves, and it erases the chasm between the two.

So at each stage of the path, we have two sources for transcendence: the push and the pull. The push results from the limitations we know about. We do not want to be limited in those ways. We want to rise above our shortcomings. We want to go beyond our animal heritage to become fully human, fully ourselves. We want freedom in front of all those limitations. So we push. We engage in the practices of the path to break the shackles we know. We push ourselves to go beyond our known limits.

The pull is what calls to us from our higher possibilities, the ones we might intuit but do not know. A deeper way of living attracts us, pulls us to engage in the practices of the path so that we may live the sweetness of the Sacred. This is the action of faith. There are realms of the spirit unknown to us, unsuspected and unimagined. They are not far off. They are right here within us. The gap is not insurmountable. And across that gap comes the intuition we call faith, calling us from beyond the limits that we do not see.

At first our path may be mostly driven by the push. We push to go beyond the personal limitations we know. We push to become better, to overcome our weaknesses. We push to compete with our fellow travelers. We push to become an ideal and perfect version of ourselves. The push impulse can be very strong and can take us a good way along the path. But one day it becomes counterproductive, because the push is all about me, about ego and personality. When our inner work starts to transcend me, then the push loses power.

In its place, the pull can appear with a renewed vigor, if we welcome it. We practice to get closer to the Sacred. We practice because faith impels us to do so. We practice to serve the Sacred. We practice because it gives meaning to our life. We practice because it is the right thing to do. Yes, our practice is personally satisfying, but that satisfaction is no longer enough to move us forward. Faith does that.

As we climb Jacob's ladder to heaven, beginning from where we are, we work to transcend one rung at a time. In the coming weeks, we will explore some of those rungs of transcendence.

For this week, please assess your current position as best you can. Look at the strength of your push to transcend your personal limitations and the quiet but persistent pull that draws you toward the Higher.

17.1 Transcending Our Materiality

(Transcendence: Part 1)

> *Lay not up for yourselves treasures upon earth, where moth and rust doth corrupt, and where thieves break through and steal: But lay up for yourselves treasures in heaven, where neither moth nor rust doth corrupt, and where thieves do not break through nor steal.* [Matthew 6:19-20]

Most of us come into adulthood believing that this material world is all that exists, or at least is what matters the most in the everyday reality of our life. We live in the material, natural world and have no reason to suspect anything beyond that. The natural outgrowth of that view is to have all our hopes and dreams, all our desires and attachments, inextricably bound to the natural and man-made world brought to us by our five senses.

But then life happens. It may be some major disappointment or some sweet success. We may lose something or someone dear to us. Or we lose out or win big at something that matters to us. Any such event may lead us to question: Is this all there is? If that question comes strongly, our search for the Sacred begins. If the question consumes us, it can even sever our attachment to the things of this world. It can grant us a measure of freedom, to know and live by the knowledge that ultimate, lasting satisfaction cannot come from the material world. In the Sufi way this is known as the first fana. In Buddhism, it is a milestone on the way to freedom in front of desires.

Even so, we are always faced with the necessities of providing for our body, for our family, and for our society. This visible, material world cannot be ignored. We are required to participate in the marketplace of life. But within those constraints we have a good deal of room for freedom. This is the arena for our inner work. How do we do what we need to do without attachment? Can we see what is necessary and do it, simply because it must be done, and without the grumbling or the feverish desire for success?

Our attitude around time gives one clue to navigating our way through. Attachment often has a component of wanting to hold onto something into the future, of wanting to acquire something in the future, or of wanting to avoid something in the future. The way through is to do what is necessary now and let the future be what it will be. We take care of the future by what we do now, especially if we do it with the appropriate degree of quality. Then we not need worry about the outcome. For this, the key is to be fully in the now, to be present. So we work to be present by applying the methods of presence. And that work helps free us from our material attachments, while also freeing us to do what is needed without the extra burden of worrying about the result.

Transcending materiality cannot be about leading a non-material life. That is not possible. This transcendence is about becoming free in the midst of all the necessities imposed on us by our body, by our life in the marketplace of the material.

The surest way to transcend our grasping after material things is to see into and live in greater contact with the Sacred, even as we continue to live in this material world, honor and respect it, and act responsibly toward it.

To be clear, we need not shun the material, we need not live in poverty or as hermits. We can enjoy the beauty of nature, the tastes and aromas of a fine meal, the warmth of close friendships, the satisfactions of working a job, and pleasures of our home. Everything matters, both our outer, material life and our inner, spiritual life. Indeed, they are not separate; we have one life to live well. The material life in itself does not interfere with, diminish, or prevent an active and ever-deepening spiritual life. The point is not to grasp and cling to things, because grasping and clinging suck all the joy out of living and sidetrack our spirituality. We end up approaching our material life with anxiety about losing what we have and not getting what we want or need. So in place of joy we have anxiety. We hardly taste the first piece of cake as we rush to finish it so we can get to the second piece.

For this week, please look at the ways you grasp and cling to material things and experiment with ways to start transcending that attachment.

17.2 Transcending Our Thoughts

(Transcendence: Part 2)

I think, therefore I am, as Descartes is often quoted. We believe our thoughts and we believe in our thoughts. They certainly seem like the most intimate and personal expression of who we are. Daydreaming, ruminating, pondering, judging, planning, obsessing, rehearsing, rehashing, and just plain letting our thoughts run on by association — it all seems to be me. Our thoughts tell us what we want and we do not want. They tell us our opinions and our goals. They tell us the story of our life. They speak to us, as us, in an endlessly changing, yet always familiar stream, driven by our ongoing experiences. The time we spend in school is mostly directed toward training our thinking mind. Given all that, it is natural that our world view and our notion of ourselves is bounded by the frame of our thoughts.

And although we have a good deal of freedom within the framework of our thoughts, it turns out that the boundaries of our thoughts are the walls of our prison. We buy into our thought frame and allow it to convince us that this is the reality of who we are and what we can know. Our belief in our thoughts limits our experience to our customary mode of awareness. Our thoughts claim supremacy in our inner world. They claim to be me. The thought "I" has us completely convinced that it is who I truly am, that we need look no further to find ourselves.

However, there is more, much more. There is a great spiritual world within us, behind and beyond our thoughts. The thought "I" is just a thought. But it does point toward the reality of who I am, which is my will.

Of the many practical methods developed to transcend our thoughts, we will look at two. The first is sensing our body. This is a matter of direct, intentional awareness of our body, first of parts and later, with practice, of the whole. This sensing practice then moves beyond body awareness to building up the sensitive energy in our body, which in turn enhances our body awareness. Thinking plays no role in sensing; it can only get in the way. Sensing is a direct perception of our body and the sensitive energy. It bypasses our thinking mind. In so doing, sensing teaches us to understand that we are not our thoughts. In sensing we have an inner action that does not involve thinking. Sensing gets us out of our thinking brain. It shows us another possibility of being in the world, of being ourselves, without being our thoughts.

Another method toward transcending our thoughts involves seeing into the gaps between thoughts. This is best practiced in sitting meditation. We begin with relaxing our body, sitting comfortably. Then we start noticing our thoughts, seeing them as thoughts. We do not try to stop them and we do not respond to them, think them, emote about them, or take a ride on them. We just sit on the sidelines of our thought-stream and let it roll on as it will, watching it all the while in a relaxed manner. During this we stay in contact with our body, which helps keep us grounded in the moment and not losing ourselves in the thoughts.

Gradually our thoughts slow down. Gaps open up between them. At first these gaps seem empty, just an absence of thought. But then we begin to see that we are still cognizant between the thoughts, that even though our mind is silent, we are still there, alive and alert. In that cognitive stillness, first revealed to us in the gaps between thoughts, we find a deeper part of our mind, we find our true consciousness. This is the awareness behind our thoughts, behind all our sensory perceptions.

With practice, with returning to this cognizant stillness again and again, with steeping ourselves in that quiet mind, we become able to open to it even when there are thoughts. We are in the great stillness while thoughts drift by like small clouds in a vast sky. Even during the day, when we are not sitting in meditation, we become able to be in that stillness, in the midst of activity, in the midst of thought.

This is transcending thoughts. And it brings a special, unexpected freedom. We are no longer driven by our thoughts. We no longer feel compelled to act on, or respond to, or counter our thoughts. We no longer necessarily believe our thoughts. And we longer believe our thoughts are who we are.

To transcend our mind means taking another, yet deeper step. It means transcending our consciousness itself. We address that in a later part of this inner work series. For this week, please practice seeing your thoughts as thoughts, seeing that you are not your thoughts.

17.3 Transcending Our Reactive Emotions

(Transcendence: Part 3)

Emotions are the spice of life, enlivening the experiences that are alive for us. In the moments of absence of a heartfelt approach to living, we are not fully alive. Emotions motivate us to do much of what we do. They also inform us, offering guidance in situations too complex or too quick for our thoughts. In short, emotions are essential for a well-lived life. But just as food is essential and wonderful, yet can negatively impact us when we allow our appetites to overcome our better judgment, so emotions can also negatively impact us.

It is not just an absence of emotion that impoverishes experience, but also, and more importantly, certain types of emotion, namely reactive emotions that overshadow and dominate experience. Something happens and our emotions react, say with anger, or fear, or greed. We all know this sort of thing and know it to be perfectly normal and appropriate. Our problem occurs when that sudden emotion does more than just inform us about a situation or prepare us for action. The problem begins when the emotion continues to dominate our experience beyond its useful life, distorting our view of ourselves and the world.

Our thoughts join in and we nurture the anger, justifying it, criticizing or even cursing the person who caused it, railing against a world that is like this. In the case of fear, our thoughts join in and we become suspicious and paranoid, fastidious or timid. With greed, our thoughts join and perseverate about the object of our desire; we obsess about our lack of what we want and how we can get it. In these moments where our reactive emotions infect our thoughts, the quality and rationality of our thinking suffers. From the standpoint of our inner work also, these emotional storms are damaging. They burn up inordinate amounts of our inner energies and they narrow and cloud our perceptions, draining our presence.

So how can we transcend these unhealthy emotions? If we notice them in their earliest stages, we may be able to just say no, to just see the emotion and let it go, to just see our thoughts starting to pile on and let that stream of thought go. But once the storm gathers strength, the direct approach to the emotion or the thoughts becomes less possible, less effective. So what then?

Notice first that our emotions and our thoughts collude

to create the problem, each feeding off the other. But we have not addressed our body and its potential role. Our body is not just a bystander in these emotional storms. Our breathing may change, our facial expression and posture express the emotion, and muscle tensions pop up. And because our body is more amenable to course correction mid-stream, this connection between body and emotion can serve as a point of leverage in abating the storm. To use that leverage we need to be in contact with a part of ourselves that is willing to let the emotion go. If we want to nurture it, to justify it, to be in it, then nothing good will happen until the storm passes and we awaken used and abused by it. But if we can find the willingness in ourselves, find that something that wants presence and peace, then we can turn to two related methods: relaxing our body and sensing it.

By relaxing our body, we change one part of the emotional pattern and that can change the course of the emotion. We relax our face. We relax our shoulders, our chest, our abdomen. We relax our whole body. Then we start sensing our body, being aware of the visceral experience of having a body and building up the sensitive energy in our body. Doing all this takes attention. In particular, it takes our attention away from the reacting emotion, its causes and ramifications. By removing some or all of our attention from the emotion that has taken us over, we weaken it. By coming into body presence, we raise our state, perhaps enough to not be lost in that particular emotion.

What then? What if we can let go and calm the storm? Do we then live with a void in our heart? Hardly. For example, equanimity is an emotion, a higher emotion. It is not dry and not indifferent. It is an alert and accepting mode of heart. It exudes peace. It is the open space of heart that allows the creative, the new to enter, that allows the old to be seen anew. Equanimity is a conscious emotion.

Other higher emotions also await us: joy, love, compassion, faith, and awe. All these come to us if we make room for them. As long as the reactive emotions occupy our heart, the higher emotions cannot enter.

For this week, please work to transcend your reactive emotions and open yourself more to the higher emotions.

17.4 Transcending Me

(Transcendence: Part 4)

Having begun to see through our thoughts, through our emotions, to see them as just thoughts and just emotions passing through our awareness, we move toward the possibility of seeing through our personality, through what we believe we are. Our thoughts and emotions run in familiar but complex patterns and rhythms. They refer to "me." But the surprising and shocking fact that slowly, and sometimes suddenly, dawns on us is that this "me" does not exist as a distinct entity, or even as a fuzzy entity. It is just a concept that we have bought into and defend at great cost.

When we can really see our thoughts as they are, we know them to be just these mental sounds or images moving through our mind. Each mental sound or image represents, refers to, or symbolizes something. Often that something exists in the material world. For example, the thought sound "table" refers to this actual wooden structure in front of me. Other thoughts, like "cold" or "justice," refer to more or less abstract concepts. We believe that the thoughts "I" and "me" refer to something as real as a table, not abstract. Yet when we look for

"I" or "me" we do not find it, we do not find something whole and indivisible in the way we assume that "I" exists. It seems that our pattern of thoughts and emotions refers to itself as "I." But no thought and no emotion is actually "I." So where am I? Or rather, do I even exist?

A major confusing factor is that sometimes when we think "I," it does refer to the reality, to who we truly are: our will. But that is only the case when we think intentionally. The vast majority of the thoughts that pass through our mind are not "our" thoughts, not intentional: they are automatic, associative, reactive, or patterned thoughts that happen on their own, that think themselves, with no involvement of our "I." Thoughts are truly ours only when we consider some issue purposely, when our attention and intention engage in the thinking process. Our problem is that we do not distinguish between these two modes of thought, between whether particular thoughts are intentional or just automatic.

So, for example, we feel shocked and ashamed when nasty but automatic, unintentional thoughts pass through our mind. We mistakenly believe that these are "our" thoughts, that they speak for us, that they represent our actual views. And so we may start a hopeless and unnecessary battle against the automatic, self-generated thoughts passing through our mind. Hopeless, because automatic thoughts cannot be banished and will always cycle back. Unnecessary, because they are not "our" thoughts and do not necessarily represent what we believe, much less what we would ever act on. Seeing through our inaccurate view of the thoughts in our mind is liberating, one less impediment on the way to being what we want to be. We are not our thoughts, whether intentional or automatic.

Our senses also collude in the illusion of "me." We see

and we assume that it is "I" that sees. Certainly there is seeing, but where is the "I" that is the purported recipient, the seer of the sights. We hear and we assume that it is "I" that hears. We feel our body and assume that "I" have a body. But that implies that I am not my body, that I am something, someone who has a body. Where is this "I"?

Again, it is like with our thoughts. If our sensory perception is intentional, if we are paying attention to what we see or hear, then it is our I that sees or hears. But the great majority of the time, we pay minimal or no attention. Our sensory stream goes on without our intentional contact with it. Life passes us by. Yet we assume that all our sensory impressions are the same, that our "I" is the seer and hearer of all these sights and sounds, even when we are not paying attention.

We can perhaps gain some clarity on this issue of I, me, or self by looking at it on three levels: the me self, the I Self, and the Divine SELF. The level of the me self is our pseudo-self, our assumed self, made up of the amorphous cacophony of thoughts, emotions, and urges that together we may call our personality and that we mistakenly assume to be who or what we are. That is the self referred to in the Buddhist teaching of no-self, that trains us to see that what we believed to be our Self is not an independent, integral Self. To transcend this me self, we must see through it, see that this mass of thoughts, emotions, and urges do not amount to an I Self, see that this supposed me self is superfluous, is just an idea, and is totally driven by our personal history and the conditions and whims of the moment.

The next level of Self is our true I, our will, the one who sees what we see and does what we do, when it is present. If our I is not present, if we are not present, then no one sees what we see or does what we do; it all just happens and streams by, moments of life lost to us. But if we are present, if I am present, then I am whole, unified, alive. There is someone at home: I am. So another part of the work of transcending our ordinary, personality self, is to be present, to be. That puts us in our I Self, in our one will. When we pay attention, we are, otherwise we are not.

Yet this I Self that we truly are, as wonderful and liberating as it is, is not the end of the story. There is the Divine SELF, the SELF of all Selves. We transcend our I Self, by opening to the Divine SELF. We will address that process in later parts of this series.

For this week, please look at the cacophony of your personality, your me self, and contrast that with the I Self of presence.

17.5 Transcending Our I

(Transcendence: Part 5)

> *The Lord comes amidst the sound of the shofar.*
> Psalms 47:6

Recently I had the good fortune to attend Rosh Hashanah services at the shul of a Rabbi who is renowned in his city for, among other things, his remarkable skill at blowing the shofar. Each passage is clear, distinct, and compelling. His single-breath blast of Tekiah Gedolah seems to go on for five minutes, resounding in the very soul of those present. In hearing such sounds, something transformative can occur. If we let the sound enter us, enter our core, if we let the sound vibrate us, if we let the sound be us, so that our self, our me, our I vanishes, then the Sacred can enter us as the sound.

This can also happen with sounds that we make, whether externally out loud, or inwardly, silently, as with a mantra or repetition. Classic examples include the Hindu "Om" and the Muslim "Hu." Unlike with the sound of the shofar, which we hear receptively, we make the sound of Om or Hu actively. So it takes further steps to let go of being the one making the sound, to letting the sound just be there, to letting the sound make itself. In making itself, the mantra becomes the Sacred vibrating us. This happens sometimes with singers: the song sings them.

Another and telling example, is the biblical phrase "I am the Lord your God." If we say that inwardly and contemplate it, then who is the I of that phrase? Clearly it is not us; it is not that we are God, not that our I is God. But if we find a way to step aside inwardly or rather grow transparent and let the I of that phrase be the One who is saying it in us, then we approach the truth of a higher reality. Our personal individuality, our true I, the I of our presence, is not separate from or different in kind from the I of the Divine. In such a moment, we are a particle of the Greatness. And because the Greatness is not divisible, in that moment we are the Greatness. But it can only happen in moments when we let go of our smallness, not just of the ego that references everything to my personal welfare, but even to let go of the greater, though still relatively small, I of presence that is individual and not all-encompassing. In transcending our true I, we step onto Sacred ground.

We can move toward that state not just in prayer. In any safe activity in which we are fully, wholly engaged, all-in, this can happen. We can go beyond ourselves. We act without a sense of being the actor, without a sense of being the doer. Though we are fully aware, the action flows through us. There can be a kind of ecstasy. Sometimes this is called being in the zone, or being in flow. Such moments are sacred. They are moments of transcending our I.

Many such moments begin, however, with our I fully engaged. We bring our attention fully to bear on what we are doing. We bring our entire mind, heart, and body into the action. We bring quality and sensitivity. We bring awareness of the whole situation and our purpose in it. And then we give ourselves over to it. We trust and give up our sense of agency, and let the action run itself. Without our interference or control, it adjusts itself perfectly. We let it flow. And in that flow, barriers drop. We transcend ourselves, we transcend time, and we become connected with all, and the All.

This may sound complicated, difficult, and elevated out of our range. But it is none of those. This transcendence is simple, easy, and natural, or rather supernatural for us. The belief that it is complicated, difficult, and out of reach is one of the barriers confronting us. If we just try to work inwardly and practically in that direction, ignoring the naysaying within us, we find ourselves progressing, slowly and surely toward the Sacred within. We learn the way by doing, by our practice and effort, by trial and error. The Ultimate awaits us, calling us home in this life. Heaven is not just for the dead. Heaven can be here and now, while we live and breathe.

Is there more possible beyond this transcendence of letting the Divine be our I? Yes indeed. But that takes us temporarily completely out of contact with the material world, whereas transcending our I does not. Rather it leaves us here, connected, not separate, living in unity and love, at least for those precious moments.

For this week, note those activities in your life that bring or could bring you closer to flow. To what extent do you give them significance? If you are inclined to prayer, practice toward transcending your I in prayer. Practice flow in other ways as well.

17.6 Transcending Time
(Transcendence: Part 6)

In 1898 George Bernard Shaw, who professed contempt for Yogis, reportedly said to the Shivapuri Baba: "You Indian saints are the most useless of men. You have no respect for time." To which the Shivapuri Baba replied, "It is you who are the slaves of time. I live in Eternity."[3]

Have you ever felt you were a slave to time? Maybe you have more things to do than time available to do them in. Maybe you are running late for work or for an appointment and feel harried. Maybe you are caught in traffic. Maybe you are facing a looming deadline. Maybe you dislike the situation you find yourself in at the moment and want to get out of it. Maybe you are bored. Maybe you are afraid of what may happen, or despondent about what did happen. Maybe you are enjoying this moment so much that you feel desperate to prolong it, to have it not end. Maybe there are two or more things that you want to do right now, but you are constrained to choose only one. In all these ways and more, we are slaves to time.

Notice that at the root of these examples is a certain set of attitudes about time, expressed and abetted by thoughts and feelings. "I must get there." "I'm going to be late." "I'm bored." "I hate this." "I love this." "Time is short." "Time is money." And so on. In these ways our thoughts and emotions tie our

3   J. G. Bennett, **Long Pilgrimage**, Dawn Horse Press, 1975, page 26

inner life to time.

Our body, being a material object with a complex set of material processes, is naturally and inextricably bound to time. Events, movements, processes — all that happens happens in time. Our body happens in time. But our inner life is different. We have the possibility of being free of time inwardly. Yet as long as our inner world is dominated by thoughts and emotions, which are events in time, binding our inner life to time, we remain slaves to time.

The more we engage in inner work, the more we come to the reality of other aspects of our inner world, aspects that are free in front of time. We begin to see attention as more fundamental than thoughts or emotions. Attention, though it manifests in time, has its roots outside of time. We begin to see awareness itself as more fundamental than thoughts and emotions. Pure awareness allows us to be outside of time, resting in the timeless. We just are. Whatever happens in time passes through awareness, while awareness abides eternal. We begin to see that when thoughts and emotions occupy the center of our inner world, then each thought is like the tick of a clock, propelling us forward in time, into our daily reality in time, the only reality we believe in.

Not so with attention, with awareness, with presence, which put us in the now. The now is independent of time. Time flows through it, but the now abides timeless. Thoughts flow through our mind. But if we are present nevertheless, if we are being here, then we abide in the now, in the always now. We can call it the Timeless. We can call it Eternity. But whatever we call it, it is the actual, ongoing experience that matters.

We can transcend time by learning to be, to be here in our body, in our mind, in the cognizant stillness beneath our thoughts and emotions. Whenever I am, it is always now. We come into consciousness, which is empty and still and timeless. We come into our attention or into our I, which are also timeless, but timeless in a different way than consciousness. Our I can be in this timeless moment, or can act across time. Examples of the latter include extending our presence from one moment to the next, repeating a particular action daily, like our morning meditation, or by deciding on a task and seeing it through to completion.

For this week, in meditation, come into your fundamental awareness, into consciousness, into your big sky mind, through which thoughts, emotions, and all your sensory perceptions pass. Notice the unchanging, eternal character of consciousness. Be in that. Transcend time, for a few beats of the clock, by being in the timeless. Practice this again and again. And as you do, you will begin to transcend time more, to live less as a slave to time, and more in the refreshing freedom of the timeless.

17.7 Transcending Consciousness

(Transcendence: Part 7)

We live and move and have our being in consciousness, our fundamental awareness. Consciousness is the cognitive screen on which all our sensory perceptions, thoughts, and emotions appear — in short, our entire life plays out within the context of consciousness. In meditation, when everything quiets down, when you are left with pure seeing, pure cognition, peace, and equanimity, with the big sky mind, it is consciousness, the conscious energy in the foreground. This is a very high state, a wonderful state, the milieu of presence. To the extent we become able to live in that big sky mind, our life is transformed.

Some even consider consciousness to be the Divine, to be God. So why speak of transcending consciousness? Is that even possible, given that consciousness is all-pervasive? And even if it were possible, why aim for that?

The first thing to recognize is that consciousness is. It does not act. It does not do anything. It is an energy, an inner territory, albeit refined and ubiquitous. On the other hand, God acts. The Creator creates. So simple logic leads us to infer that consciousness is not the Divine. The first is, while the second does.

Which in turn leads to another question: then what or where is God? Regardless of all our searching, we have not found God within the world of our senses, or within consciousness. If God is not consciousness and God is not within consciousness, a further inference of simple logic implies that God is beyond consciousness. Which in its turn, immediately raises the question of how to transcend consciousness. If we wish to approach God, or open to God, we must confront the problem of transcending consciousness.

We begin by becoming thoroughly familiar with consciousness itself. This is not our ordinary state, for usually we are lost in the contents of consciousness, in all the sensory perceptions, thoughts, and emotions that make up what we know as our life. Consciousness is underneath all that. In quiet meditation, we may come into the big sky mind of cognizant stillness, of the pure awareness that contains all that we know and see and feel. We repeatedly steep ourselves in that, to the point where we can recognize its presence in us at any time, not just in meditation but also in the middle of our busy day. When we well know the taste of consciousness, we can relax back into it at any time.

There is much that enters consciousness. What we recognize is what enters from below consciousness, namely all our sensory impressions, thoughts, mental images, and emotions. All of that comes up from the automatic and sensitive energies into the higher energy of consciousness — that is, in those moments when we are in touch with consciousness. From the side above consciousness, beyond consciousness, other elements enter. One of these is will, which we can most easily recognize in its manifestation as our attention.

So we practice focusing and sustaining our attention to strengthen it, to strengthen our will. As we work with attention, it becomes an obvious force field in our inner world. With robust attention we can reflect it back on itself, to look for where attention comes from. But we see nothing there, for attention and even more so will, do not exist in time and space, and are not part of consciousness, nor contents of consciousness. Rather attention can direct consciousness.

So instead of just looking back there, we move backward within ourselves, backward along the pole of attention. We become our attention, our will. And then we become its source. This is our direction for piercing the veil of consciousness, for coming toward the Sacred realm hidden by our consciousness. If we practice this, if we repeatedly use this method as a means of exploration, gradually we see. We find our way to open to the Sacred through the very core of ourselves. We find our way to transcend consciousness into contact with the realm of Sacred Light, which creates and feeds our being.

18.0 The Levels of No-Self
Introduction

Who am I? We may wonder about that at times, but mostly we feel that we know who we are. Yet if we look carefully at ourselves, who we are becomes a little murky, even confusing. If we look at the whole range of all we do, all we think, and all we feel, our goals and hopes, our likes and dislikes, and if we notice our assumption that "I" am the source, the author of the entire collection, the agent at the core of my life, then we may begin to doubt that assumption of identity, of agency, of a unified self that is who we are. Why? Because there is just too much randomness and too many contradictions in our inner world of thoughts, emotions, urges, hopes and dreams for it all to come from or refer to a single, unified me.

Psychologists today speak of our executive function, the part of our mental makeup that comprises a system of cognitive control, organizing and directing other processes in our mind. For a creative mind and for certain types of meditation, we need to let our executive function temporarily recede into the background; we need to get out of the way. But for a healthy mind, a thriving life, and certain other types of inner work, we need a robust executive function. So perhaps our executive function is who we are, or who we feel ourselves to be, while the rest of our mind, which the executive function may or may not control at any given moment, is not who we are.

Researchers ascribe various aspects of the executive function to particular parts of the brain. But while there may be valid psychological and neurocognitive approaches to the question of who I am, the answers they offer are not ultimately satisfying, because they are striving for objectivity, whereas our experience of who we are is totally subjective, inward. Knowing a label like executive function or knowing that a certain part of our brain has a certain purpose do not really help our personal search for ourselves, much less our search for the

Sacred.

    The Buddha's teaching of anatta, of no-self, can help illumine the subjective mystery. While the teaching of no-self contains layer upon layer of subtlety, the actual experience is direct and simple and liberating. When we first seriously encounter the notion that we do not have a self, we think about it, we apply labels and categories and logic, we consider it from the outside, not from the actual experience. Thinking about not having a self can be frightening, as if what is nearest and dearest to us were going to be taken away by the spiritual work we might embark on. But the reality is not at all like that. What we stand to lose is our illusion about ourselves, about who we are. In exchange, we are relieved of a heavy, lifelong burden that has kept us unnecessarily shackled to the promotion and defense of that illusion. And even further than that, seeing the reality of no-self opens a gateway to the spiritual depths within us.

    Many of our problems derive from the illusion of self. It constrains our happiness and satisfaction. It constrains our relationships. And it constrains our effectiveness in life. There is a telling analogy about this. Consider a substantial rock flying toward a solid object. The impact will do permanent damage. Pieces will fly. If that rock were flying instead toward a body of water, the impact would only create a splash. Then the water would settle down and no trace would be left. If the rock were flying toward air, it would just pass by with nary a whiff. If we go through life like a solid, the stones of life hurt. If we go through life like a liquid, the stones of life ruffle us but we soon settle down. If we go through life like air, the stones of life pass right through and we keep moving. The density of our illusion of self can change from solid to liquid and finally to air, as we deepen our experience of no-self. In the end, we are free.

In the coming weeks we will look at three levels of seeing and understanding the teaching of no-self, three levels of liberation from our mistaken and misguided sense of self. For this week, ask yourself "who am I?" Look at how you view yourself. Look at how your attitude about yourself shapes your approach to life and to other people. Just keep this question before you: who am I?

18.1 Not Personality

(The Levels of No-Self: Part 1)

The first liberation on the way of no-self is freedom in front of our personality. By personality we mean the whole collection of patterns of thought and emotion that dominates our inner world. To be clear, the liberation we seek is not about stopping our thoughts and emotions. They may stop temporarily in certain states, but our particular set of patterns of thought and emotion will be with us as long as we live. Yes, they do change, but they do not stop.

Liberation with regard to our personality means non-identification. We believe our thoughts and emotions define us. We even believe that they are us. That inner voice in our head seems to speak for us, seems to be me. All those emotions that arise from time to time seem to be me, a direct expression of how I feel.

But it is almost entirely automatic patterns. We know that computer programs can be very complex, so much so that they are beginning to approach being able to pass for human, as with Siri and the like. Our mental-emotional programs are even more complex, so complex that they do pass for human, which they are not. What is truly human about us lies deeper than our thoughts and emotions. But the variety and complexity of our mental-emotional programs fool us into believing that they are us, that they define what it means to be human, what it means to be me. In a word, we identify with our thoughts and emotions.

Sometimes it is clear that our thoughts and emotions result from some event in our immediate environment. Then it seems as if we are responding to what happened. At other times the thoughts and emotions seem to arise spontaneously, so that it seems as though we are thinking in a vacuum. But in almost all cases where thinking is not intentional, thoughts are the result of an associative pattern. An event causes a thought reaction. One thought leads to another, and so on, endlessly. And we identify with it.

How does this work? The central culprit is the thought I. Every one of these competing, contradictory thoughts and emotions passing through us claims to be I, simply by producing the thought-sound "I." Whenever there is a thought in us that says "I will do this" or "I want that" or "I hate this," we believe it. We believe it is I that is speaking that inner voice.

But that I is so fragmented that it cannot be our one true self, as it pretends to be. It is so automatic that it cannot be speaking for us. Rather it speaks at us while claiming to be us, claiming to be the one true agent of our life, the decider, the doer, the experiencer. Yet it is just a thought, the thought I. And from all these passing, multifarious I's, we construct our personality, believing it to be a unified whole, a something that is us. That inner voice continually saying I represents for us our personality. But it is not a whole. It is just a large collection of disparate parts masquerading as a whole. It is not who we are.

Intentional thoughts can be different. They may be

speaking for us. They may be an expression of our true I, something we are choosing to think. But even our intentional thoughts are not who we are, just as our intentional physical actions are not who we are. They are just what we choose to do, or think, in that moment. The problem with thoughts is that we believe they are all intentional, that we are somehow choosing to think every thought that passes through our mind. It is not so. The overwhelming majority of our thoughts are not intentional; they are automatic. They arise from associative interactions among our memories, tendencies, reactions, and inner habits. They are most definitely not us. We are not thinking them, they are thinking themselves. In effect, they are thinking us.

So this liberation in front of personality begins with seeing the automatic nature of our thoughts, including the thought I. We begin to see the illusion of I. Meditation certainly helps in this. We see thoughts intruding where they are not called to be. This seems simple and obvious, and it is. But its ramifications are profound, namely that we are not our thoughts, not our inner patterns of thought. And further, we are not our emotions either. What we are is a different matter entirely. But we start with what we are not. We are not our thoughts, emotions, or physical impulses. We are not the thought I. We are not this agglomeration of inner patterns and impulses that we have until now taken be ourselves.

Seeing through the pretense of our personality, of the automatic thoughts saying I, is the first level of realization of no-self. It gives us a remarkable and exhilarating freedom in front of our personality, our automatic thoughts and reactive emotions. We see our thoughts and emotions pretending to be us, and we understand thoroughly, viscerally, that they are not who we are. We no longer have to do battle with difficult thoughts or emotions. We no longer feel constrained to act on our thoughts or emotions, or to reject the inappropriate thoughts and emotions. They are all just thoughts or emotions. We let them come and we let them go of their own accord. We are free. We are free to choose which thoughts and emotions to follow up on and which to ignore.

Until we are free in front of personality, it takes control and our true I stays buried. The tail wags the dog. Yet we need our personality. We need all those patterns of thought and emotion that enable us to navigate the complexities of life. With respect to our emotions, freedom does not mean living a dispassionate life. It means having our passions belong to us, rather than us belonging to our passions. In this newfound freedom, our personality takes its rightful place, that of serving our true self, our I, which we will turn toward in the next part of this inner work series.

For this week, notice your thoughts and emotions. Notice that you are watching them, which shows that you are not them.

18.2 True Self or No-Self?

(The Levels of No-Self: Part 2)

There is a paradox at the core of how the various spiritual ways represent who we really are. Some teach that we have in us a true self, a real I, the one in us who sees what we see, does what we do, and chooses what we choose. Others, most notably the Buddhist way, teach that we have no independent self. How can we reconcile these two views that seem directly opposed to each other: true self or no self?

The easier answer looks at the question in terms of

levels, in particular at our personality that pretends to be our I, as discussed in the previous installment of this inner work series. Our personality is not a self, not our self. So the teaching of no-self is relatively straightforward to apply at that level. This approach to answering the paradox then goes on to say that at the next deeper level, beyond our personality, beyond our character, we find our true self, our real I. And that is true. However, it still leaves us with the paradox: true self versus no-self. Do we just say that the teaching of no-self only holds at the level of exposing our personality as a non-whole, a not-self, and then offers nothing further at the deeper level where we find our true I? That is not a reconciliation of the paradox; it just puts the two teachings into separate boxes.

Let's take a closer look at I, at our true individuality. First, we reiterate that this is not the I of each passing thought, not the self-referential attitudes and reactive emotions, not the I that is the subject of the stories we tell ourselves about ourselves. Rather, when we are not lost in associative thoughts or reactive emotions, our true I is one that sees what we see, does what we do, and chooses what we choose. But because our I is the subject not the object, the experiencer of what we experience, the one that sees what we see, we can never see our I directly. But we can be it.

The simplest way to begin to be our I is to work with attention. When our attention is not passive, not just absorbed into something happening around us, but is directed intentionally, it is our I that is directing our attention. Thus we can find our I in our attention, as our attention. The core practice of this consists of intentionally directing and holding our attention on something and of being the one who is directing our attention. In short, the practice is to be our attention.

Right now I am looking at a computer screen. Perhaps

you are too. The screen is there in my vision. I am putting and holding my attention on the screen. It is almost as if there is a beam of attention going from me, from my I, to the screen. I am at the source of that beam of attention. I am the source of that beam of attention.

That I, my I, seems to come from my core, seems to be my core. As such, at first glance, it seems to be centered in me. But by repeated practice, by living with it, by becoming our I, a different and unexpected picture gradually emerges, namely that our I has no center. It is our center, but in itself has no center.

One approach to understanding this is by looking in terms of dimensions. Setting aside time, the world we live in has three dimensions: up-down, right-left, front-back. Our body is at the center of our experiential, three-dimensional world. And so it seems is our I. It seems that our I is somehow at the center of our body, though we cannot quite place it. And for good reason.

Our I is our will. Will does not exist in time and space. It comes from beyond time and space. It comes from beyond consciousness, as witnessed by the fact that our will, in the form of attention, can direct our consciousness, whereas everything else is within consciousness. So our will, our I, cannot be relegated to a particular point in space, cannot be said to have a center in our three-dimensional sense. Our I comes from a higher space of unimaginable freedom. That is why, in our deepest nature, we are free and pure.

Consider an hourglass, consisting of two bulbs and a neck connecting them. Our I is that neck, whereas will is the sand. The upper glass is an infinite source of will. The lower glass is our personality, where each particle of thought, emotion, and physical impulse claims its own will. The sand passing through the neck is our individual will, our I. To complete this picture, imagine that the upper bulb is infinite and that each human being is a different hourglass neck from the same infinite upper bulb, with each neck going to a separate lower bulb. From this we see that our I, seen from below, does appear to be our center, our core, but seen from above is really an opening to a higher reality, to the world of will.

True self or no-self? It depends on the perspective, as with the two sides of one coin. Below we are separate, above we are not. The One Life flows through us all.

For this week, please practice being your attention, being your I.

18.3 Non-Doing in the Great Self
(The Levels of No-Self: Part 3)

Pure listening is a sacred act. Imagine you are in a conversation with someone. They are speaking. You are listening, just listening. Inwardly you are not reacting or judging or preparing your response or impatiently waiting for an opportunity to jump in and speak. They are speaking and you are listening with full attention. No thoughts or reactive emotions intrude between you and the person to whom you are listening. They feel heard. They feel appreciated for their own intrinsic value. But more than that, if you look carefully into yourself, into who is listening, you may see that the listening is happening through you. Yes, you are the one who is listening, but it is more than you. It is the Sacred listening through you. So if you can just listen purely enough, then the person is being heard not just by you, but by the Sacred. Such listening is an act of love. What a gift for both!

Our usual listening tends to be passive, where we let the other person speak, while we pay attention, but we are also inwardly full of reactions to what we are hearing. Pure listening begins in the wholeness of being. To just listen we need to be able to just be. Here I am. We allow thoughts to come and go. We allow emotions to come and go. We allow all sensory impressions to come and go. And all the while, we just stay here in this moment, in our body, in our mind, in our heart, in this place. We allow it all to be as it is. We are open to our life in this moment, aware of it as a whole. We are. This is the prerequisite for many wonderful things, including the ability to just listen.

Active situations, where we are not just sitting still, seem to be fundamentally different than listening. While that is true outwardly, inwardly it is possible for us to be in the wholeness of being even when outwardly active. We can begin to practice toward that by sensing our body while we are moving, for example while walking. We maintain awareness of our body by expanding our attention to include our entire body as well as our surroundings, as we walk. This act of conscious walking generates energy, enabling us to be. When thoughts arise, we notice them and we stay with the walking. Our body and surroundings engage our full attention. We let our body flow in the walk. Though fully aware, we do not feel: I am walking. There is just walking.

Just walking and pure listening are only two of the countless examples of non-doing in action that are possible for us. Creative endeavors, athletics, cooking, cleaning, making music, dancing, intellectual contemplation, meditation, and prayer are a few more categories of activities that lend themselves to such perfection in action. Their characteristics include active, full engagement of our attention and intention as well as receptivity to qualitative feedback. We make adjustments until the action comes right, and then a harmonizing wholeness allows it to continue without further interference from us.

In one sense we are fully there, fully engaged. In another sense, we are not, our self-referential sense vanishes. We effectively enter a greater Self that is the hallmark of perfection: "thy will be done." We have vanished, stepped aside to participate in a higher will. This is non-doing or true doing, where we connect with the higher and allow the higher to become us. We enter the Great Self of the universe, becoming a particle of the Sacred. We let the Sacred see through our eyes and hear through our ears, and in the case of flowing action, the Sacred acts through our body. Because our sense of separateness has disappeared, we are left in perfect unity.

In the depths of meditative prayer, we let go to open at our core, in a supplication that invites, begs the Sacred to enter our being through that opening in our will. In this most intimate act, there is obviously no room for any self, other than the Great Self, Who works both sides, as the One Who opens and the One Who enters. We take this formulation not as a fantasy or as a notion relevant only to others, but as a prescription for our own deepest inner work. In it, we directly confront the issue of who we are and Who we could be.

For this week, please practice non-doing in action and opening to the Great Self.

19.0 The Way of Wholeness

19.1 Fragmentation

(The Way of Wholeness: Part 1)

The spiritual path is a journey from fragmentation to wholeness, from time to the timeless. Beginning where we are, we look and likely find ourselves in a fragmented moment, in a multitude of processes, loosely connected at best. Here we have the major set of processes we call our thoughts, our emotions, and all that goes on in our body. Then there all the external processes. Our family, where each person has their own ongoing stories, of which we are a part. And each has their hidden depths. There is our job with all its intricacies, requirements, protocols, and people. There is our leisure, our friends, entertainment media, hobbies, and habits. There is our race, ethnicity, religion, and prejudice. There is our politics, our nation, our opinions, our passions, our indifference. There are the endless ongoing tasks of life, personal grooming, caring for our family, cooking, cleaning, and shopping. There is our home and all our possessions with their required care and maintenance, as well the utility and sometimes the joy they bring. There is the past, the present, and the future. All these and more are the fragments of our life.

But fragments, even a multitude of them, do not make a whole. We tend to feel disjointed, careening from one role to another, one task to another, one piece of our life to another. It goes from complex and bewildering to banal and boring, and every emotion in between. Can there be something that ties it all together, something that makes our life a whole rather than this endless series of fragments?

This is not just a psychological issue. Fragmentation is built into the very nature of our world, into time and space. Everything is separate in space: one thing here and another over there. Things do not occupy the same space. Events are separate in time. The gate of time severely limits us. We cannot be in two places at once. We cannot do two things at once, except for the experience-impoverishing effort of multitasking. We are separate from each other and separate from our destiny.

Not only is our life fragmented, both inwardly and outwardly, but we ourselves are not whole. We are missing something, some fundamental connection, some piece of our soul. That lack drives us. We tend to look to externals to fill it: to experiences, to jobs or money, to relationships and family. Such externals matter deeply: to be productive, to feel secure, to have the warmth of love and friendship. But even with all that, something more fundamental remains unsatisfied, unfinished. We yearn for more, for completion, for wholeness in our own being.

We cannot think or plan our way out of this. No mind-trick and no amount of fame or success will resolve our fragmentation, our separation, our lack of wholeness. Because it arises from our own nature and from the nature of our world, the only way toward completeness is to change our nature, to become a different kind of being with a different set of perceptions.

For that we pursue the spiritual path, which we can call the Way of Wholeness. In the coming weeks we will explore further aspects of that Way. For this week, look at the fragmentation of your life. See where you are amidst all that. To see how things are with us, to see what is missing is a major motivation toward the work of self-transformation, self-completion.

19.2 The Wish To Be Whole
(The Way of Wholeness: Part 2)

We might wonder what will enable us to come to a deeper level in our spiritual inner work. The primary answer to that is simple: dogged, intelligent persistence. We need to keep at our inner work practices, drop by drop, day after day, year after year. And we need to notice how things are going with us and adjust accordingly. Staying with our inner work in this way, the drops slowly accumulate to the point where we realize that something fundamental has changed in us. Then we continue our inner work, and further drops accumulate and further fundamental changes come.

That process is not linear. We go up and we come down. When we go up and new inner perceptions appear, it can be thrilling. But at first in each stage we only get a glimpse of the higher level, then we come back down to where we were, and then, by dogged, intelligent persistence, we build toward a more permanent station in that higher level. And then from that new level, the process continues in the same way, glimpsing the next higher, coming back down and then gradually building back up. It requires long persistence, but it does not disappoint, paying dividends all along the way, dividends for ourselves and for those around us.

This raises a basic question: what can be the sources of that necessary persistence? What can motivate us to stay with the Way of Wholeness, through thick and thin, through the ups and the downs, through the days, years, and decades? And how can our motivation increase to the point of urgency?

The first source is where we are coming from: seeing

our state of fragmentation. This leads naturally to recognizing our lack of and need for wholeness. Seeing how fragmented we are with our inchoate thoughts and emotions, how scattered our attention is, how the decisions a part of us makes so often fail to influence the whole of us — all that makes us want to change, makes us seek wholeness.

But the motivations for wholeness stem not just from what we do not want to be: they also come from what want to be. The more our inner work increases the depth of our presence, the wholeness and completeness of our presence, the more we love being present. We value each moment of presence. We see that living in presence is the right way to live. In presence we feel fully human, fully ourselves. As these occasional moments of presence connect with each other, they connect our life on a new level. We come to love presence and that love drives us along the Way of Wholeness. The more presence we experience, the more we love it, and the more we practice it.

As presence grows stronger and deeper, our intuition of its sacredness grows. We feel that in pure presence we are at least on the outskirts of the Divine. We understand the great privilege it is to be able to be and further begin to develop the taste of Who is being when we are, that somehow in simply being we participate in the Divine. Thus awakens our love of the sacred, our understanding of how close the sacred is to us, understanding that we could live in the sacred. And through that love, through our intuition of Whose wholeness we seek, we grow impassioned about our inner work on the Way of Wholeness.

Ultimately, these various sources of our motivation for wholeness combine into a true expression of wholeness, namely wholeheartedness. We become the bearers of a wholehearted wish for completion. But whatever the degree of our wish, we cannot necessarily say it arises from one source or another. We cannot necessarily say why we wish for wholeness. Rather that wish comes out of the depths of who we are, beyond the reach of our awareness. We just know that we need to engage in inner work, that we must, that we do, that we will.

For this week, please cultivate the sources of your wish for wholeness.

19.3 The Sensitive Energies
(The Way of Wholeness: Part 3)

To understand ourselves and to understand how to approach our own spiritual development, we need to understand how we perceive. I am here and aware of seeing these words on this screen. There is subject, I, and object, the screen, the words. What mediates between the two is a particular and important class of psycho-spiritual energies that we call the sensitive energies. They are also known as *prana* in Yoga and *qi* in Taoism.

The current scientific way of looking at visual perception is to consider the eyes, the retina, the optic nerve, and the visual cortex of our brain. But that puts it all into the realm of functional knowledge, of bits of information we can store in books or in memory. For our spiritual development, knowledge can help, but only in a secondary manner. Primary is experience, our own direct experience. And as it happens, that experience contains elements not understood or even approached by science.

So between subject and object of perception, we have these energies. You might object that true spirituality goes beyond subject-object dualism, as is certainly the case. But that belongs to a later stage of the Way. If we try to start there, without being grounded in fundamentals, our experience of those higher states will likely prove both imaginary and fleeting.

So we begin with the energies of sensory perception, the sensitive energies. We not only need to understand them, we need to accumulate, organize, and integrate them into our very being, into our soul. This takes no special aptitude. We are all equipped for this work. We need only make the effort to develop it.

The three types of sensitive energy are associated with perception of our body, our mind, and our emotions. In the body we call the sensitive energy sensation. In the perception of our emotions, we call it feeling or feeling energy, and in the perception of our thoughts, we call it cognitive energy.

To incorporate the subjective experience of our body into our spiritual practice, we become aware of having a body, of being in our body, moment to moment. Take the example of your right hand. Put your attention into your right hand and hold it there. Notice the life in your hand, its visceral aliveness. Staying with that for a couple of minutes, your experience of your hand grows vivid. Now notice the difference between your experience at this moment of your right hand and your left hand. This shows the sensitive energy, the sensation in your right hand. That energy was drawn into your right hand by your attention to that hand.

To incorporate the subjective experience of our mind into our spiritual practice, we intentionally notice our thoughts. We put and hold our attention on our thoughts, on the endless series of thoughts coming and going through our mind. By noticing them, we become aware of their meaning. We see one thought leading to another. We see that we are not driving our thoughts, that we are not usually thinking them. Rather they drive themselves. One thought inspires the next or some random sight or sound sets our thoughts off in a new direction. Usually we are only half aware of the thoughts meandering through our mind. We live surrounded by air, but we normally do not notice the air. Similarly, we live in thoughts but normally do not notice them. Our thoughts think us, drive us, pretend they are us. But when we pay attention to our mind, we bring the cognitive energy to bear, enabling us to be in contact with our thoughts, to see them as just thoughts, to know their meaning. They have their value, but they do not define us.

To incorporate the subjective experience of our emotions into our spiritual practice, we pay attention to them. When we have a strong emotion, our attention is automatically drawn to it. But we can expand the reach of our attention to include the manifestations of the emotion in our body: our facial expressions, posture, gestures, tone of voice, sensations in our chest and solar plexus, and tensions in our shoulders and abdomen. We also open to how the emotion affects our mind, how it drives and colors our thoughts, and how our thoughts feed the emotion. When our emotions are absent or mild, we just bring attention to our chest and solar plexus region, the home of our emotions. If nothing in particular is happening, then we just be there in the emotion of equanimity. In so many of our life events and interactions, a mild emotion of one type or another arises. We open our awareness to that. In all of this, we are working with the sensitive energy of feeling that enables our contact with our emotions, enables us to see our emotions as just emotions. They have their value, but they do not define us.

Why work with these sensitive energies? Doing so makes our life more vivid. Doing so provides us a measure of freedom, as we shall see. And doing so builds our soul, directly. For this week, please work on the sensitive energies in your own being, on becoming more aware of them and accumulating them. This practice proves invaluable both in sitting meditation and whenever we have spare attention as we go about our day.

19.4 Inner Body Wholeness

(The Way of Wholeness: Part 4)

Wholeness manifests the spirit. How? In the deepest realms of the spirit, there are no parts, only the one complete Wholeness. So the quality of wholeness derives from the Ultimate. Any whole on any level links, however tenuously, back to the Great Wholeness. This is why we are so drawn to a panoramic view, to the fullness of an unclouded, unobstructed, unpolluted night sky, to the sight of the full moon or a mountain, to the expanse of the ocean, to individual people and animals in their wholeness. This is why integrity means both whole and ethical, because both qualities derive from the same source.

What about the experience of our own wholeness? Despite all the fragmentation of our thoughts, emotions, and bodily systems and processes, we do at times experience wholeness and we can develop our wholeness further. For that we begin with our body.

Our body is inherently complete on its material, objective level. However, our subjective experience of our body is not unified. Though we receive myriad sensations from our body, those sensations arise in a fragmented way: a pain in some part, sights from the eyes, sounds from the ears, a rumble of hunger in the belly, the contact points with the chair we sit on and the floor we walk on. The experience of wholeness does not come from putting all these pieces together. The experience of wholeness starts from the whole.

Spread your attention throughout your body, to take it all in at once. Let your attention fill and encompass the entire body, forming a complete attention-body. Each separate body-sensation finds its natural place in this whole. Nothing is left out, nothing is extra. To strengthen this, sense your body, your whole body. Staying with that attention to the whole body and the active intention to sense the whole body, the sensation grows. The sensation spreads to every part, smoothing out its strong and weak areas to support the wholeness.

Attention carries other, deeper energies into our body. One, the conscious energy, comes to some extent as a matter of course with the attention. Another higher energy comes through the attention to the extent that we open to that energy. The sensitive energy offers a medium with affinity for attention, which rests easily in sensation. The result of the mixing of these energies is to transform the attention body into a sensation body. Then as we sit or move, we do so with our whole body. We may move only an arm, but as we do we reside in the whole sensation body. So the experience of moving the arm is not separate from the experience of being in the entire sensation body; it is all one whole. We move from the whole.

Perhaps you have practiced sensing parts of your body: hands, or arms, or legs. That is an essential preparation for this rather different work of sensing your whole body. One difference is staying power. You may have noticed the difficulty of keeping up sensing a part of your body as you go about outward activities. The effort seems to divide your attention, with part on the sensation and part on whatever else you are doing. Inevitably, you lose touch with the sensation. But whole-body sensation is different: its inherent integrity gives it greater persistence in time. Instead of dividing your attention, you have one all-encompassing attention. You act from the whole of yourself, without needing to remember to sense your arm or leg. Instead you occupy your whole sensation body and from that you do what you do. You feel complete and at peace and alive.

This is the gift of whole-body sensation: it is the first major step toward living in wholeness. For this week, please practice sensing your whole body.

19.5 Body, Mind, and Heart

(The Way of Wholeness: Part 5)

Whole-body awareness marks the first rung of the ladder of wholeness. Each step up that ladder is like moving outward in a set of Russian dolls, toward ever greater, more encompassing wholeness. To our body wholeness, we now work toward adding mind and heart. Notice that we are not referring to these as thoughts and emotions. Let's take a look at why.

Our mind is filled with thoughts. Each particle of thought represents something stored in memory, perhaps a concrete thing, an event, or some abstraction. These particles combine and recombine in rehashing the past, judging the present, pondering the future, or ruminating over ideas. Nearly all this just happens in automated, preconditioned manner without our intentional direction. To the extent that we identify with them, our thoughts so dominate our inner life that they define and delimit our world, keeping us in their narrow, confined orbit. Being mesmerized by our thoughts is an impoverished way to live.

Our thoughts do not perceive; our mind perceives. We refer to this by saying that our mind sees or cognizes. Of course the principal thing that our mind sees is the stream of thoughts passing through it. The important point is that our mind is not our thoughts, rather it sees our thoughts. When we relax back into our mind, we dis-identify with our thoughts and move beyond thought into just seeing. Thoughts may come and go, but we are here seeing. We do not try to stop our thoughts or engage with them. We let them come and go of their own accord, while we remain in the encompassing cognition of our mind. To help with this, we also abide in whole body sensation, giving us stability in the present, from which to be in our mind and see our thoughts as just thoughts.

In a similar way, our psychological/spiritual heart experiences emotions. This heart is our center of emotions and all the various emotions we have pass through it.
Most of our emotions are in response or reaction to some life event or situation. Some emotions are pleasant and some are unpleasant. We naturally prefer the former to the latter, which leads us into rejecting part of ourselves. Taking this down one level shows that our emotions themselves are mostly about our preferences, what we want and what we don't want, again rejecting part of our life. Much of our emotional life thus divides and separates rather than moving us into wholeness.

If our emotions so dominate our life as to interfere with our functioning, then we need professional psychotherapy, typically talk therapy or prescription drugs or both. That can help bring our emotional life to a range where we can function normally. Whether we start out that way or get to the normal range through psychotherapy, we very likely still have a good deal of work to do in bringing true wholeness to our emotions. At that point, rather than try to reform our emotions, to keep the pleasant and banish the unpleasant, which in any case is not possible, we seek wholeness.

Emotional wholeness means not rejecting the emotions we experience. We honor, respect, and embrace how we are, how we react. Emotional responses are part of our equipment in this life. They give us information that matters. They enable us to act effectively. They enrich our life. But this certainly does not mean we must act on every emotion. They are just as conditioned as our thoughts, set in old and sometimes destructive patterns. So, as with our thoughts, we allow our emotions to come and go, while we remain in our psychological/spiritual heart that feels our emotions. We can be in our heart, even when there are no particular emotions. In that place, we discover our heart of peace, our fundamental equanimity that allows all to be as it is. Then whatever emotions come, they arise in the context of our heart of peace. To help with this, we also remain in whole body sensation, giving us stability in the present from which to be in our heart and feel our emotions as just emotions.

Just as our thoughts pass through our mind, our emotions pass through our heart. And just as beneath our ongoing thoughts, we can remain in our all-seeing mind, so beneath our ongoing emotions, we can abide in our all-feeling heart. In both mind and heart, we rest in non-rejecting, undivided wholeness, an open-armed welcome to ourselves and everything about ourselves. Here we begin to experience the connection between wholeness and love.

Continuing our work on whole body awareness, for this week please add the welcoming, abiding wholeness of mind and heart.

19.6 Conscious Wholeness

(The Way of Wholeness: Part 6)

Each moment of life serves up a stream of impressions, inner and outer. These varied fragments of our life do not constitute a whole, nor do they render us whole. But if we can receive that stream with consciousness, then the consciousness that receives it certainly is a whole.

Why if? Aren't we always conscious, always noticing the impressions of our life? Though it seems that way, this is largely an illusion for two reasons. Firstly, much of the sensory input we receive does not rise to consciousness. Nature gave us this economy of perception to enable our nervous system to function efficiently.

The second reason, though, is more subtle and profound. We confuse and conflate detail with context: Part with whole, sensory awareness with global awareness, sensitive energy with conscious energy. The sensitive energy can bring us vivid contact with the sensory details that make up our life in any given moment. Our senses give us the stuff of life, and this seems to be all the stuff of life. But there is more.

Moments come when our inner world grows quiet. A prime example occurs in meditation when gaps appear between thoughts and we abide in the luxurious stillness of our mind. In those quiet moments, little or no content crosses our mind, just the context of our cognition, our mind knowing its own stillness. In those same moments, our emotions may be quiet as we rest in our psychological/spiritual heart. Again, no emotional content, just the context of our feeling heart. Our body may be relaxed and at ease, giving us the sensory experience of having a body, of hearing what we hear, and seeing what we see. Yet this occurs in the context of our whole body with all its senses alive. Is there something deeper behind all these various ways of seeing and cognizing, behind the surface appearances that make our life?

We have in us a kind of seeing or cognizing that goes beyond seeing with our eyes, beyond cognizing our thoughts or ideas, beyond feeling our emotions. It is the root of all seeing, all cognition. This root of cognition is like the sensor in a camera, receiving all that comes its way. We call it consciousness, a cognitive stillness made of the conscious energy. It has no content of its own and it has no boundary. It is pure awareness. Consciousness sees all, sees our thoughts, emotions and all our senses; every perception arises on the cognitive backdrop of consciousness. Because it opens to all impressions coming to it, because it does not exclude anything, and because it has no boundaries, true consciousness is complete and whole. Indeed, one of its chief qualities is wholeness.

We can and do live without contact with consciousness. But that mode of living immerses us in a two-dimensional life, confined to the surface of what we see, hear, and perceive. In our better moments in that flat world, we intuit an opportunity passing us by. Something is missing. In consciousness, nothing is missing.

To experience consciousness more, the best place to start lies in quiet meditation, allowing our mind to settle into quiescence. The pure awareness that remains is consciousness. It comes to the fore when the stream of our senses slows down. We discover that even in the absence of thought, emotion, sights or sounds, we are still aware. That gives us a taste of consciousness. With that taste, we can aspire to a more conscious life. At any given moment, we can move toward a more contextual awareness. Without giving up contact with the sensory details of our life, in fact enhancing that contact by diminishing our distractedness and identification, we open to the backdrop of awareness, the consciousness that receives all our senses, including thoughts and emotions.

Any time we can relax into the moment, we can open into consciousness. Relaxing into the moment brings us more contact with the contents of awareness, with the sights and sounds, body sensations, thoughts and emotions. All this and more is happening. Relaxing our grip on these particulars, or relaxing the grip that any particulars have on us, we look at our experience in this moment globally, we open to the entire stream of awareness now. The kind of openness that can take in the whole of our immediate experience in this moment, that can look at all of it together, is consciousness. We relax back into that cognitive stillness that underlies, surrounds and permeates everything. Even in the midst of activity and all the many impressions of life, that cognitive stillness is here. Within that stillness, we can be. Within that stillness, life is complete and we are whole.

For this week, please practice opening to the cognitive stillness of consciousness.

19.7 I Am Wholeness: Presence Meditation

(The Way of Wholeness: Part 7)

Luxuriating in the meditative and healing peace of pure awareness after our mind finally quiets down, we are so content that we may be satisfied to return to this daily for years or even decades. But repeatedly experiencing this wholeness of consciousness, the cognizant stillness, we may start to feel that somehow something is missing, that an even greater wholeness remains possible, that consciousness, though wonderful, is not the whole story, that this passivity lacks fire. What is missing is simple: it is our self. There may be consciousness in us, but is there someone here to receive what consciousness brings? Are we here in ourselves actually seeing what we see and hearing what we hear? Is our life a passing spectacle or are we participants on the field? Are we here as the one who is living our life, as the one who we are? Can we truly say "I am?"

This I of ours may seem elusive. We hardly understand what it is, what we are. This is the inherent nature of our I, for our I is our will. We cannot see our I, for our I is the one who sees. We cannot find our I, for our I is the one who looks. The only workable approach is to be our I. How to start?

There is one crucial power in us that we all more or less know. That power is attention. Often our attention is passively drawn here and there, like when watching TV or riding along a stream of self-generating thoughts or daydreams. But the power of attention comes through intentional attention, when we choose where to put our attention and hold it there. Intentional attention may be directed or undirected. We know the directed style, when we intentionally think about a problem, watch the road while driving, speak or listen in conversation, or engage in a sport. Intentional undirected attention occurs for example in mindfulness meditation, when we sit or walk while staying alert to notice whatever impressions come to us, without being carried away by those impressions: we are not passive, we are receptive.

In coming to ourselves, to our I, attention matters because it is a direct manifestation of our will, of our I. When we pay attention, we have the feeling that I am paying attention, that I am directing, steering my attention, that I am my attention. The trouble comes in our tendency to let our attention wobble, to let it wander into passivity. Then we no longer have this feeling of I, we are no longer whole.

I am wholeness means full presence. Our I must be supported and stabilized by our foundation in the sensitive energies, in our body, mind, and heart, which allows our I to penetrate our whole being. Our I must have the breadth of awareness afforded by abiding in consciousness. And finally, our I must engage in the ongoing choice to be.

If, once a day, we can experience full presence, that experience will guide our practice for the rest of the day, serving as a vivid, gold-standard for our inner work as we go about our daily activities. So we make time each day for presence meditation:

Sit comfortably with your back upright in a quiet place where you will not be disturbed. If you do not have a quiet place, consider using the modern marvel of earplugs. If your attention wanders off the meditation, gently bring it back whenever you first notice that.

Begin by relaxing into your body. Become aware of every part of your body. Let your attention penetrate throughout your body, so that you have a perception of your body as a whole. Stay with that for some time.

Begin to be aware of the life in your body, of the vibration of energy pervading your body. Let that perception grow stronger and stay with it.

You need not just be a passive observer of this sensitive energy that enlivens your body and connects you with your body. Let your attention carry your active intention throughout the sensitive energy in your body, your active intention that the sensitive energy grow stronger, more robust. Your intention, your will, you, directly support this energy in your body. It is as if the active force of your will flows from you into your body, enhancing its life, though without causing tensions. The force of will is an inner force. Stay with this.

Let the active force of your will pass from building and supporting the sensitive energy in your body to the active intention to be here, present, and fully aware. Make the active force of your will become the will to be. Here you are: you in your body, you in your heart, you in your mind, you in the cognizant stillness of consciousness. You occupy the whole of your being. Your will to be becomes active as be-ing, making the act of being into an active act, not a passive one. You become the one who is here. You feel: here I am. Stay with that.

For this week, please practice occupying the whole of your being, in full presence, so you are present, so that you feel: here I am, at the center of my life, whole and complete and in touch.

19.8 Living Wholeness

(The Way of Wholeness: Part 8)

Wholeness means that everything fits, everything belongs and has its place. Living wholeness means, in practice, that our days flow without inner obstruction. No longer is our inner life separate from our outer life: it is all of one piece. To live in wholeness means to live in awareness, in the unfragmented energy of consciousness. Behind all activity and occurrences, our life flows in peace. A current of spacious inner stillness accompanies all we do and experience. And we do not miss chunks of our day, of our life; we live it. Living in wholeness means living in presence, with a wide open, relaxed awareness that takes in everything around us and everything inside us.

Starting the day with a period of meditation that puts us in state of wholeness is the single most effective action we can take toward living in wholeness. A morning sitting sets up our entire day. We put ourselves into contact with our wish to be whole, into contact with our body, mind, and heart. We put ourselves into the cognizant stillness behind all our perceptions. And we emerge from the meditation in a state of wholeness, which we then have an opportunity to carry into our day. The sitting not only helps us have the inner peace to be present, but also the strength to meet, accept, and respond to whatever comes our way. For wholeness is not just about all the things we like about our life. Wholeness is all-inclusive and does not turn away from or reject the unavoidable experiences we wish were otherwise. That takes peace and strength.

Throughout our day we return to the inner work of wholeness. Because we start from the whole, we do not have the tension that arises so readily from partial inner efforts. We return in peace to ourselves, to our life, to our awareness. We no longer need spare attention to split between being aware of ourselves and doing what we are doing. It is all one whole. We are here in our body, heart, mind, and consciousness, and we are intentionally doing what we are doing. Being more conscious enables us to be more conscientious, the inner raises the outer. Whenever we fall or fail outwardly, even in a small way, we let that remind us to be present and whole. If we stub our toe because we were not paying attention, we take that as a reminder to pay more attention, to come back to presence right then.

Living wholeness brings the timeless to time. Our entire day becomes one large moment that we flow through, that we breathe inside of: a rich, timeless moment. We understand and appreciate the privilege of being alive. Our self-centeredness fades in the greatness of each day.

For this week, please open to spacious living, to living wholeness.

19.9 Sacred Wholeness
(The Way of Wholeness: Part 9)

Behind everything there is a sacred mountain of purpose, the unfathomable will of the world. This Divine Will is the source of all and the source of the unity of all. Its inherent wholeness suffuses itself throughout the universe and all its parts. This includes us, specifically our body and our I. Wholeness, emanating from the Divine Will and passing into our body and our I, is the source of the remarkable power of spiritual inner work. In the usual way of life, we have only superficial and intermittent contact with our body or our I. When we practice whole body sensation, we touch the sacred. When we work with attention and more particularly when we become our attention, when we become the source of our attention, we come into our I, our will, which flows from the sacred wholeness of the world.

Through this I of ours, we have a direct connection to the source of all. Yet we so rarely exercise that connection. Indeed, we block the flow by standing in the middle of that channel with our back to the source, unseeing and unhearing of anything that might be behind us and deeper. We presume to be our own source. This is called egoism. But we can drop that, at least temporarily.

Sometimes though, if intentional and conscious, standing in the middle of the channel with our back to the source is not egoism, but rather one style and level of inner work. This is "I am." We are here in our center, facing and fully embracing all our parts within the wholeness of our I. We occupy the whole of our being. This is deep and valuable practice, as through it we become fully ourselves. When we are fully ourselves, we have something of great value to bring to the sacred, namely our I.

When we open our I to the sacred, to the channel behind us, where the flow of the higher will comes down to and through us, we go beyond the practice of "I am" to the practice of "the sacred is." No longer can we say I, as we have entered a state that transcends our personal individuality.

As with "I am" this sacred, higher will has both active and receptive modes, while its essential reality supersedes those categories. It can be the timelessness of just being, just seeing. But in that case, it is the sacred that is being and seeing in us, through us. It can also be an active, dynamic, affirming presence, sourcing action, and cascading higher energies into us. In this mode, though, it is not just our presence, but rather a pure, sacred presence that subsumes and transcends our personal presence. It has no center, for it transcends space, both inwardly and outwardly.

How to come to this, an inner action that can hardly be described in words? But words are our medium right now, so... It involves first becoming fully present, fully here, awake and centered in ourselves, at least for a moment. And then looking to see that our very occupation of our center and our outward facing orientation from our center can both give way. We inwardly turn around, facing back toward what is even more inward than we are. At the same time we open to the flow of will and energy from there, from the higher, more inward side, opposite the direction we usually face. Opening to the higher, that is the practice of "the sacred is." And we do practice this daily, perhaps more than once a day. A propitious moment for this practice occurs at the end of our morning meditation, when we are more centered, more collected, less distracted. We give our best to the practice of "the sacred is." It is our prayer.

For this week, please practice sacred wholeness.

20.0 The Way of Integrity
(Introduction)

Every religion and spiritual path emphasizes the importance of morality, usually putting forward sets of rules and laws to specify what is or is not moral. On the surface this appears to be just a way of organizing a society that works well for its members. We all depend on that in many ways, which only become obvious when some lose their moral constraints. There are also deeper spiritual reasons for adopting a moral mode of living, for example the religions' promise that our entry to heaven will be more likely if we live a moral life. In this inner work series on The Way of Integrity, we will explore the spiritual motivations for morality and, more generally, for integrity.

Consider how integrity relates to morality. We could say that integrity subsumes morality and goes beyond it. The actions of a person of integrity certainly comply with the moral and legal norms of their society. But the person of integrity hews to a higher standard, that of conscience, which though seemingly personal is more than personal. Conscience is how the sacred speaks to us. And its inherent standard is love.

Between morality and conscience, nature guides us toward right action by its law of cause and effect, also known as karma or reaping what you sow. As one effect, integrity affords a person great inner freedom, enjoying the respect and trust of society, unburdened by a guilty or murky conscience, unafraid of being revealed as dishonest or self-serving. Integrity yields clarity, as many potential courses of action take little or no consideration: either they are rejected out of hand as wrong or pursued as right.

Nevertheless, dilemmas arise in the gray areas and in extending the reach of integrity. Both cause struggles. Do we keep our word when circumstances change? Do we extend integrity to actions that only affect us and no one else, such as healthy and unhealthy personal habits? How do we act when no one is watching? Do we drop our standards and principles when alone? Do we intentionally think things we would never actually say or do? These and similar issues relate to our self-respect and our respect for life, further components of integrity.

The purification that integrity brings gives us inner peace and opens doors to the sacred, doors that would otherwise stay closed. It is no accident that the Prophet Mohammed was known as The Trustworthy, for the integrity with which he managed caravans in his early career. This aspect of his character must have been a factor in later enabling him to serve the sacred as founder of one of the world's great religions.

No baggage can pass through the gate of heaven. As long as we carry the propensity for actions that lack integrity, as long as self-centered motivations and egoism rule or even lurk in us, the gate remains barred. This is not to say that purity of will suffices. Deepening of our being is also required. But the Way of Integrity does purify us.

With good reason, integrity also means unity. As long as we harbor and give voice to the many competing urges and desires in us, our actions may fall short of the standard of integrity. The unification brought by inner work: Particularly by the long practice of presence, moves us toward the unity we need to consistently and reliably act in accord with conscience.

For this week, please look at where you currently stand on the scale of integrity.

20.1 Wobbling on the Way
(The Way of Integrity: Part 1)

If we want to follow the Way of Integrity, we need to examine the forces at work in us against integrity. What drives us to do what we know we should not do or fail to do what we know we should do? How we know what we should or should not do, we leave for a later part of this series. For now, we look at the common experience of knowing that an action is wrong, knowing that we will regret it, and then doing it anyway. So why do we do what we know in advance that we will regret?

The particular sets of forces at work against integrity vary from person to person. They might include the seven deadly sins: lust, gluttony, greed, laziness, anger, envy, and pride. To these we can add common variations such as arrogance, jealousy, vanity, apathy, egoism, group egoism, misguided principles, and other desires and attachments.

Coupled to these forces, we have enabling factors that ease us into violations of our integrity. Two such factors stand out. First, we might believe that integrity itself does not matter, that we can do as some force in us pleases, without repercussions. Second, we might believe that if no one else sees or knows what we are doing, then such private acts against integrity do not matter. If we are not going to get caught, then why not do what is expedient or desirable, even if wrong, or shirk our duty and fail to do what is right?

Another anti-integrity enabling factor is having a limited view of repercussions. Several different kinds of such limitations apply. We may not reckon how the smallest thing we do, when multiplied by the billions of people who might also do the same thing, can have enormous impacts on our planet. We may not reckon how what we do now might have profound effects on our own or others' future.

We may not reckon how what we do externally will affect us inwardly. For example, failing to do what's healthy for our body or failing to avoid what's unhealthy, may, and often does, affect our inner energies and our spiritual practice. Also, we may not understand that acts against our conscience create a barrier between us and our deeper nature.

Then there is the hedonic treadmill. We seek happiness, personal happiness, by trying to get more of what we want. But the more we get, the quicker our satisfaction wanes, and the more our desires multiply. So we never quite arrive at happiness this way. Rather it condemns us to endlessly seeking external fulfillment. This desire-driven treadmill can lead us to look the other way whenever integrity raises objections. And the more we look away from integrity, the weaker its voice becomes.

All of this pushes us to wobble on the way of integrity. For this week, please look at whether and how the anti-integrity forces work in you.

20.2 Lessons of Karma

(The Way of Integrity: Part 2)

Now we turn to looking at how and why integrity matters. We begin with a particular and relatively external view, namely that of karma, or reaping what you sow. A straightforward cause and effect action applies, though the effects can sometimes be long removed from the causes and therefore hard to recognize. Yet many are easy to see. If we do not take good care of our body, we will suffer the physical consequences sooner or later. If we do not treat our friends well, we will lose our friends. If we deal dishonestly in business matters, no one will trust us. If we cheat on our spouse, we will end up without a spouse.

All that seems obvious; the causal connections are evident. Yet karma also concerns the not-so-obvious effects of morality and its lack. Greed invites greed. Anger invites anger toward us. Cheating gets us cheated. Lying gets us lied to. It takes time, and long observation of the results of our moral lapses, to learn the lesson of cause and effect, to take it to heart enough that it begins to moderate our behavior and thereby raise the level of our integrity.

We can ask whether integrity based on fear of the consequences of bad behavior is truly integrity, given that it arises from a self-centered motivation. At least from a functional perspective, though, it works. Eventually we want the deeper integrity based on higher motivations. But as a starting point, fear of consequences is a notch up from self-centered, desire-driven actions, and thus moves us in the right direction.

On the flip side, if we sow positive actions, we reap positive benefits. Generosity is a case in point. The result of an act of generosity is usually that we feel good about our actions and about ourselves, and we benefit the recipient of the generosity. If we are generous, the law of karma teaches that others and the universe will be generous toward us.

However, what if we give mainly in order to feel good or to attract generosity, and not so much to do good? Here the key factor of karma comes in, namely intention. The nature of our intentions in what we do shapes our karma. If we have positive, selfless intentions, the effects will generally be positive. If we are generous in order to feel good, then we have our reward and no further benefits accrue to us.

But as the saying goes, good intentions are not enough. Here another key factor of karma (and integrity) enters: responsibility. This entails knowing our capabilities and limits, and doing what we can and should, as needed, and as the appropriate situation and opportunity arises. Good intentions driving responsible actions form the high road to positive effects, to good karma.

The causal connection between living an unhealthy lifestyle and the resulting health problems seems clear. But the law of karma also teaches that if, for example, we cheat, and even if no one else knows we cheat, then sooner or later we will be cheated to a similar degree. If that is true, then it must be due to some mechanism buried deep in the structure of how the universe works, a mechanism we call karma.

Perhaps this is not so surprising, if we consider that another name for the law of karma is justice. We expect the universe to be just. We know that our lives are full of uncertainty and we may wonder how the universe determines which of its many possibilities to manifest to us. We hope and feel it is not just random, that there is justice, that there is karma, that what happens to us is somehow meant for us, that how we live matters.

But is it true? Does our being really attract our life? This then is part of our inner work: to notice the results of our actions and attitudes, both short-term and long, and to learn from what we notice. Certainly that can help us live with more intelligence, with more compassion, and with more integrity.

20.3 Respecting Ourselves

(The Way of Integrity: Part 3)

What do we respect in ourselves? The self-centered ego driven by greed and anger and all manner of petty desires and fears? Or the one in us who is centered in our higher nature, who pursues our fulfilling passions, nurtures our friendships and family, and can be trusted to do the right thing? Though we may often succumb to our desires and small fears, we generally do not respect those aspects of ourselves. Perhaps surprisingly, though, the way toward integrity involves respecting every aspect, every force in us, including those we should not and do not act on. If we do not respect ourselves, we are inherently divided, and lack integrity in the sense of wholeness. Self-respect is the glue that holds our integrity together.

But to put further nuance to this notion, self-respect need not lack discrimination. While we respect our body and all parts of our personality and character, we need not respect our actions, if they do not accord with integrity. By respecting our actions when we do the right thing, we promote those actions in ourselves. So respect can be a force for integrity and for action based on integrity. We do not want to feel ashamed of ourselves. We want to earn and merit our own respect, to be at peace with who we are and what we do. So we aim to act in a way that we can respect.

Yet a great part of our makeup lies beyond our control. We have only limited influence on our body. We are given this body with its genetic strengths and weaknesses. Do we reject our body, or parts of it? Or do we embrace the whole of it with full respect, even the aspects we do not like? Respecting our body leads us to take proper care of it and to inhabit it more, by way of sensing. In this way, our body becomes part of our integrity.

We have limited influence on our emotions. If we are anxious or depressed, especially if chronically so, do we reject this aspect of ourselves, and thereby heap another emotional wound on top of the underlying issue? Rather than rejecting how things are with us, if we can find compassion and respect for our emotions, we can feel whole, even if not perfect.

On the other side, self-respect does not mean arrogance; it works best with humility. Self-respect leaves room for self-improvement. Instead of trying to escape from or hide our shortcomings, we simply seek to improve, not out of self-rejection, but rather to become more completely ourselves. If we can forgo the inner war against ourselves, we can have much more energy and attention for what matters beyond ourselves: for our family, for our community, and for the Sacred.

Notice also that self-respect neither demands nor needs the respect of others. Nevertheless, others will tend to respect us, if we respect ourselves and act with integrity. Conversely, the more we respect ourselves, the more we will respect others, because ultimately what we respect in ourselves is the same as what we respect in others.

There is something very precious deep within us. The part of us that is capable of having an attitude of respect comes from what is most sacred in us. So by respecting ourselves, we invite our deeper nature to penetrate toward our surface. We connect with what is deepest in us. That is what we respect and that is what respects us. This mutual connection evokes clarity in the face of uncertainty and peace in our heart.

For this week, please notice the ways in which you do and do not respect yourself. Can you shift toward more self-respect?

20.4 Our Word

(The Way of Integrity: Part 4)

What we say matters, often as a direct expression of our integrity or lack thereof. We do not hear malicious gossip or harmful tales from people of integrity. We do not hear lies from people of integrity, though depending on the situation, they may refrain from stating hurtful truths. And above all, we do not hear empty promises from people of integrity. If they give us their word that they will do something, we can count on them to follow through and do it. To speak with integrity is certainly part of spiritual practice.

These same issues also apply inwardly, in our thoughts. Most of our thoughts are automatic, with no conscious intention behind them. They are just reactions to external events, emotions, or to other thoughts. Automatic thoughts in themselves do not impact our integrity, although if we believe them or act on them, they can have a dramatic impact. Intentional thoughts do matter, because they are our actions, albeit inward actions. Do we inwardly nurture malicious gossip or harmful tales? Do we tell ourselves lies, pretending they are true? Do we make empty promises to ourselves, promises that we fail to keep?

For our integrity to be whole, what we do inwardly must correspond to what we do outwardly and spring from ethical, kind, and forthright attitudes. We may believe we can hide our views and inward actions from others, but we cannot hide from ourselves. If we consciously and intentionally harbor attitudes of greed or hatred or shirking, then integrity can have no foundation in us. Inner integrity is the basis of outer integrity.

When we give our word that we will do something, that promise and our actions surrounding it define us. If we are to be ourselves, then we must keep our word. Otherwise, we are not anything; in a real sense, we do not even exist. If given automatically and without conscious intention, the promise has no one standing behind it. But a promise not only defines us, it can create us. When we say "I promise ...," it means something only if we are there saying it with intention. By consciously making the promise and fulfilling it, we assert our individuality, our reality, our I. An empty promise means an empty self. A real promise means a real Self. This is the spiritual reality underlying the giving of one's word.

What to do? If we never give our word, we will never break a promise. Yet this also fails to assert our I and it shirks what we need to do. So instead we are careful about what we say we will do. We only give our word with our full intention and ability to keep it. We take our word as seriously as we take our very existence. When we make a promise, we first make sure that we are actually there, present and choosing to make that promise. And then we make sure to fulfill it.

One requirement for speaking with integrity is to speak with awareness and purpose. Do we allow words to fall out of our mouth without paying much attention to what we are saying? That can lead to foot-in-mouth syndrome. At the very least, automatic talking can use up energy that could be put toward our inner work, toward our being. The second part of this is whether we talk just to take up conversational space or do we mean what we say, do we intend to say what we say? Intentions that spring from integrity usually give positive results in speech. A lack of intention, gives unpredictable and scattered speech. So in bringing our word into our spiritual path, we practice speaking with attention as well as intention deriving from integrity.

Though we may speak with attention and intention, it is no part of integrity to dominate a conversation with talk about our self and no interest in the other person or people we are talking at. That is not really a conversation. It has no give and take. Integrity understands that others matter as much as we do. Yes, we can fake an interest in the other person, and that may be a positive step in the direction away from our self-centeredness, but it still falls short of genuinely sharing our time and valuation with others.

None of the forgoing means that spiritual practice requires us to be serious in everything we say. On the contrary, our intention in speaking may be simply to enjoy the camaraderie of our friends, maybe even to say something funny. But it does mean that we aim always to be aware of what we are saying and the context surrounding it.

For this week, please look at the degree to which you keep your word and the degree to which you speak with attention and intention connected to your integrity.

20.5 The Voice of Conscience
(The Way of Integrity: Part 5)

How do we know what to do and what not to do? Of course, we stay within the laws of the society we live in and within its moral norms. And of course, we tend to our various constraints and responsibilities: working to earn our living, caring for our body, our family, and what our society needs from us. All that can be a lot, but still it leaves us enormous freedom of action, both within all those boundaries, such as in our choice of careers and in the quality we bring to our responsibilities, as well as in the areas not as constrained by the boundaries, like how we spend our spare time and how we deal with moral dilemmas. What we do with all that freedom defines our life.

A great deal of understanding what to do and what not to do comes from experience, from trial and error and watching other people's trials and errors. We learn what level of quality each of our duties and tasks calls for and how to produce that efficiently. We learn to manage our body, its needs, its appetites, quirks and limitations. We learn how to relate to the people in our life. We learn to manage our finances. One beauty of life is that all the learning never stops, even with regard to what is necessary. Situations change. We experiment and find better approaches.

But beyond the duties thrust upon us by the facts of our life, things are not as clear. Yes, we can do what we enjoy. And for many aspects of life the criterion of enjoyment is both appropriate and sufficient. We do what we like and avoid what we do not like. But these long-ingrained habitual patterns of likes and dislikes can themselves circumscribe our life. Is it really freedom to do what we like and avoid what we do not like? Or is it an inner slavery constraining us to live by our old patterns?

What is truly satisfying? One source is the satisfaction that comes from doing something well, from pursuing excellence. This can even be in mundane tasks like cleaning or doing the dishes. We go beyond the minimum required of us to move toward perfection. Many of the activities of our life, from home to place of work, can be candidates for excellence. When we look back at having done something well, really well, or at least having given the task our full attention and effort, we feel a kind of productive competence and purity, a clear conscience that is satisfying at a deep level. One reason this matters is that it teaches us the taste of conscience, when conscience is telling us the rightness of an action.

Another source of satisfaction is service, being useful for someone or something beyond ourselves. There are no boundaries to the forms this can take, but it generally builds on the golden rule of treating others the way you would have them treat you. To know that you have done something that helps someone brings a deep satisfaction; it even goes beyond satisfaction to impart meaning to our life.

It can happen that we want to do something, but a part of us knows or feels that we should not. That latter knowing, feeling, intuition may well be the voice of our conscience. It does not force us to follow it. And it is not a voice of doubt; it is the voice of truth. It offers us truth and leaves it up to us whether to act according to that truth. If we do not, and if we persist in ignoring the truth of conscience, its voice recedes and stops troubling us. But in that we case we lose what is most precious, namely ourselves, because the voice of conscience is the voice of our higher self.

So if we find ourselves wondering what to do, what choice to make, and if it is a decision with some consequence, we take the time to think about it from various viewpoints. We consider the relevant knowledge we have and how we feel about the choice. And then we look beyond, beneath our thinking and feeling, to open to the truth that is there in us. We know that truth. Our conscience knows it. That truth always has the quality of self-evident rightness about it. That inner eye of conscience is there in us. We need only open to it and accept it. We know truth.

Yes, we may be uncertain about what our conscience is telling us. So we perform reality checks. Does its prompting accord with the laws and norms of our society? Does it make sense? Is it kind? Gradually we learn to trust it, to trust ourselves. Purification follows in its wake.

For this week, please practice being open to your conscience, the truth that is you.

20.6 Having Principles

(The Way of Integrity: Part 6)

To have clear, internalized moral principles is to have a well-functioning rudder in life. This goes beyond the compass of conscience, which shows us the right thing to do. And it goes beyond the values that inform our inner world. Having principles means being able to act in accord with conscience and with our values; it means having a rudder that works. Our principles, to be effective, not only need to be acceptable to our conscience and reflective of our personal values, but also be cleanly in accord with the moral norms and laws of our society. Examples of norms include the Ten Commandments and the

Golden Rule.

This does not mean that we need to have a set of rules memorized. A person of integrity might not be readily able to articulate his or her principles of living. But those principles shine through that person's actions, because they are embedded in their fundamental attitudes toward life. Immoral and unethical thoughts may well arise, but they do not get translated into action because they do not pass the filter formed by the life principles of integrity. People of integrity can trust themselves. They need not be permanently on guard to do the right thing and avoid the rest. Rather, it comes naturally and easily.

But what if that does not describe us, as we currently are? What if we are morally challenged from time to time, tottering on the brink, and sometimes even falling? We suspect that even people of great integrity find themselves on the edge of a moral challenge at times. Temptations attack us all. If we have principles to fall back on, even if they are not firmly established, they help us let the temptations pass without succumbing to their siren song, without taking the attractive and easy, but unethical way. If we can relax back into our core, beneath the level that is tempted toward a moral lapse, we can come back to our innate purity, to the stillness of our mind and heart.

Many temptations come through the mechanism of our likes and dislikes, our desires and antipathies. We have bodily desires that, if given free rein, end in one of the myriad forms of addiction. But well short of addiction, we have work to do. For example, do we control our food intake enough to keep our body healthy? Can we relax in front of our cravings with the help of principles like "enough is enough" and by respecting our body to the point of doing what we can to keep it healthy, such as not overeating?

We have mental and emotional desires. Do we indulge thoughts antithetical to our principles? When we notice such thoughts, can we let them go, can we change the inner subject? Do we indulge emotions that drive us toward actions against our principles? When we notice such emotions, can we relax and let them subside, or can we at least refrain from acting under that influence and just ride out the storm? With perseverance, we grow stronger, more able to withstand temptations. Impulses that gave us trouble, no longer touch us. New temptations arise, but we have a practiced approach to dealing with them, to maintaining ourselves and our integrity.

Throughout our work to live a principled life and to rise above temptation, we have the remarkable tools of spiritual presence to help us. When we feel drawn toward to something we should not do, we can shift our attention to our inner work, for example to awareness of and contact with our body, with our sensation. Moving into our body in this way can raise our inner state above the temptation.

We can ride our principles to a guileless attitude to life and to people, an approach that leaves us inwardly free and thus able to experience the natural joy of living, our birthright. Living by principles declutters us: we do not need to remember lies we do not tell. We do not need to strategize ways to cheat or to avoid getting caught. We do not need to hide our actions and attitudes when there is nothing that needs hiding. We do not need to seek forgiveness for things we did not do.

For this week, please notice your own temptations. Notice also your own moral rudder and work to strengthen it.

20.7 Non-Desires

(The Way of Integrity: Part 7)

As long as we live in the mode of acquiescing to our desires and antipathies, to being unquestioningly driven by attachments and habits, by what we want and do not want, then our integrity remains at risk. Desires and antipathies generally do not care about doing the right thing. Those aspects of our psyche seek only their own satisfaction. Altruistic motivations and the promptings of conscience have little chance against the emotional power of desires. So here we are, time and again finding ourselves acting in ways we had intended not to act, doing what our desires want but not necessarily what we wish.

The resulting chaos can easily compromise our inner or outer integrity. By inner integrity, we mean the unity, clarity, and purity of our inner life, both in being and in inner actions, such as our intentional thoughts. By outer integrity, we refer to the quality of our actions in the world. Our inner integrity shapes our outer integrity.

So the tragedy of living a life driven by desires and antipathies is two-fold. Neither we ourselves, nor other people, can count on us to do the right thing, so tenuous is our outer integrity. With regard to our inner life, this conflicting mass of desires and antipathies leaves us no peace. We live continually in the hunt for the next satisfaction, which is all too fleeting. Before we have even swallowed that first bite of cake, we are looking toward the second bite.

The answer lies within us, in the realm of non-desire and non-clinging, the place of peace and equanimity. We all have that. Just beneath our thoughts, there is stillness. When we can drop down into that layer of our being, we leave desires and antipathies floating at the surface. They no longer have the same hold on us. We can breathe in peace. We can live in contentment. Instead of the desperate hunt being continuous, uncaused satisfaction becomes continuous.

To move toward that way of life, we can train ourselves to recognize and rest in the peace of pure consciousness. The classical and highly effective method of that training is through meditation. The effects grow exponentially. If we can sit in meditation for five minutes a day, that helps. Twenty minutes helps much more. An hour of meditation, though it may start with cascades of thoughts and fidgeting, tends to end with us soaking in peace, resting in the pure awareness that is whole and complete. Desires and antipathies come from a false incompleteness, as if we need something from outside to fill ourselves. That is the surface of our being. Beneath the surface, we already have all that we need. Simply being here is enough. Meditation trains us to live that way.

Sometimes we may teeter on the edge of acting in accord with a desire, as opposed to how our conscience or our more essential wishes and goals would have us act. This tends to fall toward the side of desires. But a time comes when the growing peace and equanimity within us reaches a profound enough level that we prefer that timeless state of pure being to the short-lived state of desire satisfaction.

This does not mean we live an ascetic life, forgoing all our likes and dislikes. But it does mean that our likes and dislikes come into their proper role, that of providing information about our relationship to the world, rather than driving us and keeping us on the surface of our being. It also does not preclude us from vigorous action in the world, in accord with our essential wishes, goals, responsibilities, and conscience. We can find peace in being and in action. We can be while we act.

For this week, please work to move toward non-desire, toward equanimity and peace.

20.8 Responsibility

(The Way of Integrity: Part 8)

We can imagine a person of integrity who is not a responsible person, in the sense of sometimes forgetting or neglecting or just failing to do what is required. Perhaps you know someone like that. Someone that you trust but cannot count on. Maybe that person is scattered or forgetful, but completely honest and principled. We might consider that person to have integrity, but with responsibility lacking, their integrity is not complete. Maybe we ourselves are like that in some respects.

We know that responsibility means doing what is required of us, without fail. We do our duty, our allotted tasks in life, whether small or large, mundane or magnificent. It all matters. If we have too many duties and cannot get them all done, we prioritize and cut back on what we agree to do.

Responsibilities and duties fall into three broad categories: duties to self, to society (including family and the biosphere), and to the Sacred. Although only the last category is explicitly spiritual, all categories of responsibility are fundamentally spiritual. Responsibilities give us purpose. Purpose derives from the Divine Will, which is the Purpose behind the universe. That Great Purpose imposes obligations on us. So for example, our duty to wash the dishes restores order to a small corner of the universe. The Great Purpose behind the universe appears to have something to do with the creation and maintenance of order, on all its possible scales. Another side of the Great Purpose appears to have something to do with love and compassion. Between the obligations to create and maintain order and to be loving and compassionate, our life unfolds and our responsibilities arise. The important point here is that because our obligations derive from the Divine Will, we can align ourselves with that Will, we can participate in that Will, we can allow that Will to participate in us, by being responsible.

What this means in terms of our duties to self and society we discover through the examples of people we respect, and through trial and error. What it means in terms of our spiritual duties is not so readily accessible to us. We can follow our family religion, its customs, practices, and rules. For many, that is enough and satisfies their spiritual responsibilities. For others, religion is not enough. Those do not need to leave their religion. Instead they seek religion plus, which in turn gives more meaning to and deepens their religious practices.

A person who persistently practices meditation and presence, for example, brings more clarity and better functioning into their inner life. When that person then goes to pray, in the way of their religion, their heart is more available to embrace the prayer, their attention can focus their mind and heart on the prayer, and they can pray with the whole of their being.

Yet what does this have to do with responsibility? It is not just that we are obliged to bring order to our inner life and compassion into our actions, important though that may be. Through our inner work, whether meditation, presence, or prayer, we produce a spiritual energy that serves the Sacred. Moreover, the quality or level of that energy depends on the depth of our inner work, which in turn depends on the level of our being. Not only that, but our will grows in its quality and alignment with the Sacred. The more we practice, the deeper our practice and our prayer can be, and the more useful we are, in a direct way, to the Sacred. This is a key part of why we are here, what we are made for.

By responsibly fulfilling our obligations, on all levels, we fulfill ourselves. For this week, please look at your own response to responsibilities.

20.9 Purity

(The Way of Integrity: Part 9)

We all grow up with an ego. Evolution probably put this into us as way of increasing our survival rate and the number of offspring we have. The life force in our body imposes an imperative to survive. To serve that imperative, our fabulously complex mind and emotions construct an edifice that we call ourselves. This construction is an intricate pattern of thoughts and emotions centered on the notion that I am here, separate from everyone and everything else. That is after all exactly the case for our body. Even though we depend on other people and this planet to maintain the life of our body, that dependence does not overcome the appearance of separateness, the fact that our body stops at our skin. We think as follows: this is my body, my clothes, my home, my car, my spouse, my opinion, my resume, my bank account, and so on forever. We implicitly and unquestioningly assume that the "my" in those thoughts refers to the real me and that this real me is not just my body, but is my I. This assumed entity at the center of the construction is our ego.

All that would be fine, except that it causes endless problems. In society, ego leads to crime, cruelty, and war. In our spiritual nature, ego blocks the channel between us and the Divine, preventing our true self, our true I from living and thriving in us.

The whole construction of our ego is a false one. The

fact that we say or think the word *me*, does not mean that there really is a *me*, unless we take our body as me, which we do not. We think this is my body, as if there is a *me* that resides in and owns this body. As soon as we start to actually look for this me of ours, we realize that we cannot find it. That is because it does not exist. I can direct my thoughts, so I am not my thoughts. I can to some extent manage my emotions, so I am not my emotions. I can direct my body, so I am not my body. I am not the patterns in my body, mind, or emotions.

If I am none of that, then who or what am I? We generally do not even look at that question. We just assume that I am what my thoughts refer to, what my emotions revolve around. That, however, is our ego and it focuses us on ourselves, on the endless and fruitless task of building and defending our itself.

So if ego does not really exist, how does it block our channel to the Divine? How does it keep our true I from living in us? Put simply, it distracts us. Ego orients us toward externals. When we do look inward, we do it superficially, stopping at our thoughts and reactive emotions. By meditation, presence, and contemplative prayer, we learn to set aside our self-centeredness, set aside our external and superficial orientation, and connect with our deeper nature, with our true I, and with the Sacred. This process purifies us, gradually curing us of seeing everything in terms of our ego desires. Our engagement with the world can then take on a different tone. We treat others as equals, as just as important as we are. We may even begin to see others as not separate from us.

The diminishing of our self-centered fixations is part of the process of purification. Another part resides in our increasing attraction to and devotion to the Higher. Together, these two forces open our channel to the Divine, one acting from below and the other from above. Purity means having that channel open. To some extent we can recognize this in people who do not act from self-interest.

How do we work toward purity? One way is by paying attention to and always acting in accord with the promptings of our conscience. This can be hard. It requires us to be honest with ourselves and sometimes to do things we would rather not do or refrain from things we want to do. Conscience is our eye for truth: Particularly about ourselves. Whether they harm others or ourselves, actions against our conscience burden us, clouding our hopes for purification.

Another way toward purity runs through the type of meditation that involves non-doing: just sitting and letting our inner experience unfold without trying to shape it. This trains us to forgo our desire to control, which often comes from our ego.

Gradually, through purification, we put down the enormous burden of building up and defending our ego. We can breathe freely and relax into life. We live our reality, as our true nature shines through unimpeded.

A moment comes when we stand before the Sacred. In that moment, everything depends on our purity. Traces of self-centeredness, of ego, turn us away. As Christ put it: *"Blessed are the pure in heart, for they shall see God."*

20.10 Unity

(The Way of Integrity: Part 10)

As long as every passing whim and desire can speak for the whole of us, we can have no integrity. As long as our intentions do not persist through time, we can have no integrity.

Unity, in its various domains, scales, and levels, is central to integrity. Here the other sense of integrity comes into play, not the one that refers to our moral fiber, but the one that means wholeness. Unity enables us to get things done, especially complex or difficult tasks, and especially when they require a continuing effort over time. Unity also helps us approach the Sacred.

How do we practice unity? How do we bring more unity into our inner life? Our inner work promotes unity, on all of its levels. We begin with unity of body awareness. At any given moment we might be aware of a part of our body: a pain in our leg, the coldness of an object in our hand, the tickle in our throat just before we cough, the texture of food in our mouth, the vibration of a toothbrush on our teeth, the pressure of our foot on the ground, and so on. Or we may not be in contact with our body at all. To bring us into this moment, we practice intentional body awareness. We focus our attention on an arm or a leg and hold our attention there. That part of our body gradually comes alive and vivid, as our attention awakens and attracts the sensitive energy there. We call this practice sensing. Over time, we move from sensing parts to sensing our whole body. This gives us a degree of unity: whole body unity.

Acceptance of our emotions and acceptance of ourselves, gives emotional unity. The further our inner work progresses, the more objectively we see ourselves. This can be painful, because the truth tends to clash with our prior self-image. In that pain, we may wish to reject aspects of ourselves. We may wish we were different, not like that. The problem with this approach is that it never ends. If we focus on what we do not like about ourselves, then there will always be something we do not like. The solution lies in acceptance, radical and total acceptance of ourselves as we are. We open our heart and spread our arms wide to embrace all of our self. We may still choose to work to change or improve, but we do so in the context of self-kindness and self-acceptance, not self-rejection. In this total acceptance we become whole, unified emotionally, free of inner sniping and self-judgements: a great relief and unburdening. And to the extent we accept ourselves, we find a growing capacity to accept others as they are. Emotional unity leads toward love.

Noticing our thoughts as thoughts, leads to mental unity. At one level, we may not notice our thoughts at all. At one step up, we are just lost in our thoughts, carried off by daydreams, rumination, and reaction. Beyond that, we come into contact with our thoughts, so that we are aware of their meaning, we can direct our thoughts and think purposely. Another step up, a major step, and we notice our thoughts as thoughts. We realize that we are not our thoughts, that our thoughts are not who we are, and that our thoughts do not necessarily speak for us, nor necessarily reflect our actual views. We see that the bulk of our thoughts run automatically, thinking themselves in a mechanical, reactive manner. They are just thoughts, passing by. Another step and we see the stillness, the silence beneath our thoughts. And then we know we are not our thoughts, that they are only a small part of our equipment. In so doing, we reclaim our mind, we reintegrate its component thoughts, images, and underlying stillness into one whole. Behind and surrounding our thoughts is the boundless sky of our mind. Our mind is then ours and free, with the power to see, to reflect and ponder, to plan, and to create. Its contradictions meld into the wholeness that we are.

Opening to consciousness leads to unity of awareness. We begin this opening in meditation, when we enter the stillness underneath our thoughts. We come to understand that stillness as pure awareness, as consciousness. It pervades us, not only our mind, but our entire being. It is boundless and timeless. In consciousness, we are, we can just be. And in just being, we are complete and whole, in the unity of all-encompassing awareness. Being open to consciousness, which we share with everyone else, begins to open us toward the unity of love. In consciousness, we are not separate.

The practice of presence is a central practice of our path. Presence is based in awareness of the here and now. But it is more than awareness. It requires contact with the present. And to have contact, there must be someone who is in contact, someone who is present. We must be here. Being the one who is present, being intentional about being the central core of presence, about being the one who sees what we see, hears what we hear, and does what we do, being the one who is sensing our body and noticing our thoughts, starts to give us unity of individuality, of agency, of true I. Our attention, and more generally our will, emanates from us throughout our being and is the hallmark of true presence. Thus presence embodies another level of wholeness, of integrity. Presence permeates our body, our mind, and our heart, unifying our being. Our actions and our promises do not just happen by accident, reaction, or association. They occur because we so choose, because we are here to choose. And because we are and because we choose, our choices come from wholeness and integrity.

A further step into unity, concerns the Sacred more directly. In presence our will flows from us, from our I. But from a higher perspective, all will derives from the One Divine Will. This includes our will. This step involves opening in our core, so that our will does not just flow from us, but flows through us. The higher will flows into and through us, sometimes accompanied by the energy of Sacred Light. We can practice this opening in quiet prayer. Indeed, this practice almost defines contemplative prayer.

It may be tempting to skip to the last steps in the work of unity. But to be strong in our unity, we need all the levels, we need to be unified both within and across all levels of our being. We can work at all of them, but if we neglect any of them, that will limit our progress. These levels support each other. Unified body awareness enables freedom in mind and emotion. That freedom both leads to and arises from the silence of consciousness, which in turn provides a home for the unified will of our true I, which is the core of presence and the locus that can open to the Sacred. When the energy of Sacred Light enters us, it blends with the energy of sensation to yield more conscious energy, thereby also supporting presence. So our path has its own integrity, its own unity that invites our participation. It welcomes us onto the ladder of unity. How high we climb is up to us.

21.0 Living in Flow
(Introduction)

Have you ever had hours or whole days when your life just flowed? When you were fully in contact with the details of your life and when there were no inner obstacles. When you moved easily and smoothly from one thing to the next. If you needed to think, then your thoughts were clear and concise. But mostly your mind was quiet, or at the least the inner chatter receded into the background as you went about your business. Your emotions were appropriate, relevant, and supportive to the situation, helping you fully engage in what you were doing. Your senses were alive, taking in everything relevant, and more, in vivid detail. Your body moved fluidly, efficiently, and effectively. You were fully in contact, at home in your own skin, in your own life. Your effortless attention focused on what you were doing. Inwardly you were united. Your usual self-centered concerns had vanished. Each of your activities took on value in its own right, so that you appreciated what you were doing for itself. Time stopped, while you lived within the timeless.

Flow, the state of being completely immersed in an activity, has been extensively studied by psychologists, with more research ongoing. And for good reasons, most notably the timeless serenity and happiness, as well as the heightened focus and performance that come in flow, which is sometimes called being in the zone. The research shows that the key elements for entering the flow state include being in front of a challenge that is well matched with our skills, so that we concentrate on what we are doing to such an extent that we have no spare mental cycles available to distract us.

This view of flow is outwardly oriented, dependent on an external challenge to enable flow. However, we may characterize one of the sub-goals of the spiritual path as the aim to live in flow all the time. Yet we cannot always be engaged in a challenging external task. Life requires the mundane, such as the regular care and feeding of our body, our home, and our possessions. We know how to do these necessary chores and duties, so they present little challenge to our relevant skills. This is a recipe for boredom, and apparently not for flow. So the question we pose is: can we live in flow? Is it even possible to live in flow? And if so, how might we move toward that?

Various spiritual traditions view the ideal state as flow. The Taoist teaching of *wu wei*, or non-doing, encourages this natural, effortless, fully-engaged approach to living. We learn to flow like water, continually adapting to the moment, and flowing through it. Buddhist and Hindu teachings speak of one-pointedness and of non-dual living. They teach us to flow.

At the center of this endeavor, lies an unspoken question. In the state of flow, what is it that flows? We may glibly answer that we flow. But that answer does not inform. If we flow, who are we? Our body, our mind, our emotions? What is it that flows? We understand this question by recognizing that we are our will, that what flows in flow is our will. For will to flow, it must flow through us. Thus, there is no room for ego in flow, for ego dams up the flow of will, blocking the higher will from flowing through us. There is no room for fragmentation in flow, because the conflicting fragments of our psyche hinder our will; instead we need to be unified.

There are many elements and practices that can help us live in flow, not just experience it briefly in front of appropriate external challenges. We raise our own inner challenge, that of living in flow. In the coming weeks, we will explore the elements of living in flow. For this week, notice the moments of flow that do grace your life.

21.1 Surrender to the Present

(Living in Flow: Part 1)

Tensions come in an endless variety of flavors and sizes. Many contribute directly to what we are doing, and so are both useful and necessary. Others, however, impede flow. They burn our energies wastefully. They draw part of our attention away from what we had intended to focus on, thus fragmenting our will. Depending on where we started, tensions may either pull us out of the timeless into time, or keep us stuck in time.

These tensions may be physical, mental, or emotional.

To illustrate, take the example of putting away your clean dishes and utensils after they have dried in the dish drainer or the dishwasher. Each item belongs to a particular cabinet or drawer. Your job is to put them where they belong. To accomplish this, you move around your kitchen in a purposeful manner. Your whole body is engaged: your hands to pick up the items and to put them down, your legs to move you from the unsorted collection to the cabinets and drawers, your eyes to see where you are going, your memory to indicate where to put each thing, and your ears to listen for the clinks and clunks that help you avoid breakage.

If you are in flow, this whole process becomes a kind of dance. It may occur in time and space, but you feel timeless. You are getting this small task done, with no impediments. You move fluidly and efficiently. It all goes smoothly on its own, without your conscious interference. Your mind is quiet. You give yourself to the action for its duration. You even enjoy it and end up with a sense of accomplishment, in its own small way.

But certain kinds of tensions can make this picture very different. If we are in a hurry, it will be a chore, not a dance. If we give in to attitudes of not liking the task, of resenting, avoiding, or rejecting it, of wishing we did not need to do it, of wanting it over with so we can get to the next thing, so we can go relax, then it will be a chore, not a dance. And the irony is that by wanting to get it over with so we can go relax, we miss the opportunity to be relaxed within the task itself. Wanting to get something over with is our attempt to kill that piece of time. But we cannot enter the timeless by killing time; only by accepting time can we transcend it. Only by flowing through time, unobstructed by tensions, can we flow into the timeless.

Learning to relax into our life is one of the secrets to living in flow.

Our problem is that we are very attached to our tensions. Indeed attachments are the source of our tensions. So we practice surrendering our tensions. Not surrendering to our tensions, but rather surrendering to the moment by letting go of our tensions. Say we have an ongoing, self-propelled thought-train that is inwardly loud and packs an emotional punch. As long as part of our attention stays with that, we cannot enter the flow of any other action. Our choice here is to surrender that thought-train, letting it go by releasing the hold it has on our attention, by putting our whole attention back onto what we are doing, onto where we are, into our body, into being here.

The same principle applies to any other distracting tensions, such as attitudes of wanting to get away from what is happening or of wanting to grasp something outside the present moment. These divert our attention and divide us inwardly. Can we let those attitudes go and relax back into this moment? We may have some emotion unconnected with the present moment, an emotion that takes us away or weakens our contact with the present. Again, can we let that emotion go and relax back into this moment? Mental and emotional tensions lead to unnecessary bodily tensions, which burn our energies and distract us. Can we relax our body and thereby relax into this moment?

Whatever pulls on us, whatever keeps our body, mind, heart from working together and being fully engaged in what we are doing, can we let that go and totally surrender into the present? For this week, please practice entering flow through relaxation. Relax your body. Relax your mind. Relax your heart. Surrender your tensions to the present.

21.2 Body Flow

(Living in Flow: Part 2)

We have seen an approach to living in flow that consists of learning to relax into our life. A prime path toward that begins with relaxing into our body, as a first step to learning to live in our body, to lean into our body, to be present in our body. To fully participate in life, we need to base our experience in our body. Our body is always in the present, whereas thoughts and emotions often take us out of the present. To live in flow means, among other things, to live in the present. Body presence reliably brings us here, basing us in the living now.

This is not to say that our mind and heart are inherently in opposition to flow. If we can relax our mind and heart, then our thoughts and emotions will not be obstacles to flow. We think and feel as part of our engagement with the present. The way toward relaxing our mind and heart is to begin with relaxing into our body. If we have a foundation in body presence, associative thoughts and reactive emotions do not so easily take us away from the present, away from flow.

We work at this in sitting meditation, as a way to establish a strong presence in our body, strong contact with our body. This is a learned skill. We sense every part of our body and the whole of it. In sitting meditation we can learn to open to the sensitive energy, which mediates our contact with our body. When we have a foundation of contact with our body, we can move into our body. We notice the difference between looking at our body as if from outside it, as if looking from our head brain and the other mode of being in our body, occupying, inhabiting our body. We no longer live in our mind, we live in our body, in our sensation body. This is body presence.

And we seek to carry that body presence from our sitting meditation into our life activities, which is where the opportunity to live in flow arises. Toward that, we practice being in contact with our body, being in our body, in movement. The simplest way to begin that is to practice while in a repetitive movement that does not take a great deal of attention, for example, in walking. Whenever we need to walk more than a few steps, we can practice being in contact with our body as we move. After all, when we walk, our body is flowing. If we can be in our body in walking, then we are flowing.

Walking is a microcosm of our life. We are active, needing to pay attention, but thoughts come, some from other thoughts, some from the sensory impressions we receive while walking. Can we just simply be in our body, as we walk? Not distracted by our thoughts, but here in our body.

How? We relax our body. We relax in our body. And here is the key: we relax our controlling self, to let our body move on its own, to let our body flow, from its own wisdom. This does not mean we let our body blithely walk into traffic or drive a car without paying close attention to the road. Rather when in a potentially dangerous situation, our danger sensor knows, and our controlling self kicks back in. So we practice letting our body flow as we walk. We practice letting our body walk, while we stay fully here, in our body, relaxed.

As we walk, we relax our mind. We let the thoughts pass by us, just like the scenery passing by as we walk. Thoughts become part of the scenery. We do not try to banish or control or structure our thoughts. We just be in our body and in our mind, letting everything flow as it will, including our thoughts.

We might even go fishing in the stream of our thoughts,

sometimes catching something new and creative, a solution to some issue. Flow allows new, uncensored thoughts to arise, some of which may be useful.

As a young graduate student in physics, I met Eugene Wigner, a Nobel prize winner, who at that time was researching the relationship between physics and consciousness. I asked him how to pursue such a study, thinking he would recommend that I read certain books or papers. Instead he answered, "I usually go for a walk."

So inhabiting our body serves many purposes, including simply being the right way to live. Until we actually try it though, we live with the false assumption that we are always inhabiting our body, always in contact with our body. The intentional practice of sensing and relaxing into our body dispels that illusion and sets us on a truer path.

A natural step forward from inhabiting our body is to let our body flow in movement. This, in turn, teaches us how to let go into living in flow. For this week, please practice inhabiting your body and letting it flow in movement. We can practice this in walking, in sports, in dance, and in any other workable situation.

21.3 Sensory Flow

(Living in Flow: Part 3)

The river of life, as we experience it, is an endless stream of sensory impressions. It includes the standard five senses that enable us to see, hear, smell, touch, and taste. It also includes their inner counterparts, wherein we see mental images and hear our thoughts, as well as the inner sense of touch that branches into feeling our emotions and sensing our body. Further refinements of that inner sense of touch bring direct perception of inner states and various energies.

As this river of our sensory life cascades through time, our relationship with it determines the extent to which we live in flow. There are two primary ways we stop ourselves from living in flow. The first is by putting obstacles into the stream and the second is by letting ourselves be carried away by the stream.

The second issue comes down to whether we allow ourselves to be carried along in this sensory flood so that we flow away with it, or do we stand still, like the land surrounding a river, so that it flows through us. In the first mode of living, we are buffeted and knocked around by all the stuff in the river; we live in time. In the second mode, we live in our fundamental, unchanging awareness that allows everything to flow through; we live in flow, in the timeless. The sensory river is the river of time. The timeless land is our consciousness. Instead of being a prisoner of time, such as when we become impatient, we live in the timeless. Instead of being lost in the flow of our senses, we stand in an awareness that both includes and transcends the sensory flow.

Can we stop jumping into the stream to block it, to hold onto a piece of it or push some other piece away? Can we stay present and let the river of life flow right through us, clean and unchallenged, without mistaking that river for who we are?

Training in mindfulness meditation helps. In it we practice moment-to-moment non-judgmental awareness. We begin by relaxing into our body, into full contact with our whole body. That gives us an anchor in the present, an anchor that keeps us from drifting off with the sensory flow. Then we open our sensory doors to whatever is present in this moment. And we do that without passing judgement on anything our senses bring us, without grabbing or grasping an object, without pushing away, running from, ruminating about, or otherwise engaging with an object of our senses, and without mistaking any object of our awareness, such as our body or the thought "I," for who we truly are. We let the sensory river flow unimpeded, while we abide here and at ease. When we notice that we have gotten lost in the sensory flow, we just return to our body and start again. When we can just be present, and remain in simple, immediate contact with the flow of our senses, then we are living in flow.

Paradoxically, to live in flow, we need to break our identification with the flow of inner and outer events. When our controlling ego goes at least temporarily quiescent, we can let everything in our sensory field just flow in its own time, while we flow in the timeless. Just as a river cannot be a river without its banks, we enter wholeness in flow, wholeness that includes both the sensory and cognitive levels of our mind, both time and the timeless. Mindfulness meditation enables us to enter the cognitive stillness at the base of our mind, eventually opening a wide field for awareness and being, in the midst of life. The non-judgmental awareness we develop in meditation opens out into that cognitive stillness. These two levels, the inner stillness and the simultaneous contact with our senses, together make our life more vivid.

For this week, please practice opening your awareness to the whole stream of sensory perceptions, inner and outer. Practice staying in the present and open, in the ease of letting time and sensory impressions flow on.

21.4 Fluid Mind

(Living in Flow: Part 4)

To enable the river of life to flow freely through us, we need to remove the weeds and debris clogging its path. If we turn to look objectively at our own mind, we quickly see that weeds and debris abound. At that point the battle is half won, because, as in physics, the act of observing our mind changes it. The question is whether we actually look at our mind.

We live in the world of our thoughts. Our thoughts define our reality and matter to us much more than they are worth. We identify with them, with that thin layer of inner words on the surface of our mind. Take the example of the running mental commentary that accompanies us all day. We believe that we are the one making those comments, that we are the narrator of our life. This is a subtle but crucial point. Can we see that we are not our thoughts, nor the one who is thinking them? Can we see that no one is thinking them? Can we see that our thoughts think themselves, like some journalistic software that takes in sensory data and spews out a story? It's almost all automatic.

The subtlety is in that word "almost." Sometimes we do think intentionally. At those times we are indeed the thinker of our thoughts, we are the narrator or commentator. This only happens when we intentionally consider some subject, some issue we are dealing with. We think about it. But from the fact that sometimes we clearly are the thinker, we wrongly extrapolate to believing we are always the thinker behind every thought, when in reality the vast majority of our thoughts are automatic, subject to our experience, conditioning, and sensory impressions. Can we make this distinction? Can we know when we are being intentional in our thoughts?

To the extent we believe that all our thoughts come from us, from our I, we live in the world of our thoughts. As such, we have nowhere else to turn, nowhere else to be, no place to see a different perspective other than the one offered by our thoughts. We get caught in the web of our thoughts. This world of thoughts is thin and impoverished compared to the reality around it: the external world brought to us by our senses, the deeper reaches of our inner world, and the spiritual realm.

Again, meditation helps. After relaxing into our body and establishing our background presence there, we open our attention wider to notice whatever enters the foreground of our awareness. This may be a sight or a sound or a sensation, but often it is a thought that arises unbidden and, if we can just sit and watch, the thought fades away on its own. Then the next thought comes along and fades. A fitful stream of thoughts come and go, come and go. As we see this happening, we very gradually come to understand that we are not thinking these thoughts, that they are thinking themselves. The more that understanding grows, the greater freedom we have. We are no longer in the thrall of our thoughts, no longer dominated by the vagaries of our own mental chatter. We can then say, "I am not my thoughts."

So what does this have to do with flow? Flow means freedom. We can only live in flow to the extent that we are inwardly free. And freedom in front of our thoughts is a major step toward complete liberation. What does that freedom look like? Imagine that rather than falling under the spell of and reacting to every chain of thoughts going on in your mind, you instead know intuitively and without effort that those thoughts are not who you are, that they have no power or claim over you, that they are just thoughts, just words passing through your mind, and then you return to your presence and breathe easy. If there is something useful, creative, or truly urgent in those thoughts, you may take appropriate action, but without being identified with the thoughts. One measure of our being is the extent to which we live in the deep currents of stillness beneath our thoughts, the source of true flow, rather than on the surface of our mind, where endless chatter and self-centeredness abound.

We let the thoughts go on as they will, because we know it is not possible to stop our mind from producing thoughts, that thoughts arising are just part of our equipment, like digestion, blood circulation, and breathing. We let our thoughts flow, we let our mind flow, while we abide in the consciousness, the cognizant stillness beneath it all. Our thoughts come and go, surrounded by a vast and pure awareness, untainted by the thoughts, just as the great sky is unaffected by passing clouds.

For this week, notice your thoughts coming and going. Notice the stillness beneath and around them. Live in the flowing current of that cognizant stillness.

21.5 Fluid Heart

(Living in Flow: Part 5)

Something happens that crosses us. We react emotionally and carry it around for hours or days. The mood colors everything and may even keep us from noticing much of what happens. Such emotional disturbances occur on scales large and small, with intensities major and minor. As thoughts are to our mind, emotions are to our heart, our spiritual heart. Just as thoughts often distract us from the present, emotions do too. But emotions by their very nature have an even greater power over us. A disturbance in our emotions certainly disturbs our ability to live in flow.

With thoughts, the answer is to live in more contact with the stillness in the depths of our mind. With emotions, the answer is to live in more contact with the peace and equanimity in the depths of our heart. If we can find our way into that ocean of equanimity, it leaves room for other positive emotions to arise; joy and love, compassion and commitment come naturally out of a peaceful heart. When we delve behind our associative, automatic thoughts, we find the stillness of our mind. When we delve behind our automatic, reactive emotions, we find the peace of our heart. We do not manufacture the stillness at the base of our mind. It is just there, when we let go of being taken by the surface thoughts. We do not manufacture the equanimity at the base of our heart. It is just there, when we let go of being taken by the surface emotions.

To come to that peace, we practice peace. And we do that by practicing relaxation and letting go. Our body and emotions are tightly intertwined. Emotions often manifest as tensions or discomfort in parts of our body, for example, in our chest, solar plexus, abdomen, shoulders, face, or breathing. Thus, relaxing our body, particularly those parts, helps relax our heart, our emotions. This is fairly straightforward. Our growing contact with our body through the practice of body awareness with sensation, makes us aware of those tensions, and alerts us to the possibility and need to relax them.

Letting go is another matter, though. While relaxation is a form of letting go, i.e., letting go of our tensions, another form of letting go consists of abandoning our support for a destructive emotion in its early stages. After it builds into a storm, it is too late to stop; we just ride it out and try to limit the damage. But before that, we do have a chance to quit the reaction. First we need to notice it. Mindfulness and presence enable that noticing. Second, we need to be willing to let it go, because letting go is an act of will. And we need to make that choice quickly, before the reaction engulfs us.

It often happens that our thoughts support our emotional reaction, and our emotional reaction drives our thoughts, all in a destructive, self-reinforcing loop. At such moments we mentally justify the emotion, we rehash the event, we inwardly insist on our rightness, our indignation, our fear, our desire. To let go of that, requires us not to believe in our own thoughts, or at least to consider the swarm of reactive thoughts to be less important than inner peace. When we are willing to do so, we have a great chance to find peace.

If we can establish ourselves in equanimity, then when other emotions come, they come on top of that, so that equanimity forms the conscious foundation of our emotional life. Joy comes naturally, as does love and compassion. Even fear and anger do not fully take us over, do not fully disturb us. Equanimity is not indifference, we act with vigor. Equanimity allows us to do the right thing with clarity and freedom, allows us to hear the undistorted voice of our conscience and respond accordingly. Equanimity is not a lack of passion, but the passion that does come is wholesome and life-giving, not destructive.

Peace and equanimity give us a fluid heart, ready and responsive to the moment, and without the obstacles of attachment and identification. With peace and equanimity, we can live in the fullness of flow.

For this week, please practice peace and equanimity. Relax and let go.

21.6 Fluid Presence

(Living in Flow: Part 6)

Our body, heart, and mind have differing agendas, frequently at odds with each other. Furthermore, our mind and heart often distract us from the present moment. All of that hampers our ability to live in flow. In the previous weeks, we have seen that for a fluid mind we need to abide in the stillness beneath our thoughts, and that for a fluid heart we need to abide in the peace and equanimity beneath our usual emotions. At that level the agendas align.

Indeed, the stillness beneath thoughts and the peace beneath emotions are one and the same. In the unity of consciousness we become whole. Body, mind, and heart merge. We flow through life, and life, in its fullness, flows through us. No inner obstacles, no inner divisions block the flow. What we experience, we experience with our whole being. What we do, we do with the whole of ourselves. We allow a higher unity to take root in us. Each of our parts, instead of going its own way and rebelling, takes its place in the whole to such an extent that our divisions evaporate, leaving us in the purity of unfiltered, uninterpreted, immediate perception.

But pure perception and awareness, stillness and peace, though wonderful, are not the whole story. For completeness, we look to presence. And the core of presence is us: the one who is present, the one who is aware, the one who does what we do and experiences what we experience. The most direct and immediate way to come into your own I, into your will, is through being the source of your attention, being the one that directs your attention and receives the perceptions that come back, the one who inhabits your body, mind, and heart. This is who you really are, your true center.

Paradoxically, though, it does not seem to have a center, or rather it seems to be centered everywhere. This is due to the fact that our will, our I, is not based in time and space. You might rightly protest, "I am here right now, in my center." But what's happening is that your I is entering time and space and you from a deeper dimension, thus the quality of being centered everywhere.

When we marry unfettered will with unfiltered perception, we have fluid presence. Inwardly all is quiet. Or if not quiet, then at least we reside in the stillness and peace below the surface thoughts and emotions. We reside as our I, our will, as our core. Our I reaches into and unites all our parts under its umbrella. That is presence.

But fluidity of presence goes deeper still. If our presence begins in us, in our I, then it has a static quality. If instead, we come into our I and open our I to what is above, deeper than us, beyond our I, then the sacred flows through us. Will flows. Presence, no longer seemingly our own, nor not our own, flows. Our I has become a pivot point, not just oriented outwardly toward what is below, toward our body, mind, heart, and external perceptions, but also oriented toward what is above and beyond us. Then the higher can flow through us, as us, and, at least for those moments, we live in the flowing freedom of perfection.

Our I seems to have two faces. One looks downward, toward externals, toward body, mind, heart, and senses, and seems to be centered in us. The other looks upward, toward the Sacred, toward the Source and seems to be centered nowhere and everywhere. In opening upward and simultaneously facing downward, we discover that the two faces become one, and the flow of will and energy comes from above down through us.

We can focus, for example, on inhabiting our body and at the same time opening to the Sacred, and the flow comes, as if it were the Sacred inhabiting our body, inhabiting us.

If we wish for more than a rare and fleeting taste of fluid presence, we must practice. We practice awareness of body, heart, and mind. We practice focusing and holding our attention and being that attention. We practice being in, inhabiting, our body, mind, and heart. We practice being our I, the director of our attention, the chooser of what we do. We practice being the one that is inhabiting our body, heart, and mind. And we practice letting go in our very core, pointing ourselves upward, deeper, opening to the Sacred, and living that inner freedom.

For this week, please practice fluid presence.

TOOLS AND STRATEGIES

THE WAY OF PRESENCE

ABOUT THE AUTHOR

The son of Holocaust survivors, **Joseph Naft** was born in a Displaced Persons' camp in northern Italy in the aftermath of World War II. Recovering from wartime devastation, the family soon immigrated to the United States. That legacy of unspeakable evil engendered Naft's abiding interest in how the seemingly intractable problem of human violence can be resolved.

While childhood experiences of the spiritual depths set the stage for Naft's lifelong pursuit of the sacred, he first learned formal meditation practice in 1970. In 1974-75, he studied Buddhist, Sufi and Christian practices during a year in residence at J. G. Bennett's school of spirituality in England. Subsequently he pursued a range of spiritual practices in Turkey under the guidance of Sufis from the Mevlevi, Helveti, Rifa'i, and Naqshbandi orders. He has also undertaken extensive training in Buddhist meditation. Finally, his Jewish roots remain close to his heart, both the traditional form of Jewish worship as well as meditation methods from Kabbalah.

Through his ongoing spiritual quest, Naft gradually came to see that the ultimate answer to the tragedy of violence must entail a radical change and evolution of the inner life of all humanity. The leading edge of that change lives in those committed to spiritual practice.

Joseph Naft has taught meditation and spiritual practices since 1976. His other books include *The Radiant Mountain: Presence to Go, Becoming You: Cultivating Spiritual Presence, The Sacred Art of Soul Making: Balance and Depth in Spiritual Practice* and two novels, *Agents of Peace* and *Restoring Our Soul*.

www.ingramcontent.com/pod-product-compliance
Lightning Source LLC
Chambersburg PA
CBHW071235160426
43196CB00009B/1066